D0088966

AN
ORDINARY ATROCITY

AN
ORDINARY ATROCITY

Sharpeville and Its Massacre

PHILIP FRANKEL

YALE UNIVERSITY PRESS
NEW HAVEN AND LONDON

For information about this and other Yale University Press publications, please
contact:
U.S. Office: sales.press@yale.edu   www.yale.edu/yup
Europe Office: sales@yaleup.co.uk   www.yaleup.co.uk

ISBN 0-300-09178-8 (cloth)

Typesetting by: Sue Sandrock, Johannesburg, South Africa
Printed by: NBD, Drukkery St, Goodwood, Cape Town, South Africa

A catalogue record for this book is available from the British Library and the
Library of Congress

CONTENTS

FOREWORD

Philip Frankel's in-depth and even-handed account of the events leading up to the massacre at Sharpeville – once considered a model black township – on the fatal afternoon of 21 March 1960 makes fascinating reading.

The dramatic story of the confrontation between the non-violent anti-pass protesters of the Pan Africanist Congress and the police at the Sharpeville Police Station is a tragic example of what can happen when neither protestors nor police have put in place the means with which to deal with crowd control. The official Commission of Inquiry (in its only unambiguous statement) reported that no order to fire was ever given by any police officer. Yet, in a panic chain reaction to three random shots – two from a drunken protester and one from a young constable – some 1000 rounds of ammunition were fired into the ranks of the protesters, leaving (according to the underestimated official figures) sixty-nine dead and 180 injured, many of them shot in the back.

The massacre was a seminal event in the dark history of the apartheid era, which had far reaching effects. It lead to the declaration of a State of Emergency, and a heated debate in Parliament over the Unlawful Organisations Bill which was supported by the official opposition and opposed only by the Progressive Party Members of Parliament, the three Native Representatives and the two Coloured Representatives. As a result, the Pan Africanist Congress and the African National Congress were banned and hundreds of people were detained without trial. Passive resistance in South Africa was replaced with the armed struggle and international pressure against apartheid intensified.

Robert Sobukwe, leader of the PAC, was sentenced to three years' imprisonment for incitement and this sentence was later extended by a further six years after the notorious 90-day detention Act was passed which included a section (which came to be known as the Sobukwe Clause) giving the Minister of Justice the power to continue to hold him annually. After his release Sobukwe was banned and restricted to Kimberley.

As the author has written: 'Sharpeville represents an end, a beginning, a social commentary and an evaluation. It indicated that apartheid was not sustainable except at the unacceptable human cost of irreparably damaging relations between the races.'

It should be mentioned, perhaps, that it was another twenty-six years before the pass laws were repealed, having been shown to be unenforceable even by the apartheid government.

Helen Suzman
Johannesburg

INTRODUCTION

An aerial view of Sharpeville with the police station in the centre

WHY SHARPEVILLE?

Nelson Mandela, most commentators concur, was the quintessential political leader of South Africa in the 20th century. The Sharpeville massacre of March 1960 is that century's defining event because, as Mandela the man, it represents a moment or occurrence after whose appearance on the historic landscape of South Africa nothing was quite what it had been, and nothing could quite be anticipated by even the most prescient of social commentators. Much as the extraction of Mandela from South Africa in the 20th century would leave a vast and inexplicable vacuum, to remove Sharpeville from historic memory would render what took place in South Africa in the last forty years of that century unintelligible. A South Africa devoid of either would have faced a very different set of outcomes and challenges from those which now confront it.

None of this is intended to downplay other individuals and developments whose appearance on the historic stage has profoundly shaped South Africa's route along and then away from its historically racist path. The epic struggle between Boer and Briton spewed forth its own distinguishing figures, from Lord Alfred Milner to General Louis Botha, both of whom were, in their different ways, to shape the course of 20th century South African developments. Some, in the Afrikaner mould of Botha – most notably, Hertzog and Smuts – were to stamp their particular brand of domestic and foreign policies on the Union in the half-century from its inception in 1910 to the declaration of the Republic and its expulsion from the Commonwealth. Sixteen years later the midlife struggles against apartheid were to culminate in the Soweto uprising of 1976, which once more stamped the iniquities of South Africa's racial order on the international consciousness.

Internally, Soweto 1976 encouraged dramatic shifts in the personae and wider historical processes that were to usher in the culminating period of mass mobilisation and township struggles during the 1980s – where Sharpeville was, once again, at the epicentre. Ultimately, South Africa was to make the transition to a democracy whose first Constitution, in recognition of the centrality of Sharpeville to so much of South African history, was signed by Nelson Mandela within walking distance of the site of the 1960 massacre.

This coming together of personal and community struggles, this elevation of a single seemingly insignificant black township to the symbolic nexus of the struggle for democracy in South Africa, is largely inexplicable in the light of the objective character of Sharpeville as a socio-geographic entity in the largely featureless area of the Vaal Triangle south-east of South Africa's industrial heartland in the Pretoria/Witwatersrand/Johannesburg (PWV) region. Sharpeville has always been a physically undistinguished place but on 21 March 1960 the slaughter of its inhabitants by the apartheid state propelled it into international headlines – and into a status which was to symbolise the resistance of South Africa's black population to minority rule for decades thereafter.

Sharpeville continues to occupy the emotional heights of the anti-apartheid struggle in a way which no person or place has superseded for generations, and, no doubt, even as apartheid fades away with the first century of the new millennium, Sharpeville, along with Mandela, will continue to remain inscribed in the historic memory of those who witnessed the struggle for human liberation in the 20th century on the relatively small canvas that was South Africa.

Sharpeville still has a unique capacity to evoke world-wide recognition even amongst people with little other knowledge about the struggle against apartheid. As with Mandela, this arises out of the mystique of suffering, of burdens borne either by communities or individuals who have pursued a life-long struggle for racial equality, human dignity and justice. In both cases too – be it the collective or the man – reputation is born largely but not exclusively out of remembered pain, transmogrified into symbol and then internationalised for the political purpose of liberating South Africa. At the risk of *lèse majesté* one ventures to say, there would be little to nothing of Mandela without Robben Island and little to nothing of Sharpeville without its massacre.

The Sharpeville massacre, historians concur, was not a 'benign' atrocity with few political consequences but a nefariously malignant event which instantly transformed the body politic of South Africa.[1] The sheer horror of the killings that took place around the Sharpeville Police Station on that fateful Monday made it virtually impossible for the international community to give any further moral leeway to the apartheid system, and although this did not mean an end to practical ties, after 21 March there were very few global actors who could be seen to be openly in league with South Africa, despite its heritage as a member of the Commonwealth and the Western portions of the wider global community. Within South Africa itself, the consequences of the Sharpeville massacre were manifold in the short, medium and longer term. After Sharpeville, with its ability to stoke white paranoia to a burning intensity, it became impossible for the apartheid state to tolerate all but the most innocuous (and ineffectual) forms of black resistance. In a precursor of trends for the next thirty years Sharpeville initiated a violent state reaction against black political activity to which the African National Congress (ANC), the Pan Africanist Congress (PAC), the South African Communist Party (SACP) and other opposition movements immediately fell victim. The proscription of these movements inevitably led to the armed struggle which was eventually to sap the lifeblood of apartheid and result in democratic negotiations many years later. Sharpeville was no doubt in the mind of the would-be assassin David Pratt, who, a month after the killings attempted to take the life of Dr Hendrik Verwoerd, the architect of apartheid, at an agricultural show in nearby Johannesburg. Within the decade following 1960, the major downturn in the South African economy, one of the consequences of the massacre, was to shape international transactions between the country and the wider world for years to come.

Behind these practical developments lay the enormous if more obtuse metaphoric, emotional and psychological significance of the massacre. Although when measured against massacres that preceded Sharpeville and those subsequently associated with 'ethnic cleansing' on the world stage in the years to come, the events in the Vaal Triangle were the small stuff of which the horrors of history are so often composed. But in the context of a time before the mass media had developed its capacity to sanitise or abstractify mass killings, genocides or assassinations into neat packages for public consumption, Sharpeville became part of the pantheon of the anti-apartheid struggle. After Sharpeville, which crystallised the sheer repressive horror of apartheid in the form of a tangible body count, it became impossible for the apartheid regime to legitimate its existence except to the most cynical of domestic and international commentators. The bugbear of apartheid was its complete inability to develop an ideological or moral argument to support its existence in a world after Hitler, and Sharpeville, with all its intensely subliminal associations, was decisive in undermining any future moral authority for the political system of white minority South Africa. The massacre was a critical lever which would be used over decades by the liberation movements in internationalising their struggle against apartheid.

While cries of 'remember Sharpeville' were at least partially displaced by the Soweto uprising of 1976, what took place in the Vaal was never entirely expunged from the conscience of those individuals and organisations who would have little truck over the following decades with the South African system.

The decade before the Sharpeville massacre was, on the surface, a relatively tranquil time, interspersed with subterranean turbulence. While the Afrikaner National Party had come to power in 1948 and was now in the process of unfolding its bizarre plans for racial segregation, this had little practical impact on the placid character of white society in such industrial towns as Vereeniging and Vanderbijl to the south-east of Johannesburg which abutted Sharpeville in the heartland of the Vaal region. Here, what was in many respects an extended post-Second World War euphoria remained largely undisturbed by the influx of displaced black migrants from the rural areas. There might have been some complaints about the poor quality of domestic or industrial labour, but to most whites Sharpeville or Evaton were largely anonymous communities from which the workforce appeared miraculously each day and disappeared some twelve hours later.

Township existence was of far more interest to the local and national governments. These were the years of the consolidation of the apartheid Programme which had been sold so successfully to the minority electorate in 1949. In the ten to twelve years after that, under the malign guidance of Prime Ministers Malan, Strydom and Verwoerd, the basic pillars of the new system were put in place and the 'urban Bantu' became the target of administration and control. The repressive policies that flowed from this control provoked considerable black protest, most of which, under the guidance of the African National Congress which had been formed almost forty years earlier as the primary vehicle for black resistance, was, in the circumstances, remarkably benign.

But as 1960 approached, discontent took on a sharper edge. The early fifties had seen a far more articulated (if unsuccessful) 'defiance' campaign and, in mid-decade, the mass gathering known as the Congress of the People produced the Freedom Charter, in which black South Africans laid claim to political power in the land of their birth. The fifties also saw growing impatience in the youth wing of the ANC where various factions influenced by anti-colonial struggles to the north of the Limpopo, began to question the tolerance of the ANC establishment of a system which clearly dehumanised the majority of South Africans. In the year before the massacre the ANC would split between those who still favoured a carefully deliberated and non-violent approach to an increasingly rigid racial system and those who opted for a more spontaneous and direct approach.

Much of this has been documented in works on black political protest in the fifties, many of which turn in some respect on the Sharpeville massacre. Yet, despite the general consensus that this event was a watershed in 20th century South Africa, it is quite extraordinary that so little is known about the forensics of the massacre itself – that is about the exact mechanics of that dramatic point where the forces of state repression and popular resistance met so explosively to define a moment which was to shape the political relations of the country for decades thereafter.

Much of the literature, in the form of books, articles and academic theses, adequately provides the sociological context – information about the origins of the township, the conditions of existence that eventually fuelled popular protest, and the eventual killings. Through it one can also pin down both the temporal and spatial locations of the massacre. We can, to utilise the neo-military language of the study of massacres, clearly identify the 'delivery point' (Monday 21 March 1960 at approximately 13.30 at the Sharpeville Police Station); the mode of the killing (police gunfire on a crowd composed mostly of people from the Sharpeville community); the scale of casualties (substantial) and, in the last instance, the twin constituencies of victim and perpetrator.

While certain categories of information are inexact and clearly require more investigation (the individual and collective devastation that flowed from the event for example) there is a fair amount of data on the national and international aftermath which links Sharpeville to the mainstream trajectory of apartheid history. This includes the immediate arrest of the leadership and subsequent banning of the two major African opposition groups, the ANC and the PAC; the declaration of the first of a recurring list of states of emergency which would punctuate the apartheid years; the death of Verwoerd and the malaise that was to strike the national economy as the world expressed its revulsion by downscaling its financial and trade relations with a now pariah South Africa.

Yet Sharpeville as a decisive event in history remains largely enigmatic. Like most historic massacres it was not a moment that leapt unaccompanied onto the pages of history, a sudden and inexplicable outburst of violence in the interface between state and civil society, as most of the apologist literature tends to suggest in the process of weaving historic memory. Considerable, if often subdued and largely invisible tension preceded the developments that were to culminate at the point when the SAP fired on the crowd, and although we know of accumulating popular anger about passes, rents and unemployment – all of which induced people to gather to express their discontent to the authorities – very much less is known about the 'triggers' or catalysts which immediately preceded the actual tragic confrontation. The massacre happened on a Monday but very little is known about what took place within the township on the previous critical weekend – and it is necessary to understand this in considerable depth before the massacre can be analysed or blame apportioned.

The vortex of the massacre and the eddies of social movement and transactions on its edges is, despite historic investigations, the labour of an official Commission of Inquiry, and subsequent court records, also largely uncharted terrain which compounds the problems of investigation. Virtually all the existing evidence about what transpired that day focuses on the actions and reactions of the police who were transported in increasing numbers into the township in the course of early and mid-morning to bolster their small contingent of colleagues 'besieged' in the Sharpeville Police Station by a growing 'native mob'. Although it is always difficult in retrospect to distil mobs into their discrete and individual elements, we know very little about the people who made up the crowd whose ostensible threat to authority was to result in violence.

With the exception of a tiny handful of visible leaders (who can be named but to whom little else can be attributed) there is very little on record about any of the rest of the *dramatis personae* who were present and, in some cases, became victims. There is also considerable confusion surrounding the motives and behaviour of the police, despite fairly critical if not entirely vigorous investigations of their actions in the months following the massacre.

Massacres can of course assume different forms and shapes but irrespective of their diversity of expression, they are all crucial in revealing the power relations beneath the surface of social systems, particularly in the case of persistently crisis-ridden and politically incoherent states such as apartheid South Africa. Dissecting the massacre as an explosive moment in the life of any political system provides us with vital clues to the elements which characterised that system and led to the catastrophe. Almost forty years to the day after the Sharpeville massacre, we had still not fully extracted the meaning for South African political development. Decades after Sharpeville we need to capitalise more fully on what the massacre can tell us about the workings of the early apartheid system at local level or its more general trajectory thereafter. The latter is particularly important given that Sharpeville was, on two occasions, to play a role vastly out of proportion to its size and location as a community in unravelling the monster that was apartheid. In the mid-eighties, twenty-five years into the aftershock of the 1960 killings, Sharpeville was once more to emerge as a strategic site of popular struggle within the general context of the mass mobilisation of the eighties that was ultimately to bring about the death of the apartheid state.

Part of the problem of linking Sharpeville with the broad sweep of apartheid history lies precisely in this dramatic significance. The event has been shrouded with an almost impenetrable mythology which, until very recently, with the transition to democracy, has rendered it virtually immune to objective analysis. Sharpeville has been, at once, a metaphor for both black and white brutality and writers, squeezed between a political Left and Right with their own stakes in maintaining the myths and memories wrapped around it, have found it virtually impossible to dissect it in a way that enhances our understanding of South Africa. From the very afternoon of the Sharpeville killings the various local and international players realised the enormous political capital in the event, and one consequence of the politics of memorialisation that kicked in almost instantly was an ideological moratorium on what could (or could not) be expressed for public purposes.

For much of its thirty-year existence after March 1960 the South African state discouraged investigation of what led to Sharpeville, and, perhaps more importantly, what actually took place. The reason was that any evidence other than the standard revelations produced by the Commission of Inquiry established in April 1960 could be (and was) effectively exploited by the world-wide anti-apartheid movement in its effort to internationalise its case against the South African government. Individuals and organisations who struggled against apartheid also either tacitly or implicitly connived in the suppression of further dialogue over Sharpeville because any re-engineering of the conventional wisdom carried with it a diminution of the massacre as a political tool to serve their own particular agendas.

At local level, very little evidence was publicly led by the people of Sharpeville in the immediate wake of the killings, partly because of the traumatic impact of the events and partly because they were immobilised by intimidation and fear of recrimination. In an atmosphere where the authorities were arresting any 'native' with even the slightest injuries on suspicion of public violence, it is not surprising that hardly any black witnesses – least of all credible witnesses – could be brought before the official Commission of Inquiry led by Mr Justice Wessels one month thereafter.

As my research has revealed, the handful who did eventually give evidence were carefully selected and schooled by political activists in the PAC to put forward the standard case – eventually absorbed into popular myth – that the agents of apartheid, the police, were solely, irrevocably and unconditionally responsible for the human tragedy that had transpired.

There are in fact two or three politically adversarial, monochromatic and morally unambiguous stories about Sharpeville, conjured up over the years by ideological pre-conceptions, and refined to suit particular political interests. The resistance version portrays the Sharpeville massacre as a virulent and premeditated attempt by the apartheid state to punish or intimidate its opponents, or, at least, as an example of the intrinsic brutality of the South African Police. In these narratives of victimisation the shootings were, to quote a witness before the Wessels Commission, a clear political act 'supported by hatred, *baasskap* and discrimination' – an event in which ostensibly innocent people were trapped then mowed down by the callous agents of a racist state that would neither brook interference with its segregationist policies nor, more horrifically, concede the human right of those at the Sharpeville Police Station to demand their inalienable civil rights.[2]

The other version is that Sharpeville was precipitated by a violent and bloodthirsty mob who assembled before the police station with the clear intention of slaughtering its inhabitants. This triggered the equally inalienable decision of the police to exercise their right to self-defence and preservation in the face of a threat to their own survival. Somewhere between the contrasting poles lies the 'massacre as mistake' theory which sees neither the good (the victims), nor the bad (the police), but simply the ugliness of a regrettable aberration, so common in history – of a ghastly event that was, *ceteris paribus*, 'not supposed to happen'. Since it did, Sharpeville, conceived in these terms, is less a matter of conscious decision or intention on the part of its primary actors, be they defenceless crowds or endangered agents of the state, but simply a consequence of terror and error.

It is necessary to revisit Sharpeville four decades after the killings in order to assign to the community the status it deserves within the broad sweep of apartheid history from its own foundations in the later forties to the signing of South Africa's first popular constitution a few hundred yards from the place of slaughter in the 1990s. Sharpeville has, in a sense, come full circle from death to liberation, and its massacre is a key stage in the much longer journey of South Africa from authoritarianism to democracy.

It is also important to revisit the massacre because the two diametrically opposed narratives of what took place are at odds with newly emergent historical evidence that challenges the long-standing conspiracy of silence imposed on the event by extraneous political actors with their own narrow agendas. Armed with new knowledge it is clear that the events at Sharpeville were much more than what Robert Sobukwe once deemed 'cold and calculated brutality and bestiality [in] the desperate attempts of a dying generation to stay in power.'[3] If there is one starting point for this study, it lies in the view that none of the simple interpretations does justice to what appears to have been an infinitely more complex set of social transactions. The massacre was not, in the end, simply a question of the white police 'getting at' the people (the fashionable view on the Left) nor of the black community 'getting at' the police (the view of the Right) in the context of a struggle for racial power in an otherwise obscure corner of the African continent. On the contrary, Sharpeville is an example of wider moments in the universal experience where the political rulers and their ruled have been locked into tension, antagonism and irremediable conflict, elements which so frequently form the tragic backdrop to human atrocities. Massacres, one especially horrible manifestation of such atrocities, are deeply entrenched in the sad catalogue of human experience. Massacres (and counter-massacres) were, as described in Andrew Ward's dramatic study of the Indian Mutiny of 1857, 'a kind of rite' intrinsic to the imperial purpose.[4] The last century had the dubious distinction of being an era of bloody slaughters by repressive states, idealistic revolutionaries and ethnic-driven exterminators. Even as we enter the new millennium we are bombarded with daily reports of mass killings and retributions perpetrated by the state on its subjects (or the subjects on each other) in such diverse settings as Algeria, Rwanda and the Balkans. Hence my emphasis on Sharpeville as a tool with which to explore the still largely uncharted territory of the universal sociology of the massacre as a culminating event on the extreme edge of the struggle between peoples and their governors.

Curiously, very little has been done systematically to position Sharpeville within the general context of contemporary 20th century massacres even in the limited context of South Africa where what happened on that March day has considerably more to say about the distasteful nature of apartheid South Africa. Prior to democratisation less than a decade ago, the closed political system succeeded in airbrushing most of the unpalatable aspects of Sharpeville from public scrutiny, apart from what the various political actors saw as useful for their own self-interested purposes. Even the Truth and Reconciliation Commission failed (for reasons of practicality rather than calculation) to give more than cursory attention to it. Virtually nothing has been written to situate Sharpeville within the continuum of massacres. These range from the mindless through the 'massacre by mistake' to the calculated killings of states ot their revolutionary opponents, military reprisals and revenge slaughters. They include the genocide of the Holocaust with its echoes of 'ethnic cleansing' in contemporary Africa or South-Eastern Europe.

Sharpeville, one must emphasise, was not the Japanese 'rape of Nanking', Oradour-Sur-Glane, Katyn, Babi-Yar, Josefow, Cawnpore, Amritsar, Tiananmen Square or the even more distant St. Bartholomew's Day which together form the mournful litany upon which any study of massacres must draw. But all these events provide clues to the dynamics of 21 March 1960. The complex forces that operated in Sharpeville provide evidence which, in its turn, allows us better to comprehend the universal experience of the massacre as an extraordinary event in our social, religious, economic or military experience.

The opening up of the South African political system has also generated a climate in which it has become possible, albeit within certain political boundaries that reflect the enduring capacity of memory to shape political reality, to probe what actually happened, its implications for apartheid, especially at the grassroots level, and, perhaps more importantly, for a community that has lived for decades in the shadow of a major collective tragedy. There is, one must add, a certain urgency in this project, insofar as the key actors – those who witnessed or participated in the massacre, as well as their descendants who were directly or indirectly affected – are already a diminished constituency. This is not to ignore the enormous methodological difficulties inherent in deciphering an event forty years distant and ideologically tainted in its interpretation. It is vital in redefining Sharpeville for both sociological and historical purposes to investigate the decisive human qualities and reactions in the massacre, and this involves, at least in part, talking to the participants – the perpetrators, and those between the divisive camps.

To do so raises the problem of recall that bedevils so much of oral history. The memories of some of the surviving actors, it is reasonable to assume, have been eroded by the passage of time; others simply do not wish to recall the terrible events of a day of fear, rage, pain and exhaustion. Much like survivors of long-gone battles and other traumatic events, some of the interviewees are shamed by their survival when so many others died, and have rationalised their experience through selective cognition. Still others have a continued psychological stake in maintaining the myths that are now, for the most part (though not entirely) redundant.

Then too, there is the problem of stereotyping inherent in the dialectical interpretations that have dominated the dialogue over Sharpeville for forty years. The small body of extant literature – the articles, monographs, chapters, reports and the odd book – either incline towards the victims or towards the perpetrators. In order to fully understand the sociology of the massacre, we need to steer between the simple but dangerous conventions in order to display the event and its context in all its complex richness. Only if we break through the dichotomy of violence linking victim and perpetrator so common to most writings about massacres, genocides and assassinations can we move onto the wider plain of exploring the hidden but more universal issues inherent in the event. These include, but are not necessarily limited to, the mechanics of authoritarian states, the social psychology of oppression and violence, the complex impulses that motivate political behaviour, and, ultimately, the mutating forces than turn otherwise ordinary people into killers.

At the same time the gaps in information that have inhibited systematic research into the fateful events of 21 March must be plugged. More detail is needed on the links that bound the main figures if we are to come to a higher level of social understanding. To treat the victims and perpetrators of atrocities with equality is, as Primo Levi, has pointed out, a 'moral disease'[5] – there can be no ethical equivalence between killers and killed. Having said this, the few previous studies of the Sharpeville massacre have perhaps been excessively symphatetic towards the victims, and some have been driven by what Levi calls 'the bestiality of hatred'.[6] This is to some extent unavoidable and entirely human when attempts are made to assess massacres, genocides, and holocausts, but it does not help enlighten the complex dynamics of what actually happened. Sharpeville in the end was an atrocity of international proportions, where ruler and ruled clashed in a dual and violent vortex. There was fault on both sides on Monday 21 March 1960 and we need to know much more about the sentiments and behaviour of the perpetrators within the context of their various state institutions.

If we are to strive for a 'balanced' view we need to understand much more about the political links between central and local authority and, in particular, relations within the security forces whose collective might was brought to bear on the Sharpeville community before, during and after the fatal shootings. Largely because of the silence about human rights abuses under apartheid prior to the revelations of the recent Truth and Reconciliation Commission, the current literature says very little about these matters. Notwithstanding the ongoing political incorrectness of anything that appears to justify the behaviour of the police, it is essential in order to substantiate Sharpeville and apartheid in retrospect, that we know far more about how and why the police reacted as they did – not only as anonymous organs of the state, but also as human beings with complex emotions and impulses.

The black police in the Sharpeville station have in effect been written out of history and here again, insofar as is possible, this important constituency needs to be recaptured. Even if one were to follow earlier writings by focusing almost exclusively on the crowd itself, considerably more can be added in the light of new evidence about its mood, motivations, disposition and propensity for violence against the backdrop of a highly developed theoretical literature about crowd behaviour.

Ultimately we need, some forty years on, to break free from the notion that the Sharpeville massacre was an almost inevitable consequence of struggles between different races or classes. In reading the current literature it is difficult to avoid the implicit conclusion that had the massacre not taken place in 1960, it would have occurred at some other date or in some other place because of the macrocosmic structural tensions inherent in apartheid. And indeed, the history of race relations in South Africa has not been without other massacres and similar violent clashes of far greater dimensions than the events in the Vaal region. These events however also involved prejudice, fear and anger, the interconnection between individuals acting to avert (or provoke) a catastrophe across the boundaries of different political universes and, one says with trepidation in an era of social 'science', a high degree of sheer coincidence.

A defining feature of the massacre as a sociological phenomenon is, perhaps more importantly, its innate incoherence. While in the end there are always those who kill and those who are killed, the distinction between the guilty and the transgressed is, in many cases, a legal nicety with little correspondence to social reality. Sharpeville is not a matter of intrinsically evil men involved in a modern slaughter of the innocents at the behest of a neo-fascist state. On the contrary, no-one ultimately emerges entirely untainted from the real Sharpeville story.

Sharpeville falls firmly in the category of those especially tragic historic disasters that were, in the view of participants on all sides, 'not supposed to happen'. In re-interpreting its 'real story' against the backdrop of what one author has deemed the 'scattered bones' of massacres world-wide, the following study is divided into a number of discrete but interlocking components.[7] In the short opening section I trace the historic origins of Sharpeville against the backdrop of early 20th century developments in the Vaal area. The second and main section of the book describes the events leading directly to the massacre of 21 March 1960. It then dissects the massacre itself in line with various universally recognised sociological principles regarding crowd behaviour, mass psychology, and the often violent transactions between people and government in proto-revolutionary situations. The third chapter and the postscript cover the period from the massacre to the present day, encompassing the role of Sharpeville as a focal point for popular resistance in the eighties and the last days of the anti-apartheid struggle.

The way in which people choose to remember an event – indeed how they adjust to it – is as historically important as the event itself[8] and this section is especially concerned with analysing the consequences of a community that has lived in the shadow of a major and internationally prominent political disaster. If the political and economic promises inherent in South Africa's new democracy are to be realised the enduring and still relatively intractable residues of the apartheid past must be managed; and nowhere is this more evident than in such historically ravaged communities as Sharpeville. While it is unusual in that it remained a place of mourning for years after 1960, many of its current developmental problems, dating from an act more than forty years ago, mirror those more general to other euphemistically entitled 'previously disadvantaged areas'. Sharpeville, is, in other words, a tool, albeit imperfect, for tapping into the developmental prospects of other similar communities whose names are less indelibly written in the annals of 20th century South African history.

I have attempted to deal with the Sharpeville massacre in all its ugliness: it was more terrible than described in existing accounts, and certainly far more complicated than the present histories allow. In bringing out these complexities in an admittedly sceptical and iconoclastic manner, I have been forced to navigate between what remains of carefully filtered official information subsequent to the destruction of state security documents upon the onset of democratisation, and 'populist' writings, depositions and testimonies, from victims and perpetrators, which have often been so incongruous and politically self-serving as to prove useless. In selectively discounting a proportion of the primary and secondary material I have come up with an interpretation which is, needless to say, the sole responsibility of the author. There are few useful secondary resources on the subject: hence, I have had to rely heavily on testimony and recall on the part of many individuals and organisations who, like me, aspire to as definitive a history of the slaughter as the sparse documentation and selective memory will allow.

These sources include not only an ageing but anonymous ex-police official whose peculiar description of the massacre as 'an ordinary atrocity' provides the title of the work, but many others to whom Sharpeville was either an extraordinary moral outrage or a defining personal experience. Many of the respondents about whom this is true were survivors and victims themselves and some, for many reasons, were enthusiastic in supporting a project at the interface of individual remembrance and the collective commemoration of history.

Special mention must be made of the present residents of Sharpeville, Vereeniging, Vanderbijl and the surrounding Vaal region who were, either directly or indirectly, involved in the dramatic events, as well as past residents of the area. The countless interviews with these persons, many of whom are now elderly, were essential in enriching the raw historic data drawn from secondary sources. Most of those who submitted to interviews especially the present residents of Sharpeville and ex-members of the security forces, have opted to remain anonymous. To them I can only offer thanks for their willingness to be interviewed in a way which fills the multiple gaps in the Sharpeville story.

I wish to make particular mention of a dominee in the Dutch Reform Church in Vanderbijlpark who, in response to an advertisement placed in the local media, led me to an old dusty and long-forgotten suitcase in a church basement. This, to my astonishment, contained a mass of documentation about the massacre collected over the years by one of its recently-deceased and central *dramatis personae*. As a devout Christian, it was his intention to 'set the record straight' in a book of his own, but inertia, peer pressure, and eventually death intervened before he could do so. I must deeply thank his elderly wife for allowing me to 'borrow' this confidential information.

The Sharpeville massacre typifies the fact that we cannot divide political reality into neat poles – resistors, repressors, the guilty and innocent, the good and evil. My narrative, I hope, brings out the infinite gradations of responsibility, personal weakness and moral ambivalence that are part of the Sharpeville story. It is possibly because it is so difficult, here or elsewhere, to draw a real and utterly absolute moral distinction between victim and perpetrator that there is no appropriate monument to the dead at the massacre site other than a small, misshapen and sunbleached stone. Despite the crude political trumpeting of ideologues who would hold up Sharpeville as an unambiguous example of the cruelty of which we are capable, Sharpeville has not become a place of political pilgrimage akin to Robben Island. There are, nevertheless, moves afoot in the Vaal region and wider afield to establish a more permanent, physical and fitting testimony to what occured. The 'Sharpeville 2000 Initiative' was initiated by the people of Sharpeville and other local stakeholders. Although their primary concern is less the anthropology of memory than community development, it was my contact with this group, particularly members of the Sharpeville Community Forum, that first inspired me to contemplate the present work. It will, I hope, service the eventual museum to bring about economic regeneration both in Sharpeville and the underdeveloped communities of the Vaal. In the meantime I must thank members of the Forum who endorsed my book from the outset and went on to provide me with a team of local researchers. Without their investigative efforts, their pinpointing of people to be interviewed, and the interviews themselves, the present study would have been impossible.

There are many people whom, strange as it might seem, I do not wish to thank, but who nevertheless typify certain tendencies in contemporary South Africa. These include survivors and victims who were outright liars, people with vested interests in our *not* retelling a chiaroscuro version of the standard story, and hand-wringing ex-operatives of the state who appeared surprised that apartheid had ever existed. On the other hand, there are certain key individuals and organisations who need to be mentioned and thanked. Primary research requires financial sponsorship and the current work would have been impossible without the generous input of the Royal Netherlands Embassy in Pretoria and the Bureau for International Cooperation of the Eindhoven Municipality which is 'twinned' with Vereeniging under international arrangements for development assistance. Thanks for financial assistance must also go to my alma mater, the University of the Witwatersrand, and to the Lekoa-Vaal Municipal Council.

At the individual level there are far too many people to mention. We conducted over 100 interviews with victims and perpetrators of the massacre. To those victims and perpetrators whose names have been followed by an asterisk indicating that this is not their real identity but without whose collaboration this book would not have been possible, my deepest appreciation. Less anonymously, I would like to thank the staff of the Vaal Technorama in Vereeniging who made their contemporary media cuttings available at the outset: Yunus Chamda, Mayor of Lekoa-Vaal, who has been a sustained source of support for this and other projects in his area of jurisdiction; Maretha Jordaan, who has worked tirelessly to make the vision of a Sharpeville Museum a concrete reality; Ike Makiti and other stalwarts of the local PAC, including Job Tsolo, determined to maintain the memory of Sharpeville as a key element in party and national history; Nyakane Tsolo, for his hospitality on a cold and rainy Rotterdam afternoon; Agnes Ovington in Eindhoven; Jasper van der Bliek from the University of Tilburgh, whose research interests coincided with my own and upon whose interviews I have drawn probably too liberally. Thanks must also go to Pat Tucker, past director of the Witwatersrand University Press, for her sterling editorship. On the other side of the political equation, finally but no less, I would like to extend my appreciation to Commissioner Johan Burger of the South African Police Services as well as various members of the 'old guard' of Military Intelligence without whom I would not have met many key personnel in the old apartheid security forces who arose ghost-like and nation-wide from a paper trail beginning at the SAPS Museum in Pretoria.

One does not (and cannot) normally identify the intellectual roots of any sociological project, but there have been certain people who have led me from Sharpeville to the wider literature on the inhumanity of person to person in historic memory. But in the end, I was influenced by Primo Levi; the newer literature of Zygmunt Baumann, Christopher Browning, James Young and Lawrence Langer on the intersection of atrocity and memory; the pioneering work of Maurice Halbwachs and Pierre Nora on the sociology of historic recall; and the classic crowd behaviour studies of George Rudé and Elias Canetti. Although no person other than the author carries responsibility for the material in this book, they planted the seeds out of which this project was to grow. I hope that, like them, I can begin to understand what motivates all of us in what Levi has described so simply yet chillingly as the 'mimesis' in the hopelessly complex dialectics between good and evil.

PART I

ANTE: SHARPEVILLE AND EARLY APARTHEID

Before the storm ... a convoy of Saracens moves through the streets of Sharpeville

BACKGROUND

Sharpeville owes its origins to the native 'location' of Topville which was established in the early 20th Century in what is today the Duncanville section of Vereeniging. The town of Vereeniging in turn historically supersedes Topville having been established far earlier. Vereeniging was actually the site of the Treaty which effectively ended the Anglo-Boer War and consolidated British imperial rule in South Africa for almost a decade thereafter. By the time of the creation of the Union of South Africa in 1910, Vereeniging was already beginning to display the first signs of what was later to become a vital community in the centre of the new Union's industrial heartland.

Industrial growth in Vereeniging inevitably encouraged the immigration of black rural workers, particularly those moving along the trajectory between Lesotho and the economically-expanding Witwatersrand, a few miles beyond the north-west of the Vereeniging municipal boundary. Most of those who broke their journey to find employment in Vereeniging industry as an alternative to the mines further north settled in the emerging shanty town that was subsequently named Topville. The population of the area increased with the establishment and subsequent extension of the iron and steel industry in the period after World War I which was to see the Vereeniging/Vanderbijlpark complex emerge as one of the key areas in the overall Union economy.

Life in the burgeoning shantytown was vibrant despite deteriorating conditions as population density began to outstrip the rudimentary social facilities established by the Vereeniging Town Council. As industry geared up for enhanced production to service the armaments industry with the outbreak of World War II, the shanty town experienced a massive influx of new immigrants and these inevitably strained community services of all types, particularly in the areas of public health and housing. Housing shortages encouraged wide-spread rack-renting, one consequence of which was the emergence of conflict between a landlord and tenant class that was to have various implications for the sociology of the later township of Sharpeville. In the shorter term gross overcrowding on the several hundred stands composing Topville led to a rapid decline in public health standards. By the end of World War II, when Topville contained approximately 15 000 people, there were multiple deaths from pneumonia, gastro-enteritis and tuberculosis. In two months during 1946 alone, there were 150 mortalities related to pneumonia.[1]

The Vereeniging Town Council was alarmed by the incidence of transmittable diseases on the borders of 'white' Vereeniging and these concerns were shared by the local business community which witnessed a high turnover of labour, growing absenteeism, and declining productivity at a time when the market for manufactured and steel products was at a premium under wartime conditions. Local industry subsequently became a major pressure group behind municipal policy to improve housing for the black population.[2] Yet neither the municipality nor the businessmen could countenance the physical extension of Topville, which was already, they believed, dangerously close to the suburban outskirts of the white community. A larger Topville would also intrude into valuable industrial land in the Duncanville area. Faced by these twin evils, Council and its business supporters decided that the solution to the problem lay in the creation of a new black township to which Topville residents could be relocated.

Two sites a few kilometres west of Vereeniging were purchased.[3] Fused into one – Sharpeville Native Township – the new 'location' was to lie approximately half way between Vereeniging and the neighbouring town of Vanderbijlpark. The township was to be named simply Sharpeville – after an ex-mayor of Vereeniging, John Lillie Sharpe, an immigrant Scot who had displayed considerable concern for the interests of the local black population – relative to the climate of the times.[4] It was envisioned that the relocation would be a gradual process over a number of years, and following the construction of housing facilities, the voluntary residents of the new area began to arrive during 1943. Within Topville, reactions to the new development were decidedly ambiguous, particularly on the part of landholders and landlords who had freehold land on which they could normally rent space to more than a dozen people, who would lose some £20 a month under the new arrangement and who would, to boot, be precluded from renting property in terms of the administrative regulations that governed housing in the new townships.[5] Other constituencies were also resistant: these included the local *lumpenproletariat* (the criminals, prostitutes and illegal liquor dealers) whose modus operandi required the loose and haphazard systems of social control exercised by the authorities in the slum conditions of Topville, and a broader, if somewhat more upstanding proportion of the citizenry who feared that the relatively anonymous character of the new planned township would disrupt what had been a strong conviviality of existence. Nonetheless, there were large numbers of people who welcomed leaving Topville, most notably the poorer tenants seeking upward mobility, for whom the superior housing in the more sanitised environment of Sharpeville represented a distinct social improvement.

The redeployment to Sharpeville – at least at first – was based on choice and this was not only exceptional when viewed against the background of the brutal resettlement of people that was to characterise apartheid nation-wide, but also of considerable importance, once again, to the social and cultural networks that were to emerge in the township in the fifties. The element of voluntarism in the resettlement certainly contributed to the social demobilisation of Sharpeville in its early years. During the late forties and early fifties Sharpeville was, for the most part, a relatively quiet, stable and essentially non-political community. The famous May Day stay away called by the fledgling African National Congress in 1950 essentially by-passed Sharpeville whose people also failed to rally to calls for similar action on 29 June.[6] The 1955 bus boycott in Evaton township elicited very little support in nearby Sharpeville[7], and hardly anyone in the area appears to have participated in the subsequent Defiance Campaign or in the Anti-Bantu Education Act Campaign of 1958. Ironic as it seems in historic retrospect, there was little if any material reaction in Sharpeville when the state at the time took the decision to extend the pass/reference book system to include women.[8]

But appearances often belie reality, and behind the face of Sharpeville various social, cultural and proto-political destabilising forces were at work to align the community with wider developments – far more so than is given credence in established histories which confuse political sentiments with their physical expression.[9] The environmental fatalism encouraged by a mixture of poverty and apartheid was diluted by a vibrant cultural life which promoted a diverse number of community networks. During the fifties, for example, a variety of African nationalist organisers succeeded in 'penetrating' the area where they were able to effectively disseminate resistance ideas and literature before the hand of government authority descended. The workplace, normally beyond township boundaries in Vereeniging or Vanderbijl, was also a vibrant site for political discussions which took place beyond the earshot of white officials and compliant black supervisors. Despite a fairly high level of governmental scrutiny aimed at pre-empting political activity, neither the Vereeniging Council nor the local police ever succeeded in fully insulating the residents of Sharpeville from what was, in these early years of apartheid, still relatively vigorous and critical mass media. Radio listenership was extensive, both regional and national newspapers were widely circulated, and although this did not always translate into organised or physical resistance, it still allowed the people – particularly the literate proportion – to keep abreast of popular trends and the pace of political developments.

Various cultural networks in township life were also in maintaining the flame of political opposition – albeit indirectly. As various studies have pointed out, pre-massacre Sharpeville was a mecca for sport, especially soccer and boxing, as well as for African jazz, either transferred from Topville along with its residents, or nurtured indigenously. As the universal experience indicates, both forms of activity inevitably carry political messages, particularly in small, concentrated and culturally segregated areas. Sharpeville soccer stars of the era were persistently reminded of the mechanics of segregation by the laws prohibiting inter-racial matches, and few could avoid the logic that ran from their under-equipped local facilities to the nature of the national political system. 'We played soccer because it was the only option for a black man who wanted to make something of himself while the whites ruled,' is a frequent utterance among the older generation – the initial settlers of Sharpeville – some four decades later. The protest song, 'Evaton', by a Sharpeville vocal group the Satchmore Serenaders, became, according to one commentator, 'a big hit [precisely] because it was political and banned by the government'.[10]

During the fifties a great deal of local energy was projected into gangland activities, and although much of this was focused on local struggles for control, resources and territory, there were a number of occasions when the conflict between rival gangs assumed a wider political significance. The 'Russians', groups of politically retrograde, socially displaced Basotho migrant workers, tended to dominate the Vaal gangland scene, including that in Sharpeville to which many of their less palatable members gravitated following a more strictly enforced visiting permit system introduced by the authorities in Evaton during the late fifties. Thereafter, gangland violence in Sharpeville focused on clashes between rival, and normally drunken, Basotho groups at the local Sharpeville beerhall. Yet, for many of the indigenous youth who made up a substantial proportion of the population at the time, gang participation was, as it was elsewhere, not only a means to forge identity and acquire mobility and status but also, and perhaps more significantly, a relatively low-risk substitute for prohibited political activity.

The local Sharpeville Advisory Board established to 'govern' Sharpeville under the aegis of the Non-European Affairs Committee of the Vereeniging municipality was also an important mechanism for transmitting popular opinion to the authorities and, occasionally, for influencing policy decisions in the Council. Although the white Vereeniging councillors were normally disposed to act unilaterally, disregarding 'native' opinion, circumstances often required an element of consultation, if only to make municipal policy relevant and effective. From the outset of the decision to establish Sharpeville, the Vereeniging municipality had deemed the new township a 'model' for native administration, and as it became nationally recognised as such, there was increasing pressure on the Council to ensure that governance take place with the minimum of negative publicity. This tended to work to the political advantage of Sharpeville, probably more so than in other instances of contemporary local governance, particularly when there was an inter-personal coincidence between a sympathetic councillor or municipal official on the one side, and a politically astute community representative on the other. For the most part these instances were rare: the officials (and, to a somewhat lesser extent, the white councillors) were high-handed by racist conviction while the Sharpeville representatives were compliant. Nonetheless, there were occasions, particularly crisis occasions fuelled by political events on the wider national landscape, when the Sharpeville 'advisers' could extract certain policy concessions.

Still, the opportunities for concrete political expression, particularly action, were severely constrained during the fifties. A progressively diminishing Topville survived virtually until the end of the decade, but neither its Advisory Board, nor that of Sharpeville could, with rare individual exceptions, produce community leaders with sufficient skills or gumption to exploit the limited political opportunities inherent in the relationship between the Vereeniging Council and its two black townships. Since the township boards had virtually no meaningful financial or administrative powers of their own, they were essentially dependent on their relatively gargantuan white counterpart, even at the level of enforcing basic community order. Hence the frequent and plaintive requests of the Sharpeville board that the Non-European Affairs Committee deal with the 'Russian' problem at the local beerhall once this became a community issue at the beginning of 1957. The Committee would respond vigorously with what, three years later, would be disastrous consequences.

Political mobilisation of the Sharpeville community was also constrained by the architectural configuration of the township which was planned with an eye both to cost-effectiveness and social control. As was the case with many black townships then being constructed as apartheid moved into higher gear, the design of Sharpeville involved not only the normal role players – architects, town planners, municipal officials and the like – but representatives from both the police and military who were called in once the decision was taken to develop the area identified for the new black township halfway between Vereeniging and neighbouring Vanderbijl. Various meetings were held between municipal officials responsible for (white) public safety and representatives of both the SAP and SADF during 1942/43, the purpose of which was to ensure that the design of the new community would conform to certain strategic criteria currently considered important by the agents of state security.

As was increasingly the norm, urban development was bent to political requirements, and the physical utilisation of space in Sharpeville was expressed in rigid linear lines – straight arterials designed to expose social activity, and wide central avenues to facilitate the unhindered movement of heavy armoured vehicles should future circumstances so warrant. Apart from any other considerations, the creation of Sharpeville was motivated by white fears that an expanding black Topville was dangerously intruding upon the white industrial and suburban areas of Vereeniging. In conformity with the adaptation of zoning laws to racial and strategic requirements, care was taken that Sharpeville, like most other new townships, was surrounded by a wide strip of vacant land designed both to isolate black from white and to facilitate the cordoning off of the designated black area in the event of disturbances. Altogether, Sharpeville stood in sharp contrast to the helter-skelter slum environment that was Topville. Indeed, as I have already noted, many of the latter's residents who were engaged in illicit or socially marginal activities opposed the relocation precisely because the maze of alleys and shacks allowed scope for considerably greater freedom of action and behaviour.

As was intended, the physical shape of Sharpeville would prove important in times of crisis, although the role of geography was to take a largely unanticipated form when collective violence became a facet of community existence almost twenty years later. In the meantime, the Vereeniging authorities and police were quick to nip in the bud any visible manifestations of political activity in the Topville/Sharpeville areas. Prior to the May Day stay away of 1950, for example, the authorities, in one of their more creative control exercises, called upon the Paramount Chief of the Basotho to broadcast a message calling on his Vaal constituency to ignore the planned work stoppage. This order was, however, accompanied by a ban on all meetings, addressed presumably, at those residents who were relatively impervious to ethnic appeals.[11] For the most part however, Council action to pre-empt local unrest normally involved 'consultation' with the two Advisory Boards whose members were told in no uncertain terms that marches and other actions to disrupt the 'normal' life of the townships would not be tolerated. In more potentially explosive cases police were imported from other areas of the Rand and deployed to conduct cordon-and-search operations around and within the township. Intimidation of this order was normally sufficient to deter would-be indigenous trouble-makers, who tended to step back from direct confrontation with the local state for much of the pre-massacre period. However, growing numbers of 'foreign agitators' from outside Vereeniging were detected and arrested with the progress of fifties after the Defiance Campaign. More ominously in the light of events to come, the District Commander of Police was increasingly given to warning that the police would not hesitate to use violence should their calls for order continue to go unheeded.

The general passivity of the Sharpeville community was partially encouraged by the fact that the relocation from Topville was essentially voluntary and peaceful. While Sharpeville was not especially magnetic to certain elements in Topville society, those who did eventually respond positively to the call of the municipality that they move found upon their arrival in the new development a set of living conditions which, if consciously antiseptic, represented a vast improvement on those in the Topville slum. The Council was careful to tailor the removal process to the availability of housing and this meant rigid application of the administrative rules and procedures governing admission to the Sharpeville housing scheme and the community more generally. So when people arrived in Sharpeville at various phases in the immigration process, they were almost invariably met with reasonably adequate housing which was, by any objective criteria, far superior to anything most had known in their previous existence.

Since the Council had somewhat grandly determined to make the new Sharpeville a prototype for black township development elsewhere, care was taken to supplement housing with a supportive range of social facilities – schools, clinics and the like – conducive to normal existence. In retrospect it is clear that the Council's determination to set an example was less motivated by the human requirements of the black community than by considerations of social control. As South African governors, both prior and since have recognised, 'a happy Bantu is a housed Bantu' (to quote a contemporary administrator).[12] Still, this simple view reaped returns as the progressive extension of services and facilities to meet the increasing size of the Sharpeville community over the years was sufficient to take the sharp edge off political activity – at least protest activity rooted in the incremental issues of local existence.

Sharpeville was not without its own divisions, cleavages and segmental interests which, jointly or severally, precluded a uniform community response to outside political challenges. Considerable tension arose, for example, from the very extended and periodic nature of the Topville relocation. Notwithstanding familial links between immigrants, the relatively older residents often tended to regard those who followed as antagonists in the competitive scramble for scarce employment and other community resources. Many people still recall how the older residents, even in the earlier years, 'reserved' certain shebeens or even seats in the local cinema or beerhall from which the newcomers were excluded. Tensions of this nature were inevitably irritated by the spatial concentration of each 'generation' of migrants in distinct segments of the new township which were created successively to absorb a new influx of ex-Topville people. Ultimately, in a manner not unfamiliar to many other poor communities worldwide. Sharpeville came to consist of a number of tight area-bound sub-communities or clusters, each with its own relatively distinct cultural networks for social transactions along a range from soccer to music to politics.[13]

The municipal beerhall was a recurrent site of tension and sporadic outbreaks of conflict between rival gangs of youths whose territorial struggles in the various township clusters were extended to include the only legal drinking facility. Competition for jobs between residents and the largely Basotho migrant work force housed in the local hostel was also an ongoing issue overlaid with shades of ethnic and class conflict, particularly after the influx of the Russians towards the end of 1956.[14] Thereafter the beerhall and other social venues saw periodic violence between the local gangs with their mixture of neighbourhood and criminal agendas and even between rival factions within the tribal Russians themselves.

Preferential employment policies adopted by local industry and manufacturers further compounded the problems of community solidarity and mobilisation.[15] As a number of writers on Sharpeville have pointed out, the existence of a large, transient and easily-replaceable labour reserve in the Vaal effectively hampered the development of the local trade union movement as well as ancillary political organisations who could capitalise on dissatisfaction with apartheid across the region.[16] Apart from the occasional individual who professed membership of the nationalist movement, the ANC was almost entirely absent and, throughout the fifties there were no political organisations in Sharpeville with the capacity to steer and coordinate community opinion and action should this be required in times of political crisis.

As for hundreds of local youths turned back at the factory gates in favour of migrant workers, most would either gravitate towards the gang culture or drift aimlessly around the few open areas in the township, seeking recreation, trouble (or both).[17] Because of its centrality, its shops and few trees, the wide field at the intersection of Zwane and Seeiso Streets – the nodal point of the township where the first local police station was erected in the mid-fifties – was considered a primary point for congregation.

Few of these social divisions were explicitly political or contained discernable ideological components – at least not prior to the threshold of the 1960 massacre. In the meantime however, during the relatively 'golden years' of the fifties and at the very time when Sharpeville was moving towards a cultural apogee in the diverse areas of soccer, boxing and African jazz, various forces were beginning to work on both the local and national landscape to unravel the cocoon that was the township, both in fact and in the conceptions of its original planners. These were, in the words of one commentator, 'to propel the township toward a unity it had not yet experienced'.[18]

The late fifties were, in the first place, a time of eroding standards of living, with the inhabitants of Sharpeville caught in the cleft between rising costs and increased unemployment, with local employers unyielding in the face of demands to change labour policy to the advantage of the township residents. Regional industrial and manufacturing interests were not entirely unsympathetic to the view put forward by an informal coalition of concerned councillors and philanthropic members of the Vereeniging and Vanderbijl communities that escalating unemployment could produce instability among the local black population, but a combination of economic calculations and in-built prejudice swung the balance in favour of the migrant workers. Ultimately, there was little that advocates of the Sharpeville 'model' could put forward to counter the view of the great majority of the business community that migrants were cheaper, more productive, and considerably more reliable than the increasingly numbers of frustrated (and sometimes aggressive) young people from the township who were prohibited by the pass laws from seeking employment outside the designated Sharpeville area. The Council, alone was not sufficiently empowered to rectify this situation through its own job creation initiatives, most of which foundered before even rising off the ground. Nor could the municipality alleviate the rising cost of living by reducing the rental price of houses which had risen in general proportion to overall living costs with the passing of the years.

It was at this juncture that the final removals from Topville took place. Since the initial decision in the early forties to establish Sharpeville industrial expansion in the Vaal had vastly inflated the land value of the old Topville location and this immediately confronted the Vereeniging Council with a policy contradiction. On the one hand it was committed to a gradual redeployment to Sharpeville in line with available housing, on the other, it was eager to acquire the increasingly valuable industrial land at Duncanville – and this required bringing Topville, with its last remaining 426 stands, to termination as soon as possible. By April 1951, relocations had ceased because there were 'no approved housing schemes into which [Topville] residents might be transferred.'[19] Thereafter, for much of the fifties, municipal policy wavered from one pole to the other, with different internal elements in the municipality frequently at odds with one other. Councillors susceptible to the overtures of business with its promises to buy land and broaden the municipal tax base were generally of mind to accelerate the relocation process irrespective of whether or not there was adequate housing to receive the new migrants to Sharpeville. Many officials with an eye to the local treasury were also of the opinion that relocation should be speeded up and that negative incentives should be used to persuade the already reduced Topville population to exercise their exit option. The consequence was a virtual embargo on any services or improvements to Topville in its final years by which time its residual residents were subsisting in the most appalling social conditions.

In the event, the final decision was taken by higher governmental authority after seven years of quite extraordinary bureaucratic obstruction and confusion in the network of apartheid institutions involved in the reclassification of people and the utilisation of their land. Finally, in late 1958, with the proclamation of Sharpeville Extension 1, the Council was given permission to close Topville.[20]. At this point the acquisitive urges of the municipality ran rampant and whatever the claims of the Vereeniging Council to reasonably 'progressive' status, they disappeared in a classic forced removal equal to the worst barbarities perpetuated under the inhumane rubric of apartheid. People in Topville were simply informed that they were being transferred to Sharpeville irrespective of their choices or dispositions, and, after impossibly short notice, were bundled at gunpoint into municipal police trucks along with the bare minimum of their portable possessions. When people had possessions which did not fit the specifications of the trucks, they were simply left at the roadside.[21] Thereafter, municipal bulldozers made short work of the crumbling shanties in order to clear the site for the speedy entry of the industrial developers. No adequate provision had been made for managing the social consequences of this act which effectively 'disappeared' Topville in 1959.

Its traumatised inhabitants arrived in Sharpeville's Extenion 1, known as Vuka section, to be confronted by little more than a collection of shacks and the most rudimentary of public health facilities – all on a bare piece of veld grandiosely labelled a 'site and service' settlement. This was particularly harsh on people who had previously been homeowners, who were sufficiently educated to comprehend the iniquitous workings of apartheid, and who had lost the accoutrements of a petit bourgeois township existence. Hereafter Vuka, with its displaced and angry inhabitants at various levels of social deprivation would become a cancer of political discontent within the normally calm body politic of the Sharpeville population.

Within municipal circles the final decision regarding the fate of Topville had provoked a degree of conflict. As might be expected of a racist body infused with segregationist ideas in line with the mainstream political culture of apartheid South Africa, scant regard was shown for the human consequences of such an action. The few 'progressive' councillors who had lamely argued that housing should be constructed in Sharpeville before any precipitate decision was made were largely concerned with the possibility that a forced removal would destabilise the township with various consequences for white security in the Vaal area. In the event, they were right, although the implications of the destruction of Topville were to have their impact later rather than sooner. In the meantime they gave way before an overwhelming majority of fellow-councillors and municipal officials – backed by industrial developers – who had long since tired of the inconvenience of a black slum on the borders of the town and who looked forward to its speedy elimination. Unlike many of its counterparts elsewhere, though, the Vereeniging municipality had had very little experience in the organisation of a forced removal. Previous relocations to Sharpeville, as I have noted, had been both peaceful and voluntary, and now, faced with a situation with an inherent potential for violence, the local authority was a little hesitant. Consequently, in the days preceding the initiation of the removal, there was a round of urgent if private talks between the various stakeholders, the basic purpose of which was to ensure that the process of removing Topville would take place as quickly and efficiently as possible.

Once the decision to move ahead was taken, the municipal police and other elements of the local authority involved in township administration were briefed as to their various roles in the process. Since the municipal police force was relatively small, lightly armed, and, except for a number of individuals, unfamiliar with the strategic procedures of community removals, the uniformed branch of the Vereeniging SAP was called in to stand by in a back-up capacity to deal with violence should it arise. As an added precaution, the councillors and the local police chief decided that all SAP stations in surrounding areas were to be placed on standby to deal with any deteriorating situation – even though, significantly, none was especially equipped or trained in riot or crowd control. The nearby Heidelburg SAP, who could draw on such heavy weaponry as .303 rifles and Sten guns from the armoury at the local Army Gymnasium, and who had fraternally assisted their Vereeniging colleagues on previous occasions, were among the first to be contacted.

Inevitably, these communications along the SAP chain of command attracted the attention of the security police in Johannesburg who decided that it might be in the 'national interest' to monitor a potentially dangerous action in one of the key industrial areas of South Africa. Colonel 'Att' Spengler, a seasoned official in the security services, was deployed to Topville to survey the removal from the comparative safety of the nearby main road between Vereeniging and Johannesburg. Spengler, who will resurface again as a central figure in this narrative, observed the mixture of passivity and resentment among the people loaded onto the municipal trucks bound for Vuka. There was little violence beyond the scuffles that might be expected from people suddenly evicted from their homes, yet Spengler discerned that this disoriented group were excellent candidates for 'penetration' either by the police or political activists. He decided to maintain a keen eye on developments in Sharpeville – not least because no one else was doing so, and this might afford a useful route to the higher reaches of the state security apparatus for a man who was known for his career ambitions.

The arrival of a mass of displaced persons from Topville fed into a complex of local tensions which were disturbing the hitherto peaceful Sharpeville by the middle of 1959.[22] The ability of local networks to absorb immigrants was seriously strained by the major influx at a time when many people were falling behind on their rents and turning to illicit liquor distilling and other illegal activities for survival; when the ranks of the jobless were swelling; and the marginalised township youth were moving in unprecedented numbers into gangland activity as an antidote to their frustrations at the lack of employment.

The pass system, which regulated most facets of social and private life, was universally resented as the source of all evil and, to complicate matters, increasing numbers of 'Russians' from Evaton began to arrive individually or collectively in the township as semi-permanent residents rather than casual weekend visitors. All of this, combined with the festering problems of the displaced Topville people at Vuka, implied a breakdown of social harmony and control, to the consternation of the Vereeniging Council. A number of meetings were held between representatives of the municipality's Non-European Affairs Department and the Sharpeville Advisory Board, but these proved unproductive simply because the Board had never been equipped to function as more than a powerless mechanism of communication, devoid of both administrative and policing powers. The Sharpeville Location Superintendent, at the best of times reluctant to talk to 'kaffirs' whose good behaviour he saw to be the responsibility of the local Advisory Board, was now under pressure from his superiors to alleviate a mounting community crisis and advocated more forceful measures.

Municipal police raids to stamp out criminal activity of one sort or another had been a feature of Vaal life for much of the fifties. In early 1960, for example, the residents of Boipatong and Bophelong had condemned the pass laws whose violation was turning their children into 'jailbirds' as they sought employment elsewhere.[23] Yet in Sharpeville violations of the pass and labour laws had – to a degree – been carried out with an element of circumspection appropriate to good relations in what was then a relatively stable community. Now, with the 'success' of the Topville resettlement still fresh in its memory, the Vereeniging municipality proceeded to unleash its municipal police force to eradicate the 'undesirable' and 'subversive' elements ostensibly at work to disrupt what had been, until recently, their model township.

The municipal police, a mixture of white officers drawn from the lower reaches of local society and black auxiliaries armed with batons, whips and sticks, now proceeded to act quite arbitrarily, sometimes alone and sometimes in conjunction with regular members of the Vereeniging SAP or their colleagues recruited from nearby commands for a night of 'kaffirsport'. Since their actions were largely immune from prosecution – brave (or foolhardy) was the black man who laid a charge against a white policeman – most did not even bother to hide or obscure their features. They were visible and known by name (or more often nickname) to their victims and this was to be important in the following year when many of them were to be redeployed to the area. In the meantime, the police, too, carried out their mandate in a brutal fashion which was, in the polite words of one later commentator, 'a source of considerable discontent among township residents'.[24]

The pass laws governing influx control allowed the authorities to accost any black person, anywhere, anytime – and the police now exploited these opportunities for intimidation with alacrity. There were few law-abiding Sharpeville residents who in late-1959 escaped interference on the streets, particularly after dusk in the vicinity of the municipal beerhall which had, in the wisdom of the authorities, been identified as the physical centre of all the local problems – despite the contribution of its sales to local government coffers. No search warrants were required and, in their pursuit of illegal residents, distillers, rent-evaders, and the like, the police would break into private premises at any time of the day or night, but particularly between one and four in the morning, harass and humiliate the inhabitants, smash their possessions, and in many instances subject their victims to violent beatings designed to produce passes, confessions or information for transmission to Spengler and his associates at The Greys, the ominous headquarters of the Special Branch in central Johannesburg.[25]

Since the Vereeniging Council worked on the simple assumption that gangsters were behind much of the disturbance in the normal body politic, special ire was reserved for young men, who were automatically presumed to be 'vagrants', Russians, or gang members – and were then treated accordingly.[26] This almost invariably meant arrest, preceded, accompanied and followed by physical abuse, generally conducted by 'hard' black policemen who were specially recruited for raids on the basis that they were not residents of Sharpeville. Some assaults took place in the cells of the Vereeniging Police Station, but normally it was more convenient for the wrath of the state to be exacted on prisoners at the more central Sharpeville Police Station. This had been constructed in the mid-fifties as part of the policy of the then more enlightened municipality to equip the township with a reasonably broad service infrastructure, including accessible facilities for the maintenance of public safety and general good order. In 1959 it was the only police station in the Vaal region – and one of the few throughout South Africa – to be situated in the heart of a black township. By late that year, the new structure with its complement of black personnel came to symbolise for township youth the whole repressive iniquity of the apartheid system.

The small security police contingent at the various Vaal police stations initially played no role in this process of state terrorism, partially because municipal policing was beyond its brief, partially because this élite element within SAP structures had little interest in minor community disturbances which were best left to the municipal police whom they considered barely a cut above the uniformed SAP branches in the hierarchy of police excellence.

Although the Vaal ANC were, in the retrospective opinion of a now long-retired police general, 'rubbish in these years' and could not 'even organise potatoes', after the Defiance Campaign state security policy began to focus on the protection of what were later designated 'keypoint' strategic areas such as the Free State Goldfields, the Central Highveld coal mines, the coastal refinery at Durban, and the Vaal region. Much of the work of implementing this strategy devolved on Colonel Willem Prinsloo at Kompol (Security Police headquarters in Pretoria), and it was

Prinsloo who during mid-1959 requested Spengler and his Johannesburg team to elevate the Vaal in their list of security concerns, to selectively communicate with local government in Vereeniging and Vanderbijl about the security situation, to assess the situation for themselves, and then, under the command of Spengler, to proceed accordingly. Spengler, who had monitored the ANC since the late forties, was not persuaded by assurances that the municipality and local police had the minor township disturbances under full control. He knew that Sharpeville was, in the grand scheme of things, small meat, and that the ANC presence in the area was largely nominal. Still, ever cautious since the fracas at Topville, he believed the area warranted close consideration in the light of unceasing 'Communist activities' on a nation-wide basis.

The wisdom of this was confirmed towards the end of 1959 when intelligence sources revealed the presence in the Vaal, particularly in Evaton, of a number of members of the ANC Youth League inclined towards Robert Sobukwe and other ostensibly militant 'Africanist' malcontents. A municipal police raid on a residence off Zwane Street in December 1959 had inadvertently uncovered in the roof of the house a primitive arms cache which, by its composition, did not appear linked to gangster activity. Subsequent interrogations of some prominent gang leaders at Vereeniging and Vanderbijl provided no clues regarding the ownership or use of a box containing a number of knives and razors, two small calibre pistols, and, more seriously, a .303 standard-issue SAP rifle. Following an urgent communication to the District Commander of Police, the decision was taken to move more decisively into Sharpeville and adjacent townships, to develop an effective network of informants, and to monitor apparent radicals and other members of the regional ANC.

The December interrogations are so central to the unfolding tragedy in Sharpeville that they warrant more attention. Among the interrogations the one conducted in the holding cells of the Vereeniging Police Station in the early hours of 17 December, the day after the discovery of the arms cache, is the most significant. Here the owner of the compromised house, his two terrified teenage sons, some neighbours, two or three known gang leaders and a certain 'Geelbooi' had been assembled. 'Geelbooi', a petty thief attached to a breakaway faction of one of the Rooistene gangs – the self-styled 'Buccaneers – had rounded the corner from Zwane Street at precisely the moment when the municipal police emerged carrying the sheet containing the knives, pistol and rifle. Since he appeared to be heading to the house he was immediately accosted and loaded along with ten or twelve other suspects into the back of the police truck. Half a dozen of these people were then dropped off at the Vereeniging Police Station at approximately midnight, incarcerated in a cell, and then taken, one by one, into an adjoining room for questioning.

The interrogation was carried out in the presence of two black police constables under the authority of three white officers, one of whom, a Sergeant de Bruyn, was a Special Branch operative from the Orange Free State who was visiting a relative in the Vereeniging area. De Bruyn, who had been celebrating the 16 December public holiday commemorating the Afrikaner triumph over the Zulus at the Battle of Blood River, had apparently been called away from a traditional evening 'braaivleis' to assist investigations. He arrived at the station on the edges of sobriety at approximately 1am. Prior to the interrogation, a further bottle of brandy was shared among the white officers who then began to question the suspects. All the interrogations were conducted 'vigorously', but for reasons which are not entirely clear, the interrogation of Geelbooi, which was led by De Bruyn, was especially vicious, and involved a primitive version of 'helicoptering' – one of the more extreme forms of torture that became standard procedure to be used on political detainees by the security police in later years. The unfortunate Geelbooi was tied, suspended between two chairs, spun around and repeatedly kicked and beaten with a sjambok before the inebriated torturers realised that he had nothing in the way of useful information. As a parting gesture, the now empty brandy bottle was broken across the back of his neck and he was unceremoniously thrown, bruised, shocked and bleeding profusely, out of the main entrance of the police station. Geelbooi staggered away through the dark and deserted early morning streets – and seemingly out of history.

Christmas 1959 in Sharpeville was a fairly sombre affair. While white Vereeniging residents testified later that the township mood contained nothing untoward, few had ever ventured or would ever venture into a 'native location' with its images of dirt, poverty and violence. In reality, most of the people of Sharpeville at Christmas were preoccupied with survival issues. Although the better shebeens did a brisk trade among the small township élite composed of its usual mixture of sport stars, musicians, gangsters, entrepreneurs, and a sprinkling of professional people, Christmas cheer was for the most part subdued by anxieties over rent arrears, unemployment, and the anticipation of intensified raids by a police force made more zealous in the performance of its duties by a combination of liquid and festive spirit. With heightening resistance to influx control at the national level, the pass laws were on everyone's lips – all the more so as various strangers came into the township and urged people to give vent to their dissatisfaction. In fact, as Spengler had begun to suspect, the PAC had launched a tentative campaign against the pass laws in the Vaal Triangle, first in the large metalworks which were most easily penetrable, and then in the various township communities of Bophelong, Boipatong and Evaton.

In Sharpeville itself a number of people had been hearing about the PAC's charismatic leader, Robert Sobukwe, for quite some time. Some who were to become the first PAC activists in Sharpeville claim to have first heard of Sobukwe as early as the mid-fifties, particularly in the wake of the Freedom Charter, whose promulgation in June 1955 added to the divisiveness between the established leadership of the ANC and the group of young 'Nationalists' in its Youth League. Certainly, a number of Sharpeville people felt sympathy with his 'Africanist' ideas. Among them were the Tsolo brothers, Nyakane and Job, the sons of a local coal dealer. Job, the older, had come into contact with various concepts of what would later be labelled 'black consciousness' through his association with the Unity Youth Movement. It was Nyakane however, born in Coalbrooke but schooled in the Rooistene section of Sharpeville, who had had experience organising workers on the shop floor and now took the dangerous lead. During 1958 he led a successful strike for overtime wages among workers at Vereeniging's African Cables which brought him to the attention of Z B Molete, the staunch Pan Africanist leader in Evaton. Shortly thereafter Nyakane and David Ramodibe, another young Sharpevillean, began to take the lead in linking a number of young local militants to the splinter group in Soweto.

In December 1958 the kernel of the new party officially broke away from the ANC at its national conference – and the following March a small group of young people from Evaton and Sharpeville, collectively dissatisfied with the weakness, caution, ostensible opportunism and general immobility of the local ANC, took a train to Johannesburg. Although they did not meet with Sobukwe as a group, they were favourably impressed by his closest colleagues – men such as Zeph Mothopeng and Jacob Nyaose, both of whom emphasised the need for Africans to recognise their own authenticity by igniting a political campaign with resistance to the pass laws at its foundations. Nyakane Tsolo was personally so taken with the energy and dedication of these men who were to become key members of the PAC's first national executive that he returned to Johannesburg for the foundation conference of the PAC at the Orlando Communal Hall three weeks later. Here he met Sobukwe himself for the first time. Thereafter, Tsolo and his self-elected colleagues from Sharpeville proceeded to facilitate contacts between the central office of the party and key individuals in the community. An official PAC branch was established in May 1959 led by an executive consisting of Tsolo, Ramodibe and D L Morobe (who was soon displaced as a result of 'policy differences' which were, in effect, charges of ideological inconsistency). The executive was expanded to nine persons – Nyakane, Ramodibe, Job Tsolo, Susan Mohanoe, Stefaans Lepee, Thomas More, L Koale, B Ntoampe, and, ironically, the younger sister of ANC stalwart, Adelaide Tambo. A membership drive to give the branch human substance was begun in earnest and by early 1960 PAC organisers involved in distributing leaflets or initiating quiet group discussions were a fairly standard sight at most places of public congregation. These included bus stops, schools, churches, the Sharpeville library, and the local pass office-cum labour bureau conveniently situated across the road from the municipal beerhall.

The aim (and subsequent consequences) of the 1960 anti-pass campaign have provoked considerable debate in the light of the massacre and later developments. Certain aspects that are crucially linked with the events of 21 March 1960 are fairly clear in historic retrospect and require emphasis. Firstly, the PAC leadership (and especially Sobukwe) were realistic enough to appreciate that African resistance had not yet reached the point where it could successfully engage in a full-frontal confrontation with the apartheid state, least of all precipitate its collapse in the short-term future. Sobukwe and most of the PAC leadership were impatient with the caution and lack-lustre track record of the ANC establishment which, despite a series of political campaigns during the course of the decade, appeared to be losing the political initiative.

The recapture of the political high ground, they anticipated, required far more dramatic action than the ANC conservatives were willing to risk or contemplate – but not necessarily the violence which a number of his younger and more militant lieutenants were beginning, in their frustration, to advocate. Rather than embark upon a hopeless armed struggle against the all-powerful apartheid regime, what was required was a campaign which would at once conscientise the African masses to the exact nature of their political condition, shift the moral equilibrium in their favour decisively, clog the administrative capacity of the apartheid system, and activate the international community to recognise both the evil of the apartheid system and the impossibility of reforming it through inter-state dialogue and other forms of what apologists for South Africa would later deem 'constructive engagement'. The PAC could also re-activate the principle of non-collaboration which had its roots in the All-African Convention of the mid-thirties. The key to this lay in protest against the pass system – a matter with which all black South Africans could identify at a time when an estimated one thousand people per day were being arrested under the influx control laws.[27] Strategically, it was an issue around which they could be mobilised and where collective weight would minimise individual risk.

Elements of this approach were familiar to the ANC leadership from which Sobukwe and his immediate supporters were political emigrants.

Yet a number of factors distinguished this splinter group from the bulk of the ANC establishment, and these were to be of direct significance to what was about to transpire at Sharpeville. The Pan Africanists were, in the first instance, the younger generation of the ANC. Prior to his departure from its ranks Sobukwe had been head of its Youth League, many of whose members were growing increasingly impatient with the moderate attitudes of their elders. The ANC establishment, the young militants believed, had been 'captured' by the South African Communist Party; it had departed from the 1949 Programme of Action and, in the process, it had sacrificed the African nationalist struggle on the altar of expedient multiracial cooperation. Most Pan Africanists, be they Mothopeng, Molete or Sobukwe himself, had little patience with the ANC view that the struggle was one of class, and most regarded the development of a united African front through mass action by the African people as the political and strategic priority.[28]

Secondly, unlike the ANC with its ideological roots in European conceptions of multiracialism, the PAC drew inspiration from the intrinsically African struggle against imperialism and colonialism which, at this point, was reaching its historic apogee on other parts of the continent, further to the North. This reinforced the notion of political action 'by Africans for Africans' as the means of building the collective racial identities necessary for resisting the white state.

Thirdly, and perhaps most importantly in the light of what later transpired at Sharpeville, the 'Africanists' placed far more value on individual spontaneity, human consciousness and cultural transformation as pathways to political mobilisation than the ANC whose emphasis was on planned and carefully orchestrated mass action. Although he sought a disciplined and ordered movement, Sobukwe, and most certainly his lieutenants, were no Leninists in their insistence on the key role of a leadership 'vanguard'. On the contrary, the leadership principle in PAC strategy was tentative and somewhat diminished from the outset of its foundation congress which laid down a 'disciplinary code' that was, in the words of one commentator, both 'a jumble of ideas' and a 'throwback to missionary schooling'.[29] Combining vague principles of democratic centralism with exhortations to members about rumour-mongering, back-biting and personal hygiene, the code offered the new PAC nothing in the way of practical guidelines or operational principles to be deployed in the struggle against the apartheid state. 'All that we [the leaders] are required to do,' as Sobukwe believed, and as he reminded an audience in 1949, 'is to show the light and the masses will find the way.'[30] Indeed they would – eleven years later, in the Vaal, and with the most drastic consequences.

These differences in ideological tradition, motivation and style did not constrain the PAC as they moved into the recruitment phase of their work in the tense atmosphere of Sharpeville in late 1959. On the contrary, they linked directly into what was an essentially receptive political culture. Little headway was made among the local 'labour aristocracy' – the largely migrant workers in the neighbouring iron and steel factories and manufacturing industries who were lucky enough to have employment and whose universe was shaped by narrow ethnic as opposed to racial considerations. While the older and more conservative members of the local petit bourgeoisie were also suspicious of unfamiliar and militant calls to action emanating from the agents of metropolitan Johannesburg, substantial numbers of unemployed and marginalised township youth gravitating round the pass office, the labour bureau, and the adjacent beerhall were magnetised by the spirit of assertiveness encoded in the PAC position. This stood in sharp contrast to the redundancy of the local ANC whose small membership had done little or nothing to address the social problems that had bedevilled the community for much of the preceding year. This constituency was strategically important to the PAC since it gave them access to a highly mobile and reasonably dedicated element with few social ties or preoccupations other than to roam the township and spread the PAC message.

A number of gangs were also important either as instruments for PAC propaganda, or as sources for weapons at a time when few blacks could legally possess firearms. For the most part the fledgeling Vaal PAC was chary of links with the criminal world and only a few on its lunatic fringe at that point seriously contemplated armed confrontation. However the central leadership of the PAC was still ambiguous on the critical issue of whether non-violence was the morally correct path to follow, while the gangs were of value in swelling the size of the local chapters at grassroots level. The resignation/dismissal of Morobe from the original Sharpeville executive turned on the issue of indiscipline in party ranks resulting from indiscriminate recruitment, but this had no effect on its remaining members who continued to cultivate the 'more respectable' gangland leaders as part of their strategic plan to build the credibility of the new anti-ANC organisation.

Some of these gang leaders, who had been scorned by the ANC establishment, were flattered by approaches from PAC cadres whom they saw as a new resource upon which to capitalise in their internecine territorial struggles. Others were attracted by the proto-anarchic sentiments inherent in PAC overtures. The PAC also struck a responsive chord among those of the displaced people of the final Topville relocation who had partially recovered from their recent traumatic experience and were seeking ways to even their score with the authorities. The Vuka section of Sharpeville, it was reported by police informants, consequently became an Africanist stronghold – just as Spengler and his security officials had anticipated. As events would show, some of these alliances with unreliable and unstable social formations would prove to be very dangerous.

The PAC's message that the people should refuse to carry passes and court arrest en masse was received sympathetically across the board – much as Sobukwe and the leadership had intended. As PAC cadres moved furtively through the area to avoid the ubiquitous police raiders on the prowl for 'illegals', the questions of how best to translate this concept into action and under what circumstances became the currency of guarded conversation in the local shops, shebeens and – more openly – within the relative security of private houses. Although only a very small number of Sharpeville residents actually took the dangerous step of taking out formal membership of the PAC, given the omnipresent informer network, by the beginning of 1960 there was widespread support for some sort of demonstration that would take collective feeling to the level of practical expression. To most people the passes remained, in Sobukwe's words, the 'distinctive badge of slavery and humiliation'. Social conditions had not improved markedly; the new year had brought with it all the accumulated ills of its predecessor – high rents, falling standards of living, unemployment and persistent police raids. There were no particular signs in the early weeks of 1960 – at least in the eyes of Sharpeville's residents – that the situation would improve in the months ahead. The stage was set for further and substantially more dramatic developments.

PART II

THE MASSACRE

The dead and injured lie sprawled in the road leading from the police station

THE SETTING

The great German thinker Hannah Arendt once spoke of the banal evils of authoritarianism and visitors to contemporary Sharpeville are confronted by a scene which stands testimony to the bleak but lethal legacy of apartheid.[1] Sharpeville can be entered, as it could forty years ago, by a turnoff from the main Vereeniging-Vanderbijl highway which, after a short distance brings into view a row of small and dilapidated houses, etched stark and horizon-wide across the flat, bare veld of the Vaal Triangle. To the right, in the distance lies a small patch of water, the local dam which, following South Africa's democratic transition, has become notorious as a meeting place for local 'tsotsis' (gangsters). Sharpeville houses the most violent criminals in the region and the local mafias, labelled 'the Italians', make it impossible for any upstanding citizen safely to make use of the dam which is one of the township's few recreational facilities.

The houses, situated in a sea of uncollected garbage which appears to occupy almost every piece of open land in the area, are of the uniformly cheap 'matchbox' variety constructed for the poor and ostensibly transient urban workers by apartheid's unimaginative town planners. Although some desperate attempts have been made over the years to give each dwelling a modicum of individuality – a rough portico, an incongruously green vine entwined in grey corrugated roofing here and there – it strains the imagination to envisage this prototype of alienating urban decay as the 'model' of which the white councillors of Vereeniging spoke with so much pride and enthusiasm during the late fifties.

Proceeding along tarred but potholed roads punctuated by the occasional chicken or stray goat one weaves between the main houses towards the centre. Small shacks from which local hawkers sell an assortment of goods – vegetables, combs, refreshments of cheap liquor – line the approach. The overall impression, six years into South Africa's 'liberation' is one of dull and inescapably grinding poverty. Many people stand aimlessly in small and scattered groups on the brown packed sand which substitutes for pavements in most cases. This, the visitor is told, is an indication of the conviviality of township existence, the vibrant culture of the streets. In fact these are the masses of the unemployed – men, women and youths wearing cast-off, shabby versions of designer jeans and tracksuits. They are in the streets to escape the claustrophobia of the crowded houses. They are also waiting for the unlikely possibility that a stray person will pass by and offer them 'piece work' (casual employment).

The 'centre' of Sharpeville is not a centre at all. Because it, like other townships was conceived as a dormitory town whose only reason for existence was to feed the local economy – the iron and steel industries of the Vaal, the Rand mines elsewhere – there was no apparent need to build a node (or number of nodes) where people would normally meet, shop and be entertained. The use of space in Sharpeville suggests a concentration camp without the wire. Yet, given the natural tendency of people to converge and interact, a 'centre', in the rough-and-ready sense has emerged over the years. This is in the apex of the triangle formed by the convergence of the two main arterials – Zwane and Seeiso streets. Here a fairly large open field patched with thin grass and sand stretches over several hundred yards in either direction. On its north-eastern edge there are a number of small and dilapidated shops and a filling station, behind which is the first row of houses. This is the central business district. On its north-western edge lies the Sharpeville library, constructed in the forties and today an overcrowded venue for regular visits by schoolchildren, the unemployed and anyone else seeking to escape the unremitting boredom of existence in a place with few jobs and little recreation.

Sharpeville has few trees, and grass cannot survive in this dry, crowded and poor environment where water is an expensive commodity. But the library, which gives way to the first row of densely-packed houses on its northern side, has an immaculate, if small, green lawn and a few dense acacias that immediately strike the eye. Since anything that can be stolen is stolen, the building, like any other of importance is surrounded by a high fence topped with razor wire. The grim nature of the place is emphasised by the nearby two-story community centre – one of the few 'high-rise' structures in this flat and forbidding environment, a hundred yards to the south-west of the library. Vaguely reminiscent of a church, it is a blackened and burnt-out husk, victim of the 1984 community violence and totters precariously in an easterly direction.

The western edge of the open area is framed by ubiquitous matchbox housing, the southern edge by the local clinic. Immediately to the right of the clinic, across a small street lies the dominant building on the landscape – the Sharpeville Police Station – which, forty years ago, faced directly onto the open field in front. Today, this direct access, the primary path of flight for the massacre victims, is blocked by a newly-constructed post office. Local folklore has it that it was built so that the police would no longer have to look in shame upon the place of carnage.

─── ✦ ───

CONTESTING THE VAAL:
THE POLICE AND THE PAC – 1959 TO 1960

The present police station, like the post office, is a largely post-1960 construction, although part of the low, squat brick buildings dates back to the original 'community' complex built by the Vereeniging Council to, somewhat vaguely 'attend to the welfare of the township'.[2] With the decision of the SAP in the mid-fifties to develop a number of installations within some townships as a means of intimidating their inhabitants, the Council was approached and requested to rent the set of buildings to the police authorities – not because Sharpeville was regarded as especially volatile but simply because the physical facilities were in place, largely under-utilised, and a financial liability. The Council, swayed by the argument that a police station in Sharpeville was part of SAP policy 'to establish the image of the Force as the friend and protector of law-abiding inhabitants', readily agreed.[3] The SAP was to use the new Sharpeville station for purposes of crime control, while responsibility for enforcing laws against illegal liquor brewing, rentals, local by-laws and the implementation of influx control was left to the local municipal police operating from the municipal offices at the far end of Seeiso Street, opposite the beerhall and near the 'native' cemetery.[4] But because the 'municipals' found the central police station a convenient location from which to mount intensified operations against the local population, the station failed to serve the purpose of 'fostering better understanding between the residents and the [South African] police'.[5] In fact its physical presence in the heartland of the community came to came to symbolise all the collective grievances felt by local people about 'native policy'.

Like much else in Sharpeville the police station was and is a remarkably unimpressive icon of state-perpetuated evil in its dull, anonymous and petty-bureaucratic character. There is a narrow perimeter of surrounding land sufficient to park a large vehicle (an armoured car, perhaps) but no more. This separates the main buildings from a wire mesh fence, insubstantially waist-level in 1960, but now considerably higher. Both the fence and the perimeter would, as we shall see, play an important role in the unfolding events of the massacre. The main entrance to the station is a gate leading on to the street on the west side immediately facing the clinic. Across the road to the south of the police station is a solid row of houses. From the roof of the police station there is a clear view – or a clear shot – now over the post office, into the adjoining field. In the centre of the field, roughly halfway along the rough sand path to the library stands a small and rather incongruously-shaped stone with a metal plaque attached. This is the sole memorial to the Sharpeville victims, the survivors and those members of the community who struggled for human dignity and freedom. To the passing observer, and most simply pass, it gives no clue to the cataclysmic events in this otherwise ordinary place on a sunny autumn day four decades ago.

Under normal circumstances the police station was manned by a small complement of about thirty-five to forty African policemen (including eight black sergeants) and some administrative staff. Since the SAP could rarely detect 'the necessary aptitude and sense of responsibility' required for commissioned leadership in its 'non-white' ranks, the entire complement fell under the command of a small handful of white officers – normally a single white sergeant and two white constables (all of whom, in the logic of apartheid, superseded their black counterparts, including the sergeants).[6] In accordance with national policing policy, only the white personnel carried side-arms while the Africans were armed with batons, sticks or sharpened metal poles that could be used to variously flush out covert liquor stills or non-resident 'illegals' as determined by the pass laws.

Under 'abnormal' circumstances, on the rare occasions when trouble appeared to be brewing in the township as a result of regional or national political protests, the Sharpeville complement was slightly increased by personnel drawn from the Vereeniging Police Station or, occasionally, from further afield. Police raids did not normally require an increase in personnel but fraternal relations between the Vereeniging and Heidelberg police (who had little else to do in the local township of Ratanda) sometimes led to joint cordon-and-search operations.[7]

Virtually none of the black policemen were residents of Sharpeville in line with SAP policy to deploy 'foreigners' to police different townships as far as possible. This policy, designed to insulate black personnel from the local community, actually helped to facilitate a situation where most of the community regarded the black police at the Sharpeville station as part of the 'forces of occupation'. Relations between the local police and the community were not especially close at the best of times, and by the beginning of 1960 had been further soured by the intensified enforcement of the pass laws. Not unsurprisingly in the segregated conditions of apartheid South Africa, the white officers at Sharpeville were largely divorced from the wider local community. All simply came into the township to do their duty on a daily basis, and most inter-personal contacts, in the charge office for example, were left in the hands of their black underlings. While there may have been occasional exchanges between the white police and the residents around the station or elsewhere in Sharpeville, these always took place within the established framework of 'baasskap' (literally white bossism based on the principle of race supremacy). The white officers, it appears, were not particularly vicious by the standards of the time, but they expected to be accorded the respect and deference they believed was due to people of white extraction by even the most prominent members of the black community. It is indicative of this disconnection between white uniform SAP personnel and the people they policed that the élite security police, both in the Vaal and elsewhere, tended to value the intelligence provided by their own networks of informants on political matters above that of the station commanders and their white staff.

The alienation of the black police from the wider community was also problematic from a policing perspective. Many of the Sharpeville contingent closeted in the local barracks in 1960 were Zulus from a rural background and this effectively excluded them from the urban and largely Sotho cultural networks of the township. While from the SAP perspective this was preferable for the maintenance of discipline, command and control, it also meant that the black police knew as little about the social and political movements in their immediate environment as their white counterparts. When the black auxiliaries did become participants in this environment it was normally as agents of the repressive state apparatus with all its consequent violence. Many of the older residents recall that the semi-trained black police, although prohibited from bearing firearms, were an especially unstable and aggressive component of the security forces. Intent on indicating their loyalty to their superiors and compromised in the eyes of the residents, they characteristically 'over-determined' their policing role. For the residents of Sharpeville, this meant frequent violent verbal and physical abuse under the umbrella of law enforcement.

The SAP prided itself on recruiting 'the finest young non-white men' from a constant stream of applicants available to service the security needs of the apartheid state.[8] Yet the black police in Sharpeville, as elsewhere, were also eminently corruptible. Since the apartheid laws governing virtually every aspect of black existence were highly arbitrary and lent themselves to exploitation by even the most petty of bureaucratic functionaries, the black police were encouraged to take every advantage of what was, from their perspective, a favourable repressive system. Fear of arrest or, even worse 'endorsement out of the area' under the pass laws encouraged bribery on a wide scale, and many of the shebeens (the illegal drinking dens) in Sharpeville effectively existed only because of police patronage. Police raids on a house-to-house basis afforded officials the opportunity to 'confiscate stolen goods' which were then sold back at exorbitant prices to their rightful owners. Some white officers were not necessarily immune from these temptations, prejudicial as they were to morale and discipline at the local police station. In February 1960, for example, there had been a fracas between a number of junior white officers and several black policemen over a 'kickback' from a local 'skokiaan' (indigenous beer) distillery which threatened to polarise race relations. One month later, in the run-up to the middle of March, a number of black policemen were still deeply hostile to their distrustful white superiors.

Given the dangerous nature of police work in what an official history deems 'dirty slum quarters and black townships where they [are] exposed to disease and injury', the SAP had great difficulty in competing with the private sector (or even other segments of the public sector) for the small pool of white manpower.[9] The white command structure of the SAP at the time (and for years thereafter), therefore drew heavily on poor, uneducated and often unemployable young Afrikaners from the conservative rural area and (to a lesser extent) from the urban white working class – also largely of Afrikaner extraction. By the time of Sharpeville a third of the white uniform force consisted of teenagers or persons under twenty-one[10], largely because eight years before Sharpeville the minimum recruitment age was lowered to sixteen and possession of a Standard Seven school certificate. Much of the sheer viciousness and racism implicit in the enforcement of the pass laws arose from a lethal combination of inexperience, youthful arrogance and unquestioned prejudice.[11] Township duty was considered an initiation school, with the result that the ranks of white officers at stations such as that in Sharpeville were often staffed by individuals of questionable reliability and professionalism, particularly in times of crisis.

At Security Police headquarters in both Pretoria and Johannesburg the emergence of some sort of 'extreme nationalist' faction within the ANC during 1958/59 was viewed with a mixture of glee and discomfort. On the one hand the existence of such a group was seen to constitute a direct threat to the state, on the other, it was also seen as presenting an opportunity for the state to sow discord within resistance circles. Since seminal 'securocrats' like Spengler and Prinsloo appear to have fallen into the category of those who believed that the presence of the PAC could be turned to their advantage, the informant network established in Sharpeville in late 1959 tended to turn on a complex triad involving the state security forces, the ANC, and the new Pan Africanist movement. Not all the members of the first PAC executive were entirely dedicated activists who had turned to the new movement out of frustration with the passive and ponderous attempts of the ANC to bring the white government to its knees with a minimum of confrontation. On the contrary, so many of the ANC recruits who offered their services to the local branch were suspected of being police agents that the executive initially gave preference to new members who had *not* been card-carrying members of the ANC. Still, the primary task facing PAC leadership at this point was to expand the popular base as rapidly as possible and this inevitably led to a change in policy in favour of the notion that migrants from the ANC could join but could not form part of the executive.

By mid-1959 the PAC's national target of 100 000 members was far from met and the rate of recruitment in Sharpeville was no better than the national average. Although party propaganda still insists to this day that there were 'thousands' of paid-up, card-carrying PAC members in Sharpeville by the time of the massacre, there were certainly less than a hundred by the beginning of 1960 and probably no more than 300 three months later. So embarrassingly bad was the situation in the last months of 1959 that Nyakane Tsolo and his immediate colleagues feared that the branch would suffer severe censure at the first national conference projected for December. Even the small executive was battling to keep its members in the face of personality conflicts, private agendas, and the ideological conflicts common to a new organisation at the mercy of state penetration. By late 1959 all this translated into recruitment 'policy' where virtually all-comers were made welcome, if not on the executive then at least in the ranks. This lack of discrimination in its turn inevitably increased the number of in-house police agents. It also facilitated the use of agents provocateurs from the PAC branch who were adeptly and destructively employed by Prinsloo (in Pretoria) and Spengler (on the ground) to discredit the ANC, by word of mouth or by pamphlets, issued under PAC letterhead, which were explicitly offensive in their criticism of ANC policies, both in Sharpeville and at national level. The Sharpeville branch members who attended the first national congress of the PAC in December 1959 were a shaky and discordant grouping united only by their disaffection from the ANC. As the Congress determined to launch a nation-wide anti-pass campaign, relations between the PAC and ANC at grassroots in the Vaal had deteriorated to such a point that any dialogue over the projected campaign, least of all collaboration, was well nigh impossible.

The inability of the two major black political movements to discuss their differences, align strategy or coordinate their policies, effectively precluded any possibility of joint action to head off a community crisis – if and when it arose. Even had either party managed to engineer some sort of political coalition, each was so organisationally discoordinated in itself as to render any practical collaboration unlikely. Magnetised by the anti-Communism of the PAC and the possibility of dividing the ANC, the state security forces also failed to appreciate the extent to which their manipulations contained the long-term potential for disaster. In the short term however, the situation worked to the advantage of the Security Police who, under the energetic direction of Spengler, were quick to build political capital out of local black party competition at every opportunity. Spengler, as he proudly testified at the Commission of Inquiry into the Sharpeville shootings, already knew by November – a month before the PAC national congress – that its leaders would announce some sort of mass action related to passes, and he had in his possession the names of the entire Sharpeville executive as well as those of most of the significant fellow-travellers in the local community. This was due, at least in part, to the assiduous collection of information on political activity in the township by Location Superintendent 'Lappies' Labuschagne. In part it also reflected the fact that two (or possibly three) of the handful of members in the small PAC executive were in the pay of the police and rendered invaluable assistance, along with other collaborative members, to the authorities in subverting the new organisation from its outset.

What Spengler did not know however was the exact nature of the proposed anti-pass action, nor, perhaps more importantly, the date for which it was planned. Here again however many of the ambiguities were resolved (or apparently resolved) when security policemen from Johannesburg travelled to an area on the Vaal River near the Riviera Hotel to meet covertly with a number of their Sharpeville agents in the last week of February 1960. Thereafter the police knew for certain that what the PAC had in mind was a mass gathering of the various Vaal township communities at their respective local police stations where they would state their refusal to carry passes, destroy the offending documents in the sight of the authorities, and offer themselves up for arrest and prosecution. What still remained uncertain was the date of the planned demonstration – informants had hinted at Easter – whether the police should act pre-emptively, or whether they should maintain a low profile and not react at all.

As I have already indicated, the security police held a particularly jaundiced view of their uniform branch colleagues whom they regarded, not unjustifiably, as inept and best confined to the more routine policing activities. There were also differences of a personal nature between Spengler and the Vereeniging District Commander, Major Willem van Zyl. Now that Spengler had concluded that a political problem was brewing in the Vaal, with its strategic importance for the water supply to the Witwatersrand, its metal industries, power station and mines, he decided to act unilaterally with his security police colleagues and largely by-pass established channels in the mainstream SAP, particularly Van Zyl – whom, he suspected, might hijack his intelligence coup for his own career purposes. From Spengler's point of view he was, in any case dealing with what he later described in testimony as 'a threat to the country's economy' – and this was, at least in his opinion, in a league far above the capacity of uniform branch of the SAP. Spengler also had some professional reservations about the competency of Lieutenant-Colonel Pienaar, the Divisional Inspector of Police in the Witwatersrand – not without justification as will emerge later. The information obtained at the riverside meeting was therefore passed on to Pienaar and Van Zyl only in an abbreviated form required by courtesy, while Spengler and his colleagues, backed by Prinsloo in Pretoria, moved to an independent appreciation of the situation. One possibility, they deemed, was a massive joint operation between the police and military to cordon off the various Vaal townships, comb the houses and arrest everyone suspected of even the mildest PAC inclinations. This was discounted because it would sow alarm in white society and carried the risk of popular resistance that could end, ironically, in violence. Another possibility was to simply arrest known PAC activists in the Vaal, including Sharpeville.

The local PAC claims to this day to have weeded out ANC stooges in its ranks in the first weeks of 1960 and to have 'turned' them against their police masters, either surreptitiously and without their knowledge, or by dint of physical violence. This is not entirely impossible given the complex pattern of human deceptions at work in inter-organisational relations between and within the police and the activists at the time. Either way, police agents had misinformed, disinformed or otherwise consciously misled the police into believing that the planned demonstrations were geared for the Easter holiday period when people would be off work and at home in the townships. From the police perspective, this left a reasonable time to take a low-key approach, to monitor the situation, gather additional intelligence and defer tactical decisions to a later date. It also left adequate time, or so Spengler fatally believed, to more fully brief the uniform branches of the SAP and to make any contingency plans for concentrating appropriate resources for riot or crowd control should they be required in the Vaal. As it was, such contingency plans were never made. Because of the inter-bureaucratic competition between the security and uniform branches and the belief in an Easter demonstration, no particular urgency was attached to the task of concentrating teargas supplies, riot shields and other 'soft' technologies for protest management in the Vaal region. What little existed in police circles at that time remained in Johannesburg and would remain there for the duration of the Sharpeville crisis.

In the meantime, during February, the PAC continued to activate the township for the impending anti-pass campaign while the uniform branch of the local SAP continued with their normal activities. Since the local SAP had not got wind of a rise in political temperature through its communications with the District Commander's office, the Sharpeville police were not especially alarmed, at least not until mid-month when it became apparent from national developments that even a historically passive Sharpeville might experience some sort of minor disturbance in the imminent future. This was confirmed on the local front in March by a women's anti-pass march to the office of the Location Superintendent that degenerated into a scuffle in which a few people received minor injuries. Thereafter, security arrangements in the area were partially beefed up, but not to the extent of being able to deal with a township conflict of major proportions.

By this time it appears that the PAC had become aware of a number of people from the Rooistene area who were acting as police agents. Activists on the ground pressed for violence, but when the information was conveyed to Johannesburg, the local branch was advised not to eliminate the collaborators, but rather to use them as a channel for disinformation. The consequence was that the Special Branch continued to remain secure in its belief that very little of any import was likely to take place before the upcoming Easter holidays.

The PAC's national congress of December 1959 had envisaged a series of three pamphlets to market the proposed anti-pass demonstrations, only the last of which would, as a matter of security, specify the exact date of the mass action. Whilst Sobukwe and his immediate associates had determined on 21 March as 'D-day' during secret discussions at the congress, the Special Branch had failed to penetrate these deliberations. The pamphlets that began circulating as a tool of popular mobilisation from the beginning of 1960 provided no clues as to the exact implementation of the campaign, and, in the circumstances, the SB had no reason to doubt their intelligence estimate that Easter would be the danger period. It was only in fact in the first week of March, when PAC pamphlets began to hint vaguely at an earlier date that the security police began to suspect that they had been either consciously or inadvertently led astray.

The Vaal CID had in the course of their routine activities chanced on a batch of 'number-three'-style pamphlets awaiting distribution in an Evaton house Following disclosure of their contents to the security police, a meeting, was hastily convened in Vereeniging on 14 March with the intention of reappraising the situation in the light of the new data. At the meeting, which was attended by various organisations in the police network, elements of the SADF, the local commando, the township administrations and select members of the Vereeniging municipality, it was decided to adopt a regional approach to the bubbling tensions in Sharpeville, Evaton and the smaller Vaal townships. Stations in adjoining areas of the Witwatersrand, it was resolved, should be alerted that their personnel and equipment might be required in a supportive capacity should the situation deteriorate. Such a possibility was particularly frightening to the local government officials, as one of our interviewees quipped in a phrase laden with historic irony, 'we would be in the frontline of fire'.[12] He and a group of Vereeniging Nationalist councillors, as well as Lieutenant-Colonel Pienaar of the SAP, a key figure in the eventual massacre, were vehement in arguing for a contingency plan which would allow the police to fire on demonstrators should violence reach a certain level of intensity. When other police and the military representatives pointed out that there already were specific rules of engagement to govern behaviour by the security forces in riots and other crisis situations, the councillors demurred.

At no time was any decision taken to 'teach a lesson' to the people of Sharpeville, as some anti-apartheid activists continue to allege until this day. In catering to the view that there should be a pro-active decision of some sort, the meeting concurred that should the police be required to intervene, in Sharpeville or elsewhere in the Vaal, they should be armed and ready. But there was no discussion even remotely akin to a plan for a premeditated slaughter. Indeed, much in accord with the ad hoc spirit in which the state had formulated its responses to unfolding events, there were no real plans at all. Nothing of any substance was said at the meeting about the exact personnel to be deployed should the demonstration degenerate into conflict, the firepower that might be brought to bear, supportive logistics and, perhaps most important of all, matters of command and control.

This, as we shall see, was to have tragic implications. In the meantime, two days later, a secret 'summit' of Vaal PAC branches was convened in a house in Evaton to which senior leaders from Johannesburg had been invited. After a vigorous tactical discussion chaired by Raphael Tshabalala of the Witwatersrand Regional Committee it was decided that the populations of the four Vaal townships would be encouraged to simply present themselves en masse at police stations in the area on the following Monday morning in order to indicate their rejection of the pass system and demand that they be arrested for violation of the influx control laws.

There was some debate over the selected day because many of those present were not party to the secret decisions of the PAC Congress. The majority nevertheless felt that neither Friday nor the weekend would be appropriate. On Friday most people would have the weekend in mind, and holding the protest on the Monday would allow the activists to disseminate the news of the proposed action to people who were home from the workplace. Hence the meeting settled on Monday 21 March. There was a general consensus that the demonstration would be non-violent in line with current Congress policy, and the meeting endorsed the view of other PAC branches nation-wide that Sobukwe should send a letter to the National Police Commissioner and other senior government personnel to confirm this position. An earlier decision had been taken at both national and local level to recruit as many young card-carrying members as possible into 'task teams' who would steer the proposed demonstrations. But there was little to no discussion as to what measures would be taken to actually deploy the 'task teams' to deal with any violent situation that might flower from popular passions. The matter, it appears was raised late in the evening, but discussion was terminated when news was received of a municipal police raid in the very zone of the subversive gathering. Thereupon it quickly dispersed, and with it went any arrangements to ensure some measure of effective crowd control around the Sharpeville Police Station. As later events would indicate, this failure of the key role-players in the eventual massacre to establish mechanisms for crowd control and negotiations to resolve potential conflict would prove fatal – for the police, the PAC, and not least of all, the ordinary township people.

✦

WEEKEND – 18-20 MARCH 1960

On the Friday Sobukwe formally announced that the national anti-pass demonstrations planned by the PAC would take place on the following Monday. Senior emissaries from the Vaal had apparently briefed Sobukwe about the Wednesday meeting, and one or two had expressed their concern that the training extended to the so-called local 'task teams' over the previous three months might not be adequate to contain a situation fraught with the possibility of mass violence. One still-living member of the Sharpeville executive, Stefaan Ledwaba*, distinctly recalls making the statement that 'too much emphasis was given to the task force in stirring up the people for action as opposed to what to do if the demonstration went wrong'.

Sobukwe apparently noted the bias towards mobilisation as opposed to control in the preparations for Monday – both in Sharpeville and elsewhere – but felt that the grassroots people could be trusted to exercise sufficient self-restraint to obviate the need for close monitoring. The pamphlets giving Monday as the date were in any case unrecallable now that a good proportion had hit the streets and the whole programme could not simply be geared into reverse at this late stage. Despite personal misgivings Sobukwe decided to forge ahead. But his public statements, which once more underlined the peaceful intention of the protest, were now directed at twin constituencies – the authorities with their monopoly over the instruments of coercive state control, and the people, PAC or otherwise, who might contemplate hijacking the mass action for other than peaceful purposes. The continuation of the ANC campaigns of passive resistance was also emphasised in a back-up telegram officially sent to the South African government by Sobukwe in his capacity as President of the PAC.

By midday Friday the Sharpeville PAC branch was already at work alerting the people to the plans for the Monday. Led by Emmanuel Teketsi and Stefaans Lepee, the members of the task teams began to circulate among the people with calls for a labour boycott and the burning of passes. Survivors recount the mixture of messages received from the task teams working house-to-house: in some cases they were asked to simply burn their passes, in others to surrender their reference books to the authorities and demand arrest. All however concur that the young men in particular were ordered to be ready to march to the local police station from Sunday night onwards at the sound of a whistle to be blown by Nyakane Tsolo. When some of their older counterparts expressed doutbts or fears that the stayaway might result in mass firings and loss of employment, calls for a minimum wage of £35 per month were thrown in by PAC activists as the 'sweetener' on the political agenda. Both Teketsi and Lepee also proceeded to burn their passes at the bus station in the presence of returning late afternoon commuters in a demonstrative act meant to underline their seriousness of their intentions. Meanwhile Job Tsolo was active in recruiting at the beerhall where unemployed teenage men, both respectable youths and tsotsis, intermingled in an anticipation of the normal hard-drinking weekend.

On Friday 18 March Robert Sobukwe announced a nation-wide series of anti-pass demonstrations for the Monday and, having done so, went on to emphasise that the PAC did not desire confrontation. Although the local executive in Sharpeville had no immediate organisational strategy to back up this commitment by its national leader, it quickly swung into action to give his words a tactical reality. By midday the Location Office was receiving reports that a small group of activists led by executive leaders Manuel Teketsi and Stefaans Lepee was moving from house to house to alert people to the programme scheduled for the Monday.

During the course of the afternoon the Location Office and, further down the line, the Vereeniging SAP were informed of political activity at the beerhall and, somewhat later, at the Sharpeville bus depot. At the beerhall Job Tsolo met with various groups of unemployed youths and began marketing the PAC programme. Not all of these young men were the 'tsotsis' or local gangsters characterised by the municipal administration as the major source of membership of the local PAC branch. Indeed, most 'tsotsis' tended to steer clear of formal membership on the PAC whose Sharpeville executives were inclined to lay down definite, if vague codes of social behaviour for members. Since these included restrictions on criminality and gang violence most of the gangsters preferred to maintain some distance from it. Nonetheless, the PAC programme with its emphasis on the scrapping of passes and, now, a minimum wage, opened up new socio-criminal possibilities for the various gangs, so that they were quite willing to act as auxiliaries for the new Africanist organisation. For their part, Tsolo and his colleagues were aware of the dangers for a respectable political movement of too close an association with the erratic and relatively anarchic gangs. Nevertheless, the demands of organising a mass demonstration in the short term were, they knew, way beyond the capacity of the small band of dedicated PAC in whose mainstream were some leaders who genuinely, if naïvely, believed that the gangs were a controllable coalition partner. By late Friday, activists like Teketsi and Lepee had transferred from the beerhall to the bus depot to meet workers returning from the Vereeniging and Vanderbijl factories, to urge them to strike on the Monday and to assemble at the local police station. Both PAC activists publicly burned their passbooks there and then as a means of reinforcing their commitment and underwriting their message.

Still, responses ranged from enthusiasm to non-committal on the part of many workers who feared that they would be replaced were they not to report for duty, or, worse still, arrested if they followed suit and were subsequently encountered by police patrols seeking offenders against influx control. Little of this was openly expressed for fear of social ostracism in a community which had clearly begun to gear up for collective action against the universally detested pass system.

In all of this the local ANC was conspicuous by its absence. As the semi-official ranks of the task teams were belatedly swelled by a mass of largely self-designated and some undesirable 'volunteers', the ANC remained anxiously on the sidelines. 'The local ANC,' Henry Motloadi* remembers, 'did not want to be part of the process with its hooligan element' – at least not prior to the onset of powerful forces inducing conformity in what was a small-scale community. While these forces would bring many of the bystanders (ANC members included) around in the next two days, the relatively older, privileged and politically conservative leaders of the local ANC structure remained unconvinced about the wisdom of what the PAC was doing. As the PAC message struck a responsive chord in their local strongholds – in Vuka and among the mass of township unemployed – the ANC wavered, partially for fear that the whole business would spin out of hand, but also because its small band of local leading lights could not bring themselves to lend support to a mass action whose spirit and substance they saw to lie in 'splinterist' circles. Paul Hadebe*, an old Vaal ANC stalwart candidly admits to the view in ANC circles at the time that 'should there be trouble … it would add to the political reputation of the wild young men' (who had broken free of the ANC establishment and its pacifist traditions). In the end it was a mixture of concern and political calculation that led the local ANC to hesitate that Friday afternoon.

The authorities were becoming more pro-active a little more quickly, than their more moderate black political opponents. The informant network from the community to the location superintendency quickly conveyed news of developments which were then transmitted to the Vereeniging police. One of its CID operatives, Inspector Muller, was tasked with responding with a low-key operation. Much like Spengler on previous occasions Muller decided not to stoke the fire with mass arrests – at least not before he had gathered further information. A few patrols were ordered to observe the PAC at work, to note the identity of its operatives, and to confiscate pamphlets from anyone apprehended in possession.

This produced a number of bizarre and near-farcical incidents. 'My brother Piet,' Sophie Mahlangu remembers, 'was given a good slap from the police for holding a pamphlet in his hand'. 'I thought this was unfair,' she adds 'because Piet could not read!'.

A number of informants were also 'arrested' on the pretext of failing to meet the legal requirement to report their presence in the area to the local labour bureau, and then taken to the Sharpeville municipal offices for debriefing. Unfortunately, their arrival at the office coincided with that of Teketsi and Lepee who had gone to Location Superintendent 'Lappies' Labuschagne as part of their process of informing everyone about impending events. This made it necessary for the informants to be fined a visible £1 'admission of guilt' in order to obscure their real identities – and then freed on the spot. Whether this made an impression on the PAC observers, who now returned to the bus depot to carry on work, remains a moot point.

Nonetheless, both were now of the opinion that the township was on the brink of a wave of arrests in which the PAC executive would be the primary target. When this was conveyed to the executive, the entire body, Lepee excepted, determined that the cause would best be served by the leadership going 'underground' for the forthcoming weekend. Lepee, it was decided, was to act as point man on the streets while other executive members dispersed into hiding in order to avoid what appeared to be the prospect of imminent arrest.

Nyakane Tsolo recalls being 'on vacation' in the local hostel from Friday afternoon to Sunday night, that is at the critical point at which it was essential for the PAC to establish command and control over the nascent but swelling crowds who had responded to its message. In retrospect, this represented the first breakdown in the process of politically and physically steering the crowd – the first signs of decay in the organisational capability of the PAC to enforce the intention of the demonstration as a peaceful mass action. This was not obvious at the time because both Saturday and the early part of Sunday were relatively unremarkable except for the series of house visits being undertaken by PAC organisers working on a door-to-door basis.

The scale and visibility of their activities was no doubt observed by police from the local station who reported the state of developments. Local and regional headquarters were, by this time, receiving reports from adjacent Evaton, Bophelong and Boipatong that the PAC was heavily involved in similar mobilisation with Monday in mind, but the position of the authorities remained low profile, not least because incoming intelligence indicated that the organisers of the campaign were repeatedly emphasising that it should be non-violent.

Other than discussions with the passes in their forefront, the weekend had all the appearances of a regular few days off work. In Sharpeville there were the usual sporting events in a community fanatical about the success of its boxing and soccer stars, and the streets were loud with the conviviality of usual township existence. The shebeens did their brisk weekend trade.

The authorities were, at this point, strangely quiescent in a way which merits some explanation. Clearly, the municipal officials and the police knew what was happening – at least in broad outline. They, like the general public, had heard the Sobukwe announcement on Friday and its implications for Sharpeville with its energetic PAC branch were the subject of discussions late on Friday afternoon between Inspector Muller of the local CID, Captain Cawood of the Vanderbijl SAP and Superintendent Labuschagne at the local police station. Yet the police – municipal, uniform and security – appear to have lapsed into lethargy, awaiting the outcome of events. Part of the explanation lies in the ebb and flow of the crowd at the bus station where the first bubblings of protest tended to fade away as people drifted into their normal weekend activities. This led the authorities to conclude that there was little cause for immediate anxiety – notwithstanding the warnings from Labuschagne and other officials in the township that trouble was brewing. Another reason for this extraordinary lack of energy on the part of the state also lies in the fact that there had been no destruction of property, particularly state property. Nor was the local Advisory Board being threatened despite the fact that they enjoyed very little popular support because of their inability to do anything to enhance the lot of the community. Most of the Board's members knew of the impending protest but remained silent, if only because they did not take the PAC seriously. It was this miscalculation rather than any community identification that ironically saved them from the huge wave of popular hatred that was to engulf their successors in the insurrection of the mid-eighties. For its part, no-one in the local PAC was, at this point, especially concerned with setting the community against its 'leaders' – least of all at a time when mass action required the participation of as large a number of people as possible.

Hence the authorities preferred at this early stage to stand back and attribute the first signs of 'native unrest' to the normal bonhomie of weekend township existence. This was at least part of the message conveyed to their superiors by police informants in nearby Evaton and Boipatong, some of whom appear to have been identified by the PAC and 'turned' into sources of disinformation.

Then too, it was a characteristically sunny South African weekend during which the authorities looked forward to a few days of rest and relaxation, notwithstanding Sobukwe's announcement. There was none of the vigilance that state policing was to develop at a later stage of 'total onslaught'. Quite the contrary: 'if there was trouble brewing among the natives we needed time to rest,' according to Henk Pretorius*, then a leading member of the Sharpeville municipal police force. Most of the local police and municipal officials were also not especially perturbed by Sobukwe's speech because they regarded the PAC as a still marginal political movement without the capacity to arouse the people despite its grandiose plans for the following week. Some elements in the local state were also placated by the emphasis Sobukwe had placed on non-violence and were not especially concerned about developments in Sharpeville with its historically passive reputation. So, they partook of their normal 'beer and braai', with the odd aside that the Vaal appeared a little 'onrustig' (unsettled). This was not the attitude of the security police in Johannesburg where a mixture of cynicism and circumspection drove senior officers like Spengler to act with a higher level of energy. Nevertheless, Johannesburg was another world, albeit only a few kilometres away, and its police could do little in the way of pre-emptive action without the collaboration of their considerably more restrained local counterparts. Since even the security police, with all its elaborate intelligence networks, still could not predict the outcome of Monday – at least not sufficiently so to justify putting everyone on a heightened state of alert – the entire state apparatus stood more or less still even as Sharpeville began to simmer.

And simmering there was, behind the cosmetic appearance of normality. Many people in Sharpeville were worried about what loomed at the end of the weekend, how they would respond, how they *should* respond – and some sought to alleviate their anxiety by what some later township commentators identified as an excessive consumption of liquor. If these accounts are to be believed Sharpeville tottered even more on the edges of sobriety than would be considered usual by weekend standards governing social life in the townships. ANC circles in the Vaal were also in ferment, and there was considerable discussion through Saturday into Sunday as to how the local branches should respond to the ongoing PAC campaign. Advice sought telephonically from higher up the movement's hierarchy proved equivocal and, ultimately, it was developments in the Vaal itself which lay behind the public announcement by the ANCYL Chairperson Reg Mayekiso that the planned action was both foolhardy and dangerous.

This was not a misestimation in the contemporary climate where the capacity of the PAC to maintain a grip on the situation was already being severely tested. Lepee, the only public face of the PAC leadership now that his colleagues had gone into hiding, simply lacked the personal and organisational capability to singly manage a situation involving thousands of people. By Friday night it was clear that the task teams that had been trained in anticipation of the Monday mass action were attracting an excessive number of local undesirables who had no particular connection to peaceful protest or to the PAC's agenda. Even if they did, the teams were far too small to carry out their designated role in monitoring the escalating groups of people at disparate points in various townships. As these groups developed a will of their own, the monitors shrank from their responsibilities. 'We were a people's organisation – how could we clash with the people?' plaintively asks Isaac Mthembu*, an erstwhile task team member, forty years later.

Unfortunately, not all his colleagues, in their intention to maximise mass mobilisation, shared this opinion. By late Sunday some PAC activists moving through the densely packed houses of Sharpeville and Evaton were experiencing a mixed reception to their protest message from people who preferred to spend the last hours of the weekend in a state of relaxation. Sharpeville, with its quiescent track record of defiance of state authority was especially problematic from the perspective of the militants and their gangster 'hangers-on'. Some of these now began to pinpoint and seize some of the younger male householders with the intention of forcibly taking them to the local stadium adjacent to the police station, where they would be kept for the remainder of the night before being released en masse into the veld in front of the station the following morning. It remains uncertain who devised this questionable and ultimately futile strategy, which resulted in a number of minor scuffles and a drift of people to the police station through the night, particularly women complaining that their menfolk, husbands or sons, were being 'kidnapped'. Certainly it was not the official strategy of the executive leaders – who remained committed in principle to the idea of non-violence and consensual passive resistance, and who quickly moved to try from their places of hiding to contain the self-appointed enforcers.

Unfortunately, some of the enforcers were fuelled with liquor, while the task of implementing the wishes of the covert executive largely devolved on a single man, Stefaans Lepee. He and a few immediate colleagues could not conceivably impose their authority on circulating groups of people numbering several dozen in many cases. Enlarged groups composed of activists, their associates and their often press-ganged supporters now began to form in the streets and these became the poles of attraction for others who were neither committed nor captured but simply curious. Since it was impossible or dangerous for any individual to break free from the engorging crowd pockets and simply go home, the momentum built upon itself to that fine sociological point where a crowd becomes transmuted to a mob.

By this point, early Sunday night, the churnings in Sharpeville and its immediate neighbours were so evident that even the lethargic authorities could no longer turn a blind eye to what was happening. As crowds began to materialise at various points, the state began to roll into more substantive and visibly pre-emptive action. Local police were called away from the reverie of their sundowners and telephones began to buzz. At roughly 19.00 Spengler and the Johannesburg 'experts' in the security police were summoned urgently to the Beaconsfield Street offices of the Special Branch in Vereeniging. The primary business on the agenda at this point was the possibility that the township crowds in Sharpeville or Evaton would form a large and dangerous concentration which would descend on the abutting 'white' areas. In order to prevent this, the gathering decided, black physical movement both within and between the townships had to be stopped. The protection of property in the townships themselves was not an issue. Other than municipal buildings, normally placed on township boundaries for security reasons, there were few places of strategic significance. As a participant police official put it, 'if the Vaal natives burn their houses they can then can bloody well sleep in the veld'. The one exception was the Sharpeville Police Station whose isolation and destruction, Inspector Muller reminded the gathering, would 'encourage natives to attack state installations and wreck government property in other parts of the country'. 'It was absolutely essential that we took a stand on the Sharpeville station whatever the costs,' says former Special Branch operative and now successful Vaal businessman, Attie du Plessis*. With this in mind patrols into Sharpeville from Vereeniging and Vanderbijl were stepped up with orders to disperse the gathering groups in the vicinity of the police station as quickly as possible – and with the use of force if necessary.

The amount of force that could be concentrated and brought to bear with some speed was, however, fairly restricted. Despite weeks of spasmodic deliberation, the pattern of ongoing bureaucratic wrangling between the key state role-players – the contests over who should do what, when and how in the eventuality of a confrontation – had led to precious little being done at all. Even the uniformed police lacked contingency plans on how to supplement their manpower in the event of a crisis so, when it became clear that a crisis could occur, the SAP's capacity to meet the situation with urgency was thinly stretched. The initial reinforcements it began to send into Sharpeville and other townships late on Sunday were largely young reservists, hastily mobilised and put into uniform – barring police regulation footwear which was absent from the local quartermaster in yet another display of organisational incompetence. 'Why have you sent us seuntjies [little boys] with big guns and takkies [sneakers],' Nyakane Tsolo recalls asking one senior police officer at a critical point in the pattern of rapidly unfolding developments.

The 'little boys' sent in to counter what was believed to be lethal and escalating 'groepe van naturelle'[groups of natives] were nevertheless lethal and, like their opponents, were seeking to release pent-up energy and emotion. Michael Ignatieff, in his contemporary studies of extreme nationalism, has perceptively referred to the palpable smell of male testosterone in these types of spasmodic confrontations between young men of visibly different cultural or ethnic persuasion.[13] Although that description is perhaps overly graphic in its homoeroticism for so mundane a place as the Vaal, blood was clearly in the air. 'Someone was bound to get fucked up,' says Hennie Viljoen*, then one of the 'seuntjies' on duty that night and now a retired senior member of the SAP. Despite the fact that their officers had emphasised that their role was to intimidate and bisect the crowds rather than arrest their members, conflict was already largely unavoidable with the approach of midnight when the ramshackle PAC executive deigned to emerge from hiding. The first violent confrontation actually took place, not in Sharpeville, but in nearby Evaton where police patrols encountered a number of groups, largely composed of young men, assembled on side streets adjacent to the arterial roads of the township. The police patrols were reluctant to move into the dark and pitted sand roads between the squat houses and in some cases the assembled groups simply filtered phantom-like into the night when called on to do so – or when assisted to do so with a canister or two of teargas. In other cases however groups refused to disperse or break up immediately and the patrols were forced to act with short, sharp baton charges. The police were also armed with sjamboks whose vicious welts produced the desired effect when used at close quarters. There were some perfunctory attempts to use teargas, but the police quickly desisted once it was realised that the gas in the canisters was either too light or erratic for use on a largely windless night in the more open spaces. Teargas as a means of crowd control was not to be used much again, either that night or the next day, with tragic consequences.

In Sharpeville itself trouble flared intermittently throughout the night as small groups of PAC organisers and their less reputable cohorts approached houses with their demonstration agenda, forced entry in the face of frightened inhabitants, and pulled men and boys into the street demonstrations. Some of the more conscientised went willingly and from about 20.00 onwards the township was networked by bands of roaming men. Some gravitated towards the area near the beerhall which the PAC had designated in their latest pamphlets as one of the sites for a post-midnight pre-demonstration meeting, others simply wandered through the township in an inchoate expression of political resistance. The first outright clash occurred in the early evening when a unit of about thirty policemen under Captain Cawood encountered a group of about 150 men armed with stones and lengths of iron. In a fashion that was to set the pattern for the night and next morning, the police requested the gathering to disperse, and baton-charged them when they failed to do so. Later at the football stadium, another designated meeting point, Ruben Raputsoe remembers the presence of known police informers who, when threatened, departed quickly only to return with police reinforcements. Frederick Batkani and Albert Mbongo recall, 'the police came and asked us what we were doing. When they [the PAC leaders] replied that they had come to talk 'about the bad rules of the passes ... the officers started to hit us with whips.' This was, they add whimsically forty years later, clearly 'the wrong answer'.[14] In an atmosphere of mutually declining tolerance casualties began to mount. By 3.00 on Sunday morning the police had officially encountered and dispersed over seventeen demonstrations in Sharpeville[15] amongst which was one of about 500 persons who were stopped near a row of houses on the township border.

Hit-and-run incidents involving protestors and police continued for some hours in a spiral of mounting violence and reciprocal antagonism. By one or two in the morning emotions against the police were rising. This was evident as police patrols now began to encounter groups armed with sticks, pikes, scythes and lethal knobkerries (a long-handled club-like weapon fashioned from a sapling with a bulbous root at its end). A handful of shots had allegedly emanated from the depths of the crowd during the late night and early morning. This legitimated the police dispensing with dispersal warnings and simply surging into the various crowds with whips and batons flailing.

These initial clashes were not especially murderous and, in historic retrospect, there was considerable mutual restraint in the overwhelming majority of cases. Despite the chanting of what could best be described as groups rather than crowds of people there was no apparent instance where a full-scale attack was launched on a police force considerably unnerved by the baying protestors. Nor did the SAP bring its full power to bear on the protestors in the face of considerable provocation – in part because they were under strict orders not to fire except in the most exceptional and life-threatening circumstances, in part because their targets were roaming entities of a dozen to a hundred individuals who appeared and then suddenly disappeared into the all pervasive darkness. Although several dozen protestors sustained minor injuries from the batons and whips, there were hardly any police injuries resulting from what contemporaries described as 'self-defensive' cases where the police actually charged to reinforce their message. There were certainly no more than a handful of gunshots insofar as anyone can recall, and the police casualties were mainly minor and caused by stones finding their mark. According to the conventional wisdom woven around Sharpeville, there was little to nothing on Sunday night that portended the horror that followed. In reality however, that night was of enormous significance in setting the tone for the subsequent tragedy by defining the relationship that developed between victim and perpetrator.

'We were fighting blacks in the black,' as one denizen of a Vaal outehuis (old-age home), once a young police-reservist active in 1960, now puts it. Sharpeville is still a dark and lethal place at night and it was even darker in the absence of street lighting some forty years ago. For the most part the clashes that raged through the night into the early morning of 21 March were conducted in unrelieved darkness except for the dull halogen lights of police vehicles or the odd hand-held spotlight hastily commandeered from police armouries for pin-pointing demonstrators. Low technology riot control is notoriously a nightmare for any police force even in the light – and so it was on the Sunday before the massacre. The absence of lighting meant that the police were forced into close-quarter monitoring of the groups they encountered and it was impossible to estimate the size of the crowds whose edges faded imperceptibly into the dark. Since the most militant members of these groups inevitably surged to the front, it was only natural for the younger and relatively less experienced policemen to conclude that there were large numbers of potentially violent people behind those they could see. In fact, the crowds they encountered were essentially composed of ordinary and, for the most part, entirely lawful persons in the process of being swept up in the momentum of a dangerously escalating situation.

In the consequent atmosphere of mutual threat the crowds were, here and there, forced, or so they believed, into self-defence posture. Once the anxious police produced batons and whips, violence became imminent for the simple reason that a certain proportion of the crowd saw it as imminent. 'The police were going to "*donder* [beat] us",' Siphiwe Mbuli* recalls, 'but we were going to act first'.

'We were terrified by the dark, the natives and their howls against us,' then Constable Jaco Jacobs* remembers. 'We knew they would kill us.' So there was a spiral of confusion, fear and hostility, there were whippings and stones, as the contestants sought to pre-empt each other, and, inevitably, there were casualties on both sides which, however minor, reinforced the mutual psychologies of destruction. By midnight when the PAC executive emerged and Tsolo blew his whistle to signal the formal beginning of the mass demonstration, both the crowds and the police were convinced that the dawn would herald a day of violence. The crowd, batoned and whipped, were angered, and the police believed they were perched on the edge of a vortex. By early Sunday morning the first casualties – blacks bleeding about the head and scarred with whip welts, the odd white victim of a stoning – were being admitted to the still hollow wards of the Vereeniging Hospital.

There were, in this deepeningly self-reinforcing situation, some quite extraordinary acts of individual compassion and heroism. There was Captain Cawood, who testified before the later Wessels Commission of Inquiry that he, alone among SAP officers, was frequently forced during the course of the night to cross the narrow line separating police from protestors, to reason with enraged people who appeared to be the leaders. On the opposite side of the political equation there were also a number of historically-forgotten people among the crowd who, like reverse-Cawoods, approached the heavily armed police and urged them to desist from using violence on people of peaceable intentions. Several black police with minor wounds caused by stones were taken into nearby houses and offered water and bandages by their occupants. One of them remembers the political debate that ensued between him and the inhabitants of a house but was, in the end, unresolvable. And so, in a sense, was the situation outside, where efforts on both sides to moderate the position declined drastically after a police patrol in the early hours of Monday came across a single rusted pistol in the veld, presumably dropped by some fleeing demonstrator. So intense was the feeling among the SAP of an imminent racial bloodbath, even at this early point, that the decision was taken to regroup most of the patrols at the Sharpeville Police Station from which urgent messages would be sent to secure reinforcements.

Unfortunately, shortly thereafter the single telephonic link between the station and the outside world went dead. This raised the level of dread among the occupants to new heights since most of the police attributed this development to PAC saboteurs intent on isolating the installation as an overture to a full-scale attack. The fact that the line was notoriously inefficient and had been reported to the local telephone authorities on a number of occasions in recent weeks was either unknown or ignored in the conditions of mounting panic. For the next few hours the small police contingent 'besieged' in the station remained convinced that at any moment they would be stormed by huge mobs from the outside. In retrospect, this was an irrational expectation given that the crowds were essentially aimless in their behaviour. The regular firepower already contained in the station would, in any case, have been adequate to dissuade the demonstrators from taking any more radical action. Nonetheless, internal relations within the station were tense, and made worse by some sort of fracas between two black and one equally anxious white policeman over a minor administrative matter.

A motor vehicle had been dispatched to Vereeniging once telephone communications had been severed and at 3.00 the first reinforcements began to arrive by truck. The township was then divided into a northern and a southern segment. By early morning most of the confrontations in the streets had tapered out as both sides fell into exhaustion. A blue-grey dawn saw small clutches of police vehicles parked on the two main entry roads and peppered over the empty veld along Sharpeville's boundaries. Despite the battering and confusion of the night, the day began in total silence.

PAC plans for the Sunday night were based on the principle of mass dispersal and were designed to exhaust the police through persistent hit-and-run tactics. For this reason the team leaders were determined to keep as many people as possible on the streets, but to ensure that they were configured in relatively small and mobile groups which would harass and confuse the SAP by their sheer presence. Despite the unavoidable incidents of pro-active or retaliatory stone-throwing in the subsequent tense environment, the local PAC leaders continued to insist as a matter of both strategy and principle that there be no crowd violence against the police.

While some parts of Sharpeville were relatively untainted by the disturbances and people slept on peacefully others, especially those on the township margins, were occupied by noisy crowds whose size and actions effectively met the PAC requirement to wear down and disorientate the police. By morning many of the police manning the roadblocks were dead-tired, and contemplated the proposed demonstration at the Police Station a few hours later with dread. Many recall being extremely stressed and agitated. Inadvertently, the very success of PAC policy to provoke, harass and tire the custodians of law and order as part of a pre-demonstration 'softening up' had also produced a hard siege mentality in which many policemen were 'trigger-happy'.

——— ✦ ———

21 MARCH – MONDAY MORNING

At 6.30 on Monday 21 March, Sobukwe and six of his closest associates began the 4,5 km trudge from the home of the PAC leader in Soweto to the Orlando Police Station – a breeze-block single story edifice roofed by corrugated iron, not unlike its Sharpeville counterpart. Here Sobukwe and his small band intended to surrender their passes and demand arrest in an act of exemplary self-sacrifice intended to mobilise the masses.

In Sharpeville two to three hours earlier the first commuters had begun to arrive at the bus station to meet their normal early morning transport to the factories of Vereeniging and Vanderbijl, only to find that the buses had not arrived on schedule. The local leadership had calculated in its original plans for the demonstration that an exfiltration of commuters from Sharpeville would seriously weaken the whole initiative, and this was underlined by the events of Sunday night when it became evident that large numbers of people, though sympathetic with the campaign, would nevertheless go to work as usual. Since the buses normally arrived in Sharpeville from the white areas, it was essential to stop their drivers, most of whom lived in the township at addresses with which the activists were acquainted. PAC supporters had taken the additional precaution of covering the main roads leading into Sharpeville in the event that transport was being manned by substitute drivers. One single bus seems to have partially evaded the restrictions, but on entering Sharpeville it was stoned and its driver made a hurried departure. By early morning the PAC's mission had been accomplished so that when the first commuters arrived at the depots they found nothing except a number of PAC members. The latter proceeded to address the swelling crowd and one or two scuffles ensued as some frustrated travellers realised that they would not be going to work after all.

Most members of the congregation were compliant, however, either because they welcomed the prospect of an extended weekend or because of the fear of violence and social ostracism implicit in the speeches of the PAC cadres. For the most part, it seems that peer pressure played the dominant role in convincing people to adhere to the stayaway, although a number of the more recalcitrant members of the crowd who made their opinions felt also recall clear threats to themselves and their families. Some people simply went home to wait out the day. Others went to the Police Station under the illusion that its commanders could explain the lack of transport – and there they waited throughout the course of the morning, forming the 'core' of the eventual mob.[16] Still others remained in the streets to form potential crowd pockets and supplements to the group at the police station, because they feared that should they be found at home they would be accused of collaboration with the state and defiance of the boycott. The PAC message of Sunday night had obviously sunk home, although small numbers of individuals still went to work on foot via various circuitous routes through the veld. As they later recalled, they met many groups of people – men, women and children – who were coming into Sharpeville from the neighbouring townships – either to observe events or, in some cases, following PAC instigation to make their presence felt.

Most of the larger crowds of the previous night had dispersed during the early hours of the morning. Shortly thereafter, at first light, Carlton Monnakgotla recalls, 'people were lifted from their beds by the PAC' and moved into the streets. These people soon intermingled with the large numbers of people gravitating back from the bus station.[17] By Monday at 8.00 the crowd of the previous evening was in the process of reformulation on an even grander scale, swelled by those who had gone to the bus depot in the hope that there would be some late transportation to their workplaces. The growing crowd became an increasingly vast, inchoate and mobile throng moving from the outskirts to the epicentre of the township. Some were simply on their way home to sit out events, others had heard of some event at the police station and were moving in that direction. Inevitably, mobility changed to stasis under the force of numbers, and a little after 7.00 a group of about 5 000 had gathered at the far eastern end of Seeiso Street, the opposite end from its junction with Zwane Street – the site of the police station.

This early morning gathering was in many respects decisive in what was to happen several hours later at the police station. First and foremost, the crowd had congregated near the municipal offices on the township boundary, dangerously close in the estimation of the police, to the side-road leading up to the main arterial into 'white' Vereeniging. Like the police station, the municipal offices physically represented the state and whereas the station alone had been previously designated a crucial location to be defended at 'all costs', the shabby one-story buildings out of which emanated life-and-death administrative decisions for the people of Sharpeville were also now designated 'strategic'.

The concerns of the police in this regard were not unfounded. Titus Molapa* of the PAC task team on the spot and the advocate of a march on Vereeniging itself, recalls that 'we needed to go up Seeiso Street and past the beerhall [directly opposite the municipal buildings] ... we needed to carry our anger and struggle into the white houses (and) not just to the police station.' Although this was not part of the PAC game plan – Titus had in fact been admonished for this suggestion by the executive some days before – this was the nightmare that the authorities feared above all. They thus decided to make a stand outside the beerhall – to prevent the invasion of both the municipal buildings and the 'white civilisation' that lay beyond.

Most of the crowd did little to assist with the stockpiling of stones which young PAC militants now began to pile in heaps in anticipation that the SAP would desperately defend the route into Vereeniging. Many shared the view of the local executive that acts of this nature would degenerate into violence and actually sought to leave the scene as unobtrusively as circumstances would allow, but could not be seen to be doing so. From the perspective of the police however, these were minor distinctions, particularly when the relatively small squad of eighteen white and thirty-five 'non-white' personnel arriving on the scene under the command of District Commander, Major van Zyl, was met with a barrage of projectiles from all sides. As protestors sprang out of nearby houses to swell the crowd, the inevitable baton charged followed. But when this failed to disperse the crowd and the police found themselves 'omsingel' (outflanked) on all sides, they reacted in what was to be a grim forerunner of what was to follow on a much larger scale several hours later. They fired with pistols and rifles, discharging forty-two rounds and, as Van Zyl was to admit in testimony at a later stage, they did so out of fear for their lives, without orders, and entirely on their own initiative.

In this instance, fortunately, there were few casualties – partly because some of the police still had the circumspection to fire over the heads of their tormentors, partly because the group under Van Zyl were local police with relatively more compunction about killing Sharpeville people than the more callous 'imported' reinforcements who arrived later. Only one policeman, Constable Coetzee, was lightly injured on the head (despite later police references to a massive 'hail of stones'). Nevertheless the volley included a lethal discharge from a Sten gun carried by Constable van Rensburg which felled six of the crowd on the spot. Rifle fire from Constables Kallis, Coetzee and Els brought down several others, but whether these people were killed or merely wounded remains unknown and these figures were not added into the eventual official arithmetic of the casualties. (The police subsequently admitted that two people had died in this incident).[18]

The gunning down of these anonymous people broke the relative moratorium on the large-scale use of firearms that had prevailed throughout the crisis up to this point. For many in the early morning crowd, the combined thunder of police pistols, rifles and the single Sten severely shook the ethic of non-violence – so much so that someone secreted in a house nearby fired back two shots, probably with a small calibre pistol. Again, the bullets missed any mark. But for the already shaken police, many of whom were exhausted from the night's work and their fear of imminent slaughter, the shots signalled incontrovertibly that the 'Bantoe' were intent on a racial *Götterdämmerung* that very day.

Van Zyl failed to mention these initial killings to the eventual Commission of Inquiry which, in turn did, not probe too deeply. Yet friends of the now-deceased District Commander report that he felt a mixture of fear and cold rage that blacks should fire on white men – as if the waving knobkerries, the provocative chants and the ear-splitting whistles were not enough. As the crowd swarmed around the police – but now at a healthy distance – he immediately radioed Colonel Lemmer in Vereeniging for urgent additional reinforcements from beyond the borders of the district.

The local commando was already on standby, but Van Zyl also suggested that air support be brought in so that the demonstrators could observe the full power of the apartheid state which they had the temerity to confront.

Most of the mid- to late morning was punctuated with running clashes between police and demonstrators at various points throughout Sharpeville and other townships. In a few instances the police used teargas to disperse the crowds but this was mostly ineffective because of its light consistency and the mild wind which had sprung up from the Vaal River and the Free State backveld to the South of the various black communities. The police were forced to resort to baton charges, and teargas was implicitly ruled out as a medium of control should the disturbances escalate in the course of the day. Evidence to this effect was presented to the Commission of Inquiry when questions were raised as to why there were no teargas canisters in the complement of weaponry delivered to Sharpeville Police Station during the course of the morning.

By dawn patrols were at work both within the four Vaal townships and along the roads linking one to another. Most of these patrols consisted of police cars, vans or trucks with black policemen loaded at the back. When a number of open police vehicles carrying reinforcements into Sharpeville were stoned between 8.00 and 9.00 a vigorous discussion ensued at the District Commissioner's headquarters as to how to manage a clearly deteriorating situation. Two representatives of the SADF who had arrived early in the morning to liaise between the police and armed forces advocated that – even at the risk of escalating the situation – more energetic attempts be made to control the crowds using military technology.

During the fifties the exigencies of riot control had forged a closer relationship between the SADF and the police. One consequence of this was the progressive use by the SAP of military vehicles, including heavy protected 'army lorries' acquired from the Department of Defence and then converted to transport police to crisis points as circumstances required. In 1959, the SAP had also purchased forty-seven Saracen armoured cars from their colleagues in the armed forces and, at the time of Sharpeville, some sixty of these were operational in both the Union and South West Africa.[19] A small number were dispensed to the Vaal early on the Monday and, by mid-morning the security police then on site or in the vicinity of Sharpeville, notably Captain Willers and Senior Sergeants Wessels and Muller, decided that the situation in Sharpeville warranted a concentration of these heavy vehicles in the area.[20] Following clearance from Colonel Prinsloo who had recently arrived at Vanderbijlpark Police Station, a three-Saracen unit under the command of Captain Brummer was immediately deployed from Bophelong where the police had the situation in hand. The Saracens, it was reckoned, could provide protected transportation for reinforcements moving from the township boundary to the Sharpeville station. They were precautionary in the event of more violence and, above all, were meant as a signal to the ululating crowds that the police meant serious business. Other Saracens in the area, for instance at Evaton where thousands of demonstrators were also in the vicinity of the police station, were not transferred since the situation there seemed every bit as serious as that in Sharpeville. Nonetheless, arrangements were in motion to further enhance police capacity by a transfer of Saracens from the SAP depot of the Eastern Witwatersrand Command at Springs.

Major van Zijl and a number of officers were at the municipal offices near the beerhall on the Sharpeville border when the first Saracens under Captain Brummer arrived at approximately 10.30. Their first task was to help ferry reinforcements and to escort various persons and cars gathered at the office of the Location Superintendent on the border of the township to the central police station. These persons included some white officials from the local Non-European Affairs Department who had innocently arrived to find out why their black employees had not reported for work, as well as members of the media who had been alerted to the Vaal demonstrations, had arrived at the Location office to go through the normal procedures of seeking permission to enter a black area, and now wished to be taken to the heart of the action. Most were refused permission and advised to leave an area which was fast becoming dangerous. Among those who secured permission were Jan Hoek, a photographer from Johannesburg's *Rand Daily Mail*, his colleague, Benjamin Pogrund, and Ian Berry and Humphrey Tyler representing *Drum*. The cars of the *Rand Daily Mail* journalists were stoned as they proceeded in convey towards the police station behind the three Saracens. The latter two reporters however enjoyed a more peaceful journey, albeit on a circuitous route through a noisy, gesticulating and dense crowd which spilt into the roadway from the adjacent pavement.

The general mood of the crowd and their response to the appearance of the Saracens and their convoy of cars was to become a key point of contention in the official inquiry into the shootings. Basically two stories emerged – both ideologically-driven and, in time, to become part of the different mythologies woven around Sharpeville. In the first (apologist) version, the general mood was largely celebratory – the majority of people on the streets were happy, if noisy, and their shouting was for the most part festive, if not entirely non-political. Cries of 'Afrika' punctuated the air along with the raised thumb salute that denoted the national anti-pass movement, but there was little in these gestures to suggest uncontained anger, repressed or impending violence. In most instances during the night the various crowds had stood down from confrontation and scattered when confronted by the armed might of the police. There was no reason to believe they were actively seeking a violent clash. Quite the contrary, as government critics were later to point out, the arrival of the Saracens was greeted with friendly African-style ululations, particularly from the women who made up a large proportion of the crowds. Certainly, no one tried (or was foolhardy enough to try) to stop these heavy armoured vehicles.

The official version of popular feelings is quite different. From the testimony presented to the Wessels Commission by police personnel, it appears that the crowd was violently enraged and that hostile utterings, curses and various other forms of verbal abuse were directed at the security forces, accompanying officials, and even sympathetic journalists. In the opinion of some of the latter, later conveyed to the Commission, the expression of the crowd was 'grim, savage and ruthless' – a perception with which the SAP would then and later identify. Interestingly enough, though they agreed that the crowd was dangerous, there were subtle divisions between the local officials and their police counterparts as to the cause of their disquiet. To most of the police, some of whom were reinforcements called into Sharpeville and were unfamiliar with the township, the crowd was simply another anonymous black mob like anti-pass demonstrators they had encountered before.

Many of the officials of the local Department of Bantu Administration and Development however had worked with individual members of the crowd, albeit from positions of arbitrary authority, and some iota of humanism had rubbed off. Many, including Labuschagne, saw people with whom they interacted on almost a daily basis and whom they could not conceive of as genuine 'subversives' with a resistance agenda. The Superintendent himself had always regarded Sharpeville as an intrinsically 'vreemdeliewende gemeenskap [foreign community]', 23 000 of whose members, he documents paternally, were members of established churches.[21] Even though PAC activists had experienced a number of inevitable confrontations with Labuschagne in the months leading up to 21 March he was, from the wider community perspective, certainly no worse and in some respects, far better, than his counterparts in other 'native locations'. A well-meaning man and devout Christian Labuschagne continued, to his dying day, to insist that the events of Sharpeville were a 'mistake', an aberration, or a particularly tragic case of otherwise innocent people led astray by insidious external agitation.

In reality, the truth lies at some indefinable point between the popular antagonism which the apartheid police took as a given in their relations with civil society, and the somewhat condescending 'liberal' view of the crowd as a happy-go-lucky and relatively playful group. It is indisputable following years of intensified apartheid enforced by the SAP, that the force had taken on the characteristics of a political police and that 'at the time of the Sharpeville tragedy increasing numbers of Africans concluded that they were living in a Police State'.[22] Yet, apartheid in 1960 was still in the process of articulation and its most vicious instruments of social control were not to become fully operational until several years later. One of the consequences of Sharpeville was, in fact, to alert the state to accelerate construction of the security architecture of full-blown apartheid.

The crowd would have included a diversity of people who, if bound by an overweening sense of general wrong incarnated by the police, functioned at different levels of political mobilisation. The nature of 'the crowd' as a sociological entity is, in any event, inherently multifaceted, and between its layers and segmentations are different agendas, levels of consciousness and propensity to expressive political behaviour which adjust according to shifts in its surrounding environment.[23] At a more concrete level, some people in Sharpeville still drew distinctions between the municipal police who had functioned at the leading edge of state repression in the events leading up to 21 March and what others regarded, in unfortunate retrospect, as the more benign members of the SAP's uniform branches.

During the course of the evening and early morning the crowd had composed and recomposed and, as its internal order and homogeneity began to decompose, the PAC found itself battling to control the dispersal and actions of its loosely connected constituents. By the time the Saracens entered Sharpeville, the situation had become anarchic to the extent that what might be true in one context – the negative experiences of one set of journalists or police in one area of Sharpeville – was patently less true in another. There were patches of violence or combustible violence in various places and much ultimately depended on the increasingly minimal influence exercised by spontaneous pockets of leadership that sprung up among different sub-crowds in different zones or places. So it was quite possible that the Saracens were met with low levels of hostility at their point of departure near to the location offices, but then ran into deeper levels of popular antipathy in the heartland of the township where, from all accounts, the more militant supporters of the anti-pass campaign had begun to occupy the strategic high ground.

Cultural networks in a society deeply divided hy race, culture and ethnicity must clearly be taken into account in understanding the different meanings which traditionally segregated people attach to the same set of social transactions. Apart from a few individuals with a smattering of the 'fanagalo' patois normally used to give orders, none of the police understood the vernacular Sesotho language of the local people. Expressions which formed part of the normal verbal intercourse of township life were beyond the understanding of those whose very role it was to administer the 'native locations', and were automatically assumed to be belligerent. The relative absence of black personnel among the reinforcements in the Saracens precluded the police from making informed use of translators. In one significant instance where a black constable was asked by his white superiors to identify what the crowd was saying he first feigned an absence of hearing, but then took malicious delight in explaining that the shouts were intrinsically hostile. This was hardly reassuring to an increasingly paranoid police force, some of whose members had already reached the conclusion that even passive onlookers in the crowd were simply waiting for the right moment to strike at their oppressors.

To most residents of Sharpeville the traditional 'Afrika' salute was a non-pejorative and generally acceptable form of acceptance and greeting. But to the police, the officials, and even some of the journalists to whom the very notion of 'Afrika' carried connotations of the deepest black barbarism, the salute was replete with intonations of threat and violence which added into the siege mentality of the white minority at both national and local level. Some harried journalists who had come from Evaton, where violence was much more in evidence by mid-morning, inadvertently assisted the transposition of these sentiments to already anxious security personnel deployed to Sharpeville even before the latter had entered the township. One widely respected journalist from Johannesburg's *Rand*

Daily Mail when questioned by police officials outside the Location Office labelled the Vaal crowds of the day as the 'most vicious' in his experience. Many of the police who subsequently ran the gauntlet from the office to the central police station were therefore understandably terrified by what they perceived as an imminent threat to their lives though it was, from a purely township perspective, an exuberant but ultimately non-lethal public demonstration.

Many regarded the entry of the Saracens as a bizarre indication of the importance being attributed to the people of Sharpeville. The young and the children were especially intrigued by the enormity of these unfamiliar vehicles and moved forward in their innocence to appreciate their nature by touching their cold armour. Older people were less intrigued but were nevertheless curious, and the slow progress of the Saracens through the main streets encouraged them to come forward. Some of these people were inevitably pressed from behind into the path of the Saracens to form the dense mass of 'hostile' protestors whom the anxious occupants of these vehicles believed they had encountered.

But behind the cultural and physical dynamics of misperceptions there was trouble brewing on both sides. In the first place, the Saracens were the thin edge of the wedge of increasing numbers of heavily armed police personnel moving to supplement the normal police contingent at the Sharpeville Police Station. With few exceptions, all of these police were white and had no previous experience of the 'softer' aspects of crowd or riot control. They were armed with Sten guns and .303 rifles more suitable for fully-fledged warfare or hunting expeditions and their sense of anxiety increased with each metre that they proceeded into the townships.

The system of communication, command and control, as I have noted, was already haphazard. Because of the inadvertent failure or conscious decision of the security police not to fully appraise the uniform branch of the nature and extent of the disturbances, most of the personnel moving into Sharpeville believed that they were being deployed into an intensely dangerous situation where racial violence was inevitable. Among those who thought this way was Lieutenant-Colonel G D Pienaar, who for some months had been monitoring Sharpeville from Divisional Headquarters in Johannesburg. He was ordered to Sharpeville to participate in the management of the mounting crisis and was to emerge as a critical role player at the height of the crisis.

There were other forces at work which augured an eventual violent outcome. Some of the crowd had fallen under the influence of various township marginals, particularly some of the gang leaders who, fuelled with liquor (or headaches) in the aftermath of the weekend, were urging people to adopt a more adventurous stand than simply to watch the progress of the police forces. Given the work stoppage and the restrictions imposed by the PAC on people leaving the township, there were few vehicles on the streets by mid-morning other than those of the police. Of those, several black drivers and passengers who had been foolhardy enough to defy the restrictions were apprehended by groups of youths and forced to alight and return, amid jeering, to their homes. There were sporadic assaults and, in one or two cases, severe beatings for the non-compliant, including a father seeking to rush his ill child to the Vereeniging Hospital. For the most part however, local drivers were simply threatened and some had their keys confiscated as did the handful of white civilian drivers – mainly the small body of journalists wending their way to the police station in search of a story.

There were also weapons about, but most of these were sticks, knobkerries and other 'cultural weapons' (to use more contemporary terminology) though some of the PAC organisers had managed to acquire a number of small calibre pistols from criminals. In the course of the weekend there had been some wild talk about assassinating the more hated police officials or mounting an insurrection, but the more mature PAC members had been quick to rein in this quixotic element with its dangerous mixture of political motives and personal vendettas. However, there was a limit to the extent to which everyone could be monitored all the time. Shots were fired, as the police alleged, but these appear to have been largely symbolic (and badly aimed) gestures of popular antipathy emanating from a minority section of the restive crowd. In at least one instance a psychologically-unstable youth in possession of a pistol was disarmed before he could do any serious damage and then confined to a house on the edge of the township along with a number of equally disturbed (or naïve) acquaintances who talked of direct confrontation with the authorities. It must be conceded that the stones being thrown at police and other vehicles were real and certainly unfriendly, particularly when they 'rained down', as described by one journalist who later complained of 'serious damage to his car's paintwork'.

Officials of the Non-Europeans Affairs Department who rashly came to collect their 'native' employees also ran into trouble with stone-throwing demonstrators who broke their windscreen, causing damage amounting to £96.[24] They wisely gave up their search. Still, the impact of the stones was muted in most cases and the passage between the Location Office and the police station was hardly tantamount to the running of a genuinely life-threatening gauntlet, at least for most of the early and mid-morning.

As the Saracens shuttled back and forth with their reinforcements Lieutenant-Colonel Pienaar arrived from Divisional Headquarters in Johannesburg. A senior officer, then a few years short of retirement, Pienaar was an archetypal by-product of the SAP bureaucratic establishment. He had risen methodically through the ranks with no particular accomplishments over the years apart from his claims to being a white man in an organisation with a white command system. Now, he was known to be looking forward to his severance pay and a future as a small-scale farmer. He did not 'need' Sharpeville or its problems, as he made abundantly clear in his testimony to the Commission of Inquiry. Nonetheless, during the course of Sharpeville's violent Monday he was tasked by his immediate superior, the Witwatersrand Divisional Commissioner, Brigadier Els, with management of the mounting crisis. He had apparently been present in the Vaal somewhat earlier in the weekend but had returned to his home base at Marshall Square to emerge once again late on Monday morning at the office of the Location Superintendent, along with the ubiquitous Colonel Spengler. Both entered the township, now accompanied by the shuttling Saracens, with a view to making an *in situ* assessment at the Sharpeville Police Station.

Spengler, it appears from available evidence, had had a busy week, most of which was devoted to security police operations in various areas of the Witwatersrand and the Vaal where the anti-pass campaign had developed momentum. Sharpeville had not been at the centre of his attentions, at least not prior to Sunday. He and Prinsloo apparently conversed on the Sunday night and early on the Monday morning Spengler and a number of his colleagues travelled down to the area. By late morning they had assembled at the municipal offices at the entrance to Sharpeville. Here they met with a number of local senior SAP personnel, the town clerk of Vereeniging, Labuschagne, Colonel Holmes and Lieutenant-Colonel Pienaar. After a brief conversation Spengler and Pienaar indicated their wish to have their cars escorted directly to the Sharpeville Police Station by the attending Saracens in order to deal with the situation 'directly'. The time was just after 13.00.

There is to this day no consensus as to the size of the crowd that had gathered around the police station when Spengler and Pienaar arrived. Like much else in the Sharpeville saga, problems of recall, distortions of perception, and political agendas play havoc with various estimates. As a generalisation, the perpetrators, most notably the SAP, have inflated the figures as part of the process of legitimating their behaviour, while the victims have downplayed the numbers in order to reinforce the image of a reasonable body of innocents congregated at the place of their killing. There is also some evidence to suggest that some of the aerial photographs sent to police archives and subsequently presented to the Commission were carefully doctored to increase the size of the crowd, particularly at the epicentre of the eventual shootings, the west side of the station. Ultimately however, most observers had difficulty in making any estimations at all because the terrain around the station was so flat, and because groups of people came and went throughout the period up until midday. Several key witnesses before the Commission of Inquiry escaped the massacre because they had decided to leave the site for refreshment or to go home for lunch after a long morning during which nothing appeared to be happening. In justification of their actions, the police who came before the Commission referred to figures from twenty to thirty thousand adults and a number of children, although the total population of Sharpeville at the time was estimated to be no more than thirty-five thousand – of whom about 20 000 were children. Even if account is taken of non-residents who had been encouraged by the PAC to lend their support to the demonstration or had come of their own volition, these estimates seem excessive. Ultimately, most persuasive calculations settle in the region of eighteen to twenty-five thousand, many of them children.

It is conceivable that the police overestimated the numbers precisely because the terrain was flat. None of them was acquainted with exact local demographics and most, it appears, believed Sharpeville to be far more densely populated than it was. It appears that it it did not occur to anyone in the station to make an aerial observation of the behaviour and size of the crowd by, for example, climbing on to the roof. This, together with the fact that the arriving reinforcements spoke of shifting, vicious and hostile crowds who thronged the main streets and were ostensibly on the way to the station, and it is quite conceivable that the police contingent quite genuinely believed that they were a small group under direct threat from an enraged mob of tens of thousands.

How 'small' was small? Here again there are inconsistencies between myth and reality. We know for a fact that the Spengler/Pienaar convoy consisting of a number of police cars and their Saracen escort was the last body of men to enter the station prior to the massacre. But what we do not know with absolute certainty is the number of personnel who were actually deployed within the station at this point – partly because of the racial peculiarities of contemporary police record-keeping, partly because of the intentional destruction of official documents in the wake of the massacre (and before the Wessels Commission), and ultimately because the SAP had a clear political interest in deflating the arithmetic in justification of their actions. For one thing, the official documents that still exist on Sharpeville either entirely overlook the presence of the 'native' police, or condescendingly refer to them by their Christian names. With casual references to 'Bantoe-Konstabel Edmund' or 'Amos', it becomes exceedingly difficult to sort out who is who and who was where.

Certainly there were far more police in and around the Sharpeville station than is represented in the official version of events which portray 130 white police confronted by a bloodthirsty mob of tens of thousands. Although the notion which exists in the minds of many of the survivors of thousands of police and troops swarming around the station is equally exaggerated, there were considerably more police in place than appears the case from the standard arithmetic. Close scrutiny of the correspondence from various police commanders across the Witwatersrand who were called upon to comb their stations for reinforcements reveal, for example, that there were at least 160 heavily-armed white personnel at the station. Official statistics also conveniently ignore (or downplay) the further presence of 130 black police armed largely with assegais and knobkerries. These included large contingents trucked in from Newlands and Moroka – both of which, along with other Witwatersrand divisional stations were half emptied of their complement in the desperate rush to send additional personnel to the Vaal. Finally, the standard versions, by referring only to 'reinforcements', also bypass the presence of local personnel from Vereeniging and Vanderbijl as well as large numbers of police in the immediate environment – in lorries to the north of the veld bordering the station; in adjacent streets; on the township boundaries and, above all, in the Cape Stands (a collection of houses on the south-west corner of the police station so-called because they were occupied by coloureds not by Africans). Here alone, a further ninety police, including twenty-nine heavily-armed white personnel, had been deployed to provide covering fire should an attack on the police station occur or appear to be imminent.[25] In fact there were about 400 police (almost half carrying firearms) in and around the Sharpeville station at the time of the slaughter. Taken in conjunction with the Saracens, three of which were parked with their heavy Browning machine guns in the yard of the station, this gives the lie, in large part, to the notion that a small and isolated body of men was faced with an overwhelming threat from a gargantuan mob.

Much would have depended, though, on the structure of the crowd and its internal dynamics, both of which were to determine the nature of the process which led to the confrontation. In this regard it is relevant that the crowd was not the undifferentiated mass, implanted in the minds of the police, and, indeed, the subsequent Commission of Inquiry. On the contrary it contained a diversity of sub-sections and social fragments whose individual and collective agendas would shape the course of the day. It does not appear that any of them foresaw the possibility of storming the police station, partly because of the emphasis that had been placed on non-violence by the organisers of the demonstration, more fundamentally because of the deterrent posed by the concentration of firepower behind the fence of the station. Even had there been some agenda of this sort among certain individuals in the crowd, the progressive arrival of armed police reinforcements during the course of the morning would have been sufficiently dissuasive to all but the most foolhardy.

Unfortunately this was not the perspective from across the low fence separating the police from the crowd, particularly as their numbers swelled and those in front became densely packed against the thin wire barrier. Inside, where 'cultural weapons' were perceived as lethal weapons of assault, there was an imminent sense of threat which escalated with the progress of the morning. Participants in the garrison recall that the police believed, almost to a man, that elements in the crowd were also heavily armed with either pistols or rifles which they had every intention of using should the opportunity present itself. This calculation was apparently confirmed by the reinforcements who had run the gauntlet from the edge of the township to its centre, and who had heard (but had not actually seen) shots being fired in the general tumult accompanying their passage.

Was the crowd then truly aggressive and armed – as the police were to insist at the subsequent Commission of Inquiry – or was it essentially a peaceful gathering with some individuals carrying sticks, as defenders of the victims were to assert? This brings into play a third element – the local 'tsotsis' who had thrown in their lot with the PAC activists. Some would certainly have carried the tools of their trade – knives, chains and so on, and it is quite possible that some carried some form of small calibre weaponry. There is also a possibility that there were bullets among the stones that rained on the approaching Saracens – it would have been difficult for even the most acute ear inside the vehicles to differentiate between the thud of a rock and the impact of a bullet on protective armour.

Former gangsters confirm that there were weapons although they claim that the small proportion of shots that were fired were aimed not at the police but into the air. It would, in fact, have been extremely difficult for township residents to access high-power weaponry, particularly in the face of the ongoing police raids that had led up to March 1960. There is no evidence that the PAC was intent on building arms caches and the single rifle discovered by the police in the previous year was never linked to PAC activity, despite the brutal efforts of the security police to do so. According to police reports the rifle was, in any case, an antiquated and poorly maintained firing piece which could not conceivably wreak much in the way of destruction, even had it been aimed at the police station. The purpose of the little weaponry in the crowd appears to have been to bolster the morale and sense of power of certain of its individuals rather than to wound or destroy the personnel in the police barracks.

But the police did not know this. In an era when the notion of an armed 'Bantu-onluste [uprising]' connoted demonic violence for most whites, any shot (or a sound resembling a shot) would have been sufficient to confirm the perception that the crowd lusted for white blood. And many people heard, or thought they heard shots among the cries from the engorging crowd as it surged and swelled around the station. The events at Cato Manor, 'a particularly troublesome black township in the Port Natal Division', were still fresh in the minds of most policemen.[26] Here, some weeks before, a number of police had been slaughtered after one of their number had accidentally trodden upon a black women's foot during the course of an otherwise 'normal' police raid to deal with such apartheid crimes as violation of influx control, the selling of illegal liquor, destruction of pass/reference books, ANC incitement, the burning of schools, factional tribal conflicts and the destruction of livestock dipping tanks. In a situation not dissimilar to that brewing in Sharpeville, the small police force had been obliged to barricade itself in two adjacent huts which were eventually stormed by more than a thousand rioters.

The more fortunate of the nine police who died had simply been stoned to death, but there were cases of disembowelment flowing from 'the naked aggression and bloodlust of the rioters'.[27] 'We took great delight in shouting "Cato Manor" ... because we knew it would disturb the boers,' says Samuel Ntshona*. It certainly did!

The fighter planes requisitioned by Major van Zyl had made things worse in a number of unanticipated ways. The Vereeniging District Commander had come up with the idea that the crowd would be cowed and dispelled by projecting the power of the state in the form of the South African Air Force. Consequently, just before midday, a number of aircraft appeared over the scene and 'buzzed' the crowd from a dangerously low level – for the pilots if not the people they sought to intimidate. The response was not what the authorities had expected. Rather than fleeing the scene in anticipation of imminent bombing, the crowd, and in particular its young, simply waved at what they still term 'the flights' in friendly acknowledgement. Some may well have lifted their sticks to the sky in mock hostility, as the police alleged in their evidence before the Commission, but for greater majority the noise and sound of the aircraft appeared to feed what many on the ground appear to have seen as the semi-festive nature of the day. There were cries of glee from the children, none of whom had actually seen a fighter aircraft in flight. Among the adults, the appearance of the aircraft seemed an affirmation of the importance of the occasion. 'We were,' in the words of one old survivor, 'honoured that the government had blessed us with its presence in the air.'

Apart from the intention to intimidate the crowd, the rationalisation behind this essentially pointless aerial display remains inexplicable. From interviews conducted with old police commanders it appears that there was no intention to bomb or machine gun the assembling crowds, while a reconnaissance of their numbers could have been achieved just as well with some careful observation at ground level. If the purpose was merely to cow the demonstrators, the result was the reverse. Not only were they not especially impressed by the message of serious intent symbolised by the aerial flypast, the very fact that they were not increased the sense of anxiety among the ground-based state forces. The failure of the crowd to flee at the sound of the warplanes reinforced the view that this was a bloodthirsty mob intent on destruction. 'Some of us ducked as the planes flew over us,' a constable recalls, 'but the mob knew no fear.'

Developments within the Sharpeville station were also becoming untenable in a way that was to further fuel police fears. Relative to the black complement, the number of white police was small, though better armed, even after the arrival of reinforcements. While the white SAP could normally count on the loyalty of their black subordinates who had compromised themselves through their service in the organs of state security, the recent differences within the station had soured race relations. The PAC had also been at work in the previous weeks to market their cause to the local police and, though none had positively responded, the fact that such potentially dangerous contacts had taken place at all was a cause of concern to the authorities. Directives from the Johannesburg security police during February had in fact advised the Vaal police commanders to keep their black auxiliaries under close surveillance as a means of countering their 'contamination' by the local communities. While this surveillance produced nothing concrete to suggest that the black police in Sharpeville or elsewhere in the Vaal would mutiny or defect under pressure, the very existence of a racial link between the police in the station and the crowd outside was sufficient to convince at least some of the white SAP members that they faced a dual threat.

During the course of the morning some of the black police in the station had also begun to display what their white colleagues perceived as an unhealthy interest in the motivations of the crowd. A number of them appear to have identified with the rejection of the pass system, and this was especially disturbing to the one or two white policemen who understood a smattering of the indigenous language spoken by their black counterparts. Although the latter were as perplexed as the whites as to how the situation might be resolved – and probably as frightened, from the perspective of at least one white SAP member, the black police appeared to be 'lax', as if in possession of some sort of intelligence to which only they and the crowd were privy.

By midday it was fairly clear that the crowd was not diminishing and would not dissipate of its own accord in the near future. This was partly the result of the crowd momentum that was progressively carrying people into the field in front of the station, and also partly the result of PAC efforts to prevent its dissolution by spreading rumours. One of these was that senior *administrative* officials dealing with influx control policy in the Department of Bantu Administration and Development would arrive at the police station at about 14.00 to make a momentous (if unspecified) announcement regarding the future of the pass system. This was not entirely untrue – the police had also been informed of an impending important arrival – Brigadier Els from SAP headquarters in Pretoria who had been designated to take charge of the overall situation and who would, they presumed, make a speech of some sort to the gathering crowd.

Through the course of the morning the police, both black and white, had periodically, if fruitlessly, worked the wire fence to request the crowd, over the roar of noise, to move away from the vicinity of the police station in favour of the nearby football stadium. Here they could expect to be addressed at some later stage by a senior *police* official. In the face of these mixed messages the crowd was confused and, at its edges, shuffled around aimlessly. Most of its members, inclined towards the PAC activists and tantalised by the prospect that government officials were coming to announce the abolition of passes, remained ranged around the police station under the delusion that the campaign was on the brink of victory. As this notion spread the crowd at the station grew. Some, perhaps the more sceptical, drifted vaguely towards the stadium and the PAC acted immediately to reverse the movement. The real intention of the police, its activists argued, was to disempower the people by corralling everyone in the stadium where they would then be shot indiscriminately.

Benjamin Twala* distinctly recalls that he and his friends were told by a suspected black police agent that they should leave the station and go to hear the 'big white baas who is coming to the stadium'. Moments later their path was blocked by a PAC organiser who warned them that to do so would be to risk life and limb. Carlton Monnakgotla and Simon

Mkutau similarly recall being ordered by the police to 'march to the football stadium', but then being turned back on the basis of a message that 'if we go to the football grounds they will shoot us all'. 'So we turned around and went to stand in front and around the police station once more.'[28]

PAC strategy during the morning was formulated on an *ad hoc* basis. No specific plans had been laid down for the members of the executive committee to communicate as events unfolded, nor were there any planned channels for liaison running between the committee and its task force leaders in the field. People simply met (or failed to meet) according to the flow of events, and this meant total confusion in which it was left to individuals to interpret and convey the party's agenda as they saw fit, as it coincided with their personal interests, or as the needs of the immediate situation at grassroots seemed to dictate. While all the PAC organisers understood that the primary purpose of the demonstration was to steer the crowd to the police station in some fashion or another, no particular attention had been given to how this was to be done, or when and what to do should the crowd, in its collective logic, decide otherwise. In accord with the populist spirit of the PAC this was a truly spontaneous mass action – at least once it had been ignited. Thus it was quite possible, as many survivors note, to be told by PAC organisers to take one course of action at a particular moment, only to be advised to act in a contradictory way, minutes later.

Since most of the PAC organisers were not wearing readily identifiable caps or badges people had to rely on people they, or their friends knew personally be committed members of the PAC. This, in turn, created vast opportunities for poseurs, *agents provocateurs,* and people who might have only limited connections with the PAC to exercise their sway. In the circumstances – whatever later claims were made by the PAC – the local leaders had very little information as to what was happening at any point, while their constituents acted in a vacuum which was, in the end, essentially leaderless.

The police were almost equally disorganised. While the Vanderbijlpark Police Station was officially designated the centre of operations, most of the strategic personnel were scattered between Vanderbijl, Vereeniging, the edges of Sharpeville, different locations within the township, and in the Sharpeville station itself. Radio and telephone communications somewhat plugged the gap, but none of this technology could override the urgency and momentum with which the crisis developed towards its apogee after midday, nor could it compensate for the impact of bureaucratic and personal considerations upon overall police strategy. Officially, Captain Theron was the commander *in situ* at the Sharpeville station (under the overall authority of Vereeniging District Commander, Major van Zyl), but as the security police poured into the area, his authority was gradually subverted by Captain Willers and his seniors, none of whom appeared enthusiastic about leaving what was fast becoming a major operation in the hands of the uniform branch. The tensions between the two branches of the police were recognised by Prinsloo in Pretoria and it was largely with a view to establishing a better coordinated system of crisis management that he decided to personally come down to the Vaal on the Monday morning.

The decision to send other outsiders to manage the situation – Pienaar and, above all, a very senior officer like Brigadier Els – was similarly motivated by the need to impose a firmer overall system of authority. But by midday, Sharpeville still awaited Els, while Pienaar was locked an argument with Van Zyl and Spengler both of whom, to a greater (Spengler) or lesser (Van Zyl) extent were inclined towards continued efforts at negotiation while Pienaar emphasised a hard and, if necessary, confrontational line. Their discussions at the municipal offices during the late morning had been punctuated by these tactical differences and it was largely because of irresolution and disagreement on all sides that Spengler and Pienaar had decided to go to the police station to make an on-site assessment. There were also manifest policy differences running the line between the Vanderbijl station and its counterpart in Sharpeville. While the 'defenders' of Sharpeville were increasingly desperate to diminish the surrounding crowd as quickly as possible, their Vanderbijl counterparts were less than enthusiastic about the crowd being diverted to the football stadium. Captain Van der Merwe, who was at Vanderbijl at midday, recalls that the staff at the local station emphasised the proximity of the stadium to the white suburbs of the town. There had been disturbances in Vanderbijl that very morning when large crowds of township dwellers from Evaton, Bophelong and Boipatong had assembled in a threatening manner before the local police station. By mid-morning they had been 'driven out of town' by the police, but there was still fear that they would congregate again.[29] Captain Cawood and his men who had been in Sharpeville throughout Sunday night were recalled to Vanderbijl to remain on standby at about 11.00. Armed white vigilantes had also appeared to 'assist' the police during the morning and were itching to unleash their firepower on the 'swartes'. The police had politely declined their help and then established roadblocks on the routes to the various townships in order to segregate the various racial factions. This would be considerably more difficult were the Sharpeville crowd to move to the stadium. Ironic as it might seem, Van der Merwe emphasises, it was probably better in principle that the Sharpeville crowd remain outside its own police station.

Notwithstanding the politics of crowd gravitation and the internal dynamics of the main role players, the situation by midday had developed an innate momentum that was increasingly irreversible by either the police, the PAC, or indeed, by the crowd itself. The police and the PAC now faced a common dilemma. The small police contingent could not peacefully disperse the mob and the mob was not likely to dissolve of its own volition. This was confirmed by verbal contacts across the low station fence during which the front-ranking members of the crowd called on the police to arrest them for violations of the pass laws. They would not go away, they indicated, and would, if necessary, remain through the day and into the night until the police took them into custody. This the police could not do. The cells in the station were simply too small to accommodate a group of these proportions and none of them had, in fact, technically violated the pass laws. Nor were the police disposed to move outside the relative safety of the security fence to carry out the routine checks of who did or did not have a valid pass in their possession.

The PAC was equally befuddled in a standoff situation which was not, in many respects, of its making. Having mobilised thousands of people to surrender their passes and suffer arrest they now found, to their consternation, that the police were not prepared to react by arresting anyone. In the circumstances, the whole situation contained the potential to degenerate into a complete farce at one end of the continuum, or violence at the other.

———— ✦ ————

LUNCH AND SLAUGHTER

By 13.00, on the lip of the drama, the key role players were all firmly in place. Some people in the crowd had left for lunch and, in doing so, were able to avoid the catastrophe that was about to engulf their fellows, friends and relatives. Vincent Leutsoa, the librarian at the Sharpeville library diagonally opposite the police station to its north-west across the veld, took a lunchtime tea only moments before bullets shattered the library windows.[30] Carlton Monnakgotla, the former South African middleweight boxing champion, who was nineteen at the time of the shootings, remembers how he felt thirsty, left the crowd at the fence, and went to buy a drink at the nearby shops a few seconds before the shootings. 'A can of coke saved my life.'[31] Many others, less fortunate, did not leave the scene. Despite its ebbs and flows the crowd was swelling and, by 13.00 had grown to about twenty thousand people. Some of its members had climbed onto the roof of the clinic on the west side of the station while others were perching on the roofs of nearby houses in Zwane Street. While their motivation was simply to secure a better view of developments, some of the police in the station were so fearfully paranoid by this point that they believed that these people were carefully positioned snipers. About a third of the ground-based crowd was concentrated around the main gate of the station with the remainder running down its north and south sides. There were relatively few people – either demonstrators or police – on the east.

Half an hour before the killings there were about 300 men in or near the police station drawn from nineteen commands across the Vaal,

Johannesburg and the East Rand (See Table 1). This formidable force was armed with an assortment of pistols, .303 hunting rifles and Stens. Across the way from the station in the Cape Stands were the heavily-armed railway police from Kaserne with their hand-held light machine

TABLE 1
POLICE DEPLOYMENT AT SHARPEVILLE – 13.00, 21 March 1960*

Command	White	Black	Total
Sharpeville-Uniform SAP	3	27	30
Sharpeville -Municipal	4	1	5
Vereeniging	21	39	60
Vanderbijlpark	11	3	14
Johannesburg Central	18	–	18
Johannesburg Radio – Kaserne	14	–	14
Bezuidenhout Valley	4	5	9
Jeppe	9	–	9
Hospital Hill	13	–	13
Bramley	3	–	3
Parkview	4	2	6
Rosebank	4	2	6
Norwood	5	–	5
Ferndale	5	4	9
Yeoville	1	–	1
Craighall	–	6	6
Newlands	10	21	31
Moroka	2	19	21
Kliptown	2	–	2
Springs	17	9	26
Boksburg	6	–	6
TOTAL	156	138	294

* Excludes some members of Vereeninging CID and Special Branch

guns. The largest contingent (sixty men) was from Vereeniging; the smallest, a lone constable with a Sten gun who had been deployed in mid-morning from the Craighall police station in the leafy suburbs of Johannesburg. Three Saracens as well as a number of other assorted police vehicles were parked at the ready in the compound.

Three men now arrived centre stage – each of them, in his own way, was to catalyse the looming catastrophe. Spengler and Pienaar passed through the station gates at roughly 13.00. There was a general cacophony in the area as people shouted a mixture of African chants and political slogans at the approaching convoy. A number of stones were also thrown but these bounced harmlessly off the Saracen armour. The car carrying Pienaar was less fortunate: much to the irritation of the already testy colonel, its paintwork was damaged and its windscreen cracked. Confronted by the overweening physical presence of the Saracens, the crowd nevertheless parted as the armoured cars moved carefully forward into the station compound. The gates were then quickly closed behind them and Spengler alighted to survey the scene prior to determining some future course of action. What this might have been remains an historical mystery now locked incontrovertibly into the mind of a deceased man.

A small delegation of the crowd led by the local PAC leadership under the authority of the two Tsolo brothers had passed through the fence slightly earlier in the morning and Spengler appears to have decided that talks with this group about their immediate objectives, if not long-term aims, offered the best way out of a dangerously escalating situation. Unfortunately, the delegation had either been rebuffed by Captain Theron, who abjured responsibility for any negotiations prior to the arrival of more senior officers, or had refused to assist the police to disperse the crowd without direct orders from Sobukwe himself. When Theron refused to arrest them they left the scene and melted back into the surrounding crowd. Spengler and Pienaar were briefed on what had transpired by Theron who also pointed out that he had recently used a hand-held loudspeaker to attempt to communicate with the crowd. This had proved futile, partly because of the high volume of noise, and partially because the loudspeaker was relatively low-powered.

Intending to make closer physical contact Spengler now proceeded to the fence to see if he could observe any sign of leadership among the chanting and amorphous mass on the other side. It was at this point that Nyakane Tsolo came forward and requested readmission into the station to speak with Spengler.

A strange situation, inexplicable to this day, then ensued, with Spengler requesting Tsolo to identify himself and Tsolo replying that he was the leader of the PAC named 'Zero'. This was peculiar, since there is evidence that Spengler knew exactly who Tsolo was, if not through personal dealings, then at least through the photography sections of security police files. It is curious that Spengler should have asked the man he knew to be the local leader of the PAC branch who he was, and its even more strange that Tsolo should have used a *nom de plume*. Either the two enjoyed some sort of 'relationship' which neither wished to make evident to the assembled crowd, or Spengler misheard Tsolo in the noisy atmosphere. In any event Tsolo was requested to ask the crowd to disperse. When he repeated that only Sobukwe could call off the demonstration, Spengler placed him under arrest and ordered Sergeant Wessels who was at his side to take the prisoner into the station.

The ubiquitous Colonel Prinsloo awaited Tsolo. Prinsloo had not accompanied the main security police contingent under Spengler that had arrived in the Vaal earlier that morning. Briefings with senior government officials on the unfolding pass demonstrations had apparently delayed his departure and, on the way to Sharpeville, he had also detoured to Evaton where the police station was also 'omsingeled' (surrounded) 'deur sowat 15 000 Bantoes'.[32] In consequence, Prinsloo bypassed the meeting of municipal and police officials at the administration offices and proceeded under his own steam directly to the Sharpeville Police Station where he commandeered Theron's office. Tsolo and Prinsloo now engaged in a quick discussion. Neither knew the other, and Prinsloo began the dialogue badly by insisting dismissively that he wished to speak to a person more senior that the mere secretary of the local branch of the PAC. Tsolo was offended, and within seconds the exchange had degenerated into outright confrontation. Like Spengler, Prinsloo urged

Tsolo to recognise the danger of the situation and call his people off. When Tsolo once more insisted that only Sobukwe could issue such a directive and was unlikely to do so until 'freedom' was attained, the Colonel was inflamed and broke off any further communication. Wessels was instructed to throw Tsolo into the cells. In the meantime Captain Willers, Prinsloo's immediate aide, was directed to go back to Spengler in the sun-drenched compound and find some other more amenable 'Bantoe-leier'.

Spengler had, in the meantime approached Pienaar. A short terse conversation ensued which, according to a nearby constable, dwelt on the issue of how to proceed in resolving what both senior officers clearly recognised as a potential conflagration. During the quick and chaotic mobilisation of the SAP for duty in Sharpeville, neither officer had been fully briefed on the firepower available to the police. When Pienaar had suddenly been dispatched from Johannesburg early that morning to take command in Sharpeville, he was given the barest details of whom he was to command and the weapons his men would have at their disposal. Given the poor lines of communication between the uniform and security branches of the SAP, Spengler was equally unaware that the police were more than equipped to deal with the situation. In the event, both men were anxious about police capacity to disperse the crowd.

Spengler, it appears, believed that a salutary burst of fire would soon have the crowd in full flight, but Pienaar, determined to 'bring matters to a head' as soon as possible, demurred. A short enfilade, he believed, would only further inflame the mob and, should they launch an attack across the low and leaning fence, the station's defenders would lack sufficient time and space to project their fire. If there was to be shooting, he concluded, it was better to do it quickly.

Neither officer appears to have given any consideration to whether the line of fire should be into the body of the crowd or over their heads and Spengler remained convinced that negotiation was still the best possible way of surmounting the crisis. So, dissension prevailed. Spengler turned abruptly from his more aggressive counterpart, talked briefly with Willers about the outcome of the interrogation of Tsolo, and then walked quickly back to the station perimeter. From his vantage point near the gate, he once more scanned the baying crowd in the hope of detecting another leader more amenable to discussions. His eye alighted on Thomas More, another member of the PAC executive, who was screaming wildly near the entrance. With a hand movement Spengler invited him to enter the compound. More did so and, like Tsolo, demanded arrest while firmly rejecting any suggestion that he assist the police to disperse the crowd. Faced with this violent outburst, Spengler placed him under arrest in accordance with his wishes. Like Tsolo More was led down into the main building to meet with Prinsloo. When the conversation proved equally unproductive, More was also taken to the cells.

A critical conversation (which eluded the later Commission of Inquiry) now ensued between Willers, Prinsloo and Pienaar, who had entered the room sweating profusely from a mixture of heat and irritation after his frustrating encounter with Spengler. Willers was summoned from the cells where he had had further brief discussions with Tsolo and More. His report that he had made no headway with either was received with considerable dissatisfaction. According to a young sergeant, Prinsloo and Pienaar conferred. There was, he recalls, some sort of 'message from government', some talk about 'the extreme militancy' of the crowd, 'flare-ups', and words to the effect that 'this business be brought to an end as soon as possible'. Prinsloo, who appeared enraged, called for Tsolo to be brought up again from the cells: he had no interest in More whom he described in Afrikaans as 'a bloody idiot'. Pienaar was dispatched outside to convey some sort of communication to Spengler, whose contents remain tantalisingly unknown but which probably contained his and Prinsloo's concern that the crisis had reached a point of imminent explosion. Tsolo appeared in the room with Willers and he and Prinsloo again discussed the possibility of crowd dispersal.

Spengler had in the meantime been working the fence in search of another negotiator and had stopped here and there to attempt to speak with various individuals pressed against the station perimeter. He now decided, somewhat foolishly in some respects, to order that the gate be opened so he might move to the edge of the assembled crowd in his now increasingly hopeless endeavour to pinpoint a mediator who could still the 'oproerig'(restive) masses. As he did so, a man in a red shirt, unknown to this day, came forward to surrender his pass and partake of the honour of joining the PAC leaders under arrest in the station. By then Spengler was losing patience. He placed his hand on the shoulder of the man in the traditional manner of police apprehending suspects and the man, reassessing the consequences of incarceration, shrank back. Spengler began to 'jerk him about'[33], the man resisted and in the midst of the melee, the colonel stumbled over a hidden object on the ground in the vicinity of the half-open gate. As he lurched to his feet, his victim still in hand, a nearby police constable, Sten gun at the ready, rushed forward to help him …

It was at this moment that Colonel Pienaar, though he had not seen the incident, concluded that the time was ripe for some sort of pre-emptive gesture – to 'save' the station along with his personal reputation. He observed that the security fence was leaning dangerously inward at some points under crowd pressure and believed that should it give way it would be too late to avert the crisis which he and Prinsloo believed to be imminent. Some of the police, discomforted by their inability to maintain a distance between themselves and the crowd, were using their rifle butts to push people back, some of them recoiling with distaste as members of the mob reached through the mesh to touch them. One policemen in short sleeves moving up against the fence was slapped fairly heavily on his bare forearm, several were scratched or gashed by small sharp implements which they believed to be knives or razors though they were in fact, for the most part the sharp edges of the fence. There was a deep sense of dread among the police, a veritable psychosis of fear. So all were receptive when Pienaar, in 'an attempt to exercise a sobering effect', ordered the formation of a defensive line along the west side of the station.[34] In response to his orders, amid a cacophony of 'Cato Manors' emanating from the crowd, weapons were loaded as an added precaution.

Geelbooi, last seen staggering away into the night after his brutal interrogation at the Vereeniging police station some months before, now made an unlikely, brief, and ultimately disastrous reappearance upon the stage of history. Having spent much of the weekend with his petty criminal associates, he made his anonymous way to the station much the worse for a Sunday night bout of drinking. At the police station he was, by all accounts, near the fence at the west gate where he spied (or believed he spied) his erstwhile interrogator, Sergeant de Bruyn among the white policemen immediately to the left of Spengler. 'Ek sal die vark skiet,' (I will shoot that pig) he slurred, producing a small calibre pistol. A scuffle followed as a friend attempted to inhibit his intention. Arms were raised and two shots ricocheted harmlessly into the air ...

The time was 13.29 and there was, at that precise and tiny moment of history pregnant with disaster, a inexplicable lull in the noise that had risen all morning long from the throats of the crowd. Clouds had gathered through what had initially been a crystal clear Highveld morning and by 13.00 black cumulus loomed in the backdrop. There was a soft roll of thunder in the very far distance and some of the crowd had fallen silent as they pitched their ears to the disturbances in the upper atmosphere. At that very moment, as Spengler stumbled, the shots from Geelbooi's gun – two small cracks – reverberated through the air. The crowd in the street between the station the clinic – the only portion to witness events at the gate – did not know that what they were seeing was an information-gathering exercise which might lead to negotiation. What they thought they saw was the 'arrest' of one of their leaders and the manhandling of others – two inside the station, one at the gate.

Many, including the beleaguered police, heard Geelbooi's shots. Some of the crowd, incensed or curious, leaned inward along the fence line, adjacent to the undefended gate, to better observe the spectacle. Others, frightened that the fracas involving Spengler was a precursor to trouble, began to turn away but were prevented from moving by those behind them who still believed that a 'groot baas' from the government was coming to speak about the pass laws. A few pebbles – seen by the police as a 'rain of stones' – were cast in frustration at the gate where the spiral churning of the crowd created the impression that it was about to move forward. A pebble harmlessly struck the constable trying to defend a tottering Spengler and he instinctively raised his Sten gun. He heard

Pienaar (or someone else, possibly a nearby sergeant) shouting something akin to 'skiet' (shot), 'daar was 'n skiet' (there was a shot), or an apparently imperative, 'Skiet!' (shoot). Spengler almost intuitively sensed the imminent descent into the vortex and reached upward to deflect the firearm now over his head. A shot was fired but the rifle bullet skewed harmlessly into the air and out of the story. The moment, though, was in the vice of history. The rifle report travelled along the line of the nervous police to both left and right, releasing the forces of death with grotesque simultaneity.

———— ✦ ————

SOCIOLOGY OF A MASSACRE

It had taken precisely two shots to provoke the firepower of the police at the 'battle of Seeiso Street' earlier that morning. Men had acted unilaterally. There had been no formal order to fire in the street then, and, it appears – notwithstanding the dispositions of Prinsloo and Pienaar – there was no order to fire from the station now. In the preceding hours the capacity for violence on the part of the police had been viciously upgraded. By 13.30 the SAP at the police station had disposed of approximately 4 000 rounds of fire, variously distributed between .38 calibre revolvers, .303 rifles, hand-held light machine guns (Sten guns), .25 pistols (largely held by members of the security police and the Vereeniging CID) and, to crown the massive armoury, an additional 2 000 rounds distributed between the Browning heavy machine guns mounted on the Saracens in the police compound.

It was a measure of the restraint on the part of the police – according to evidence presented to the subsequent Commission – that the totality of this slaughter machine was not brought to bear on the pressing crowd. Many police did not immediately respond to the panicked chain reaction – not it seems, because of any feelings of humanitarianism mixed with doubt and confusion, but simply because 'things happened too quickly and were over before they began,' according to one old 'konstabel'. A constable armed with a Sten gun fired into the ground in panic – and was hit by a ricochet in one of the dozen minor police casualties of the entire incident. Other weapons jammed, and some made a conscious choice in the fleeting moment not to join the ranks of the perpetrators. Others followed their own logic or the momentum of the day and the result was a huge discharge of well over 1 000 rounds – at least a quarter of the potential fire-power of the police – first into the face of the crowd, and then into their fleeing rear – all within the course of less than a single frozen minute.

The impact was, by any standards, devastating, and the devastation was, in large manner, dictated by the physical deployment of the police up the sides of the Saracens and along the line formed by Pienaar on the west side of the station near the gate. The Saracens within the station perimeter, having emptied their personnel, had parked at various points within the fence with their gun ports still largely closed.

Because of their internal heat, most of their crews had alighted and some, along with members of the station contingent, had climbed with their pistols, rifles and Sten guns onto the vehicle platforms. This elevation enabled them to improve their surveillance of the surrounding crowd but also, to a degree, cut them off from the line of command, control and communication that centred on Pienaar and Spengler in the noisy vicinity of the gateway that faced onto the clinic on the west side of the station. In addition, their emplacement on the Saracens rendered them more vulnerable to any flying missiles, be they sticks, stones or even bullets. As it was, one or two policemen were struck by the odd small stone. None of these caused injury, but they intensified fear, anger and the sense of threat.

The volume and intensity of the police fire was cataclysmic, yet the sheer horror of Sharpeville lies in the fact that it was, as apartheid's critics allege, a largely gratuitous act of violence inextricably connected with the whole system of racial violence in South Africa from its modern foundations to its democratic transition almost 350 years later. In the end, the question of whether the crowd had the means, motivation and disposition to turn an already fast decomposing peaceable demonstration into an act of armed propaganda against the state pales into insignificance

TABLE 2
POLICE FIREPOWER DEPLOYED AT SHARPEVILLE*

Command	.25 Pistol	.38 Pistol	.303 Rifle	Sten Gun	Total Rnds Fired
Sharpeville – Uniform SAP	4	3	–	–	21
Sharpeville – Municipal	3	–	–	–	–
Vereeniging	–	21	13	2	110
Vanderbijlprk	–	10	1	1	7
Jhb – Central	–	9	1	–	94
Jhb -Radio (Kaserne)	–	12	1	7	425
Bez Valley	–	–	4	–	–
Jeppe	–	3	4	2	–
Hospital Hill	–	1	12	–	85
Bramley	–	1	–	1	63
Parkview	–	–	4	–	13
Rosebank	–	–	4	–	18
Norwood	–	–	5	–	47
Ferndale	–	–	5	–	34
Yeoville	–	–	–	1	–
Craighall	–	–	–	–	–
Newlands	–	5	3	3	213
Moroko	–	1	–	1	64
Kliptown	–	1	1	–	–
Springs	–	14	11	2	118
Boksburg	–	6	4	–	32
TOTAL	7	87	73	20	1344

As per number of weapons. Excludes 4 Browning heavy machine guns mounted on Saracens with total of 1 800 rounds (not fired), sidearms held by CID and Special Branch members, and the assegais, knobkerries and bayonets of the black police.

when seen against the fact that once the firing had been initiated, all restraints on reason were broken. All massacres, barring those planned, premeditated or sanctioned by policy, are a 'mistake'. They represent, it has been suggested, a 'triggering' or unleashing of deep-seated fears, anxieties and even feelings of primary hostility which are then projected willy-nilly and uncontrollably onto unfortunate out groups who happen to be in the wrong place at the wrong historic moments.[35] Once this took place at Sharpeville, as it did at 13.35 that Monday, there was a clear intention on the part of the police to wreak the maximum damage.

At a much later date, Sydney Kentridge, the noted South African barrister recruited on behalf of the dependents of the victims to appear at the subsequent Commission of Inquiry, observed that there had been no order to shoot and hence no need to fire. This perfectly logical conclusion takes no cognisance of the fact that a massacre is not for the most part a rational event in the broad sweep of history, but rather a moment within which long-repressed individual and collective pressures, some well beneath the surface of consciousness or personality, are explosively released in an orgy of destructive energy. The crowd, as the Commission of Inquiry later noted, was denied the luxury of a baton or bayonet charge, a warning shot, or even an instruction to disperse: it is a measure of the intensity of emotions at work in the minds of the police that – by their own admission – this extraordinary flouting of the universal police procedures for riot control did not even occur to Pienaar and his commanding officers. Given the proximity of the police to the crowd – a few metres in places – it is questionable whether it was not already too late to use some (if not all) of the more conventional techniques of soft control: both gunshots into the ground or teargas overhead would have had a ricochet effect that could have endangered both targets and users. Geelbooi, who died in the first hail of bullets, was not 'responsible' for the horror, but his 'twee skote [two shots]' (frequently alluded to, if unsourced at the Commission) were the inadvertent trigger for the release of a flood of subterranean racial tensions, prejudices, fears and hatreds intrinsic to apartheid, the totality of Sharpeville history and the events of that day. The two shots essentially swept aside all the established boundaries and reasonable norms of behaviour binding people to the state, the rulers to the ruled. In effect, the Lockean 'social contract', embracing both victim and perpetrator, was broken.

Was a rupture of these dimensions premeditated by the state and its agents as alleged by the most vehement of apartheid's critics? Forty years after the event, the martyrology of Sharpeville continues to include the notion that the national government, the police, the local authorities, acting in some sort of loose coalition of opinion, conspired consciously, and with premeditated intent to 'teach the people a lesson'. This view was expressed at the Commission of Inquiry and it remains the bedrock of the various narratives about 21 March spun by the victims decades later. Not surprisingly, there are few who attribute the death of friends or family to the more charitable 'massacre by mistake' theory, the panic of the police, the dangerously escalating momentum of developments or any conception with the vaguest hint of condonation for police behaviour in any form whatsoever. Yet there is very little evidence to support the view that the killings were pro-active, repressive or specifically planned in advance to quell the persistent anti-pass and passive resistance demonstrations that continued to disturb the country. Even had such atrocious plans existed, it remains difficult to explain why the authorities would have chosen so patently obscene an act as a massacre in favour of less politically risky punitive techniques such as arrests (or even the odd assassination), or, for that matter, why the site of punishment should have been such a relatively low-profile area as the 'model' township of Sharpeville.

Having said this, there are some disturbing aspects of police behaviour just prior to the killing which suggest that a 'demonstrative' act, if not a massacre, would not have been viewed askance in some security circles. There were officers in the higher ranks of the uniform branch of the Vaal SAP who felt that the time had come, after months of successive raids into Sharpeville, to 'convey the seriousness of intent [of the authorities]' as one of the surviving officers now puts it, and ways of doing so, such as the detention of PAC leaders, were in fact discussed with senior security police personnel such as Spengler after the first national convention of the PAC at the end of 1959. A number of meetings along these lines were held in the opening months of 1960, but most appear to have ended inconclusively on the note that the PAC should be allowed to carry out its planned anti-pass campaign, and should be challenged should its efforts degenerate into violence and disorder. In other words, by 21 March there was no specific strategy to shoot anybody although some tactical contingency plans were discussed between the police, the SADF and the local authorities in the Vaal, the purpose of which was to deal with any disturbances that might arise. Given that the PAC advertised a nation-wide demonstration at some point in early 1960 as part of the process of mass mobilisation, it is perfectly natural that governmental and security force leaders would respond with some thoughts about how to manage the political consequences of such an event. The problem was that the uncertainty until the last moment as to when the campaign was to take place tended to obscure the debate about how the state should react to it, both politically and militarily, when it did.

Most of the officials who are alive today speak of their personal frustration at their inability to pinpoint the date of the campaign, of the conflicting estimates that came from various intelligence sources in the police and local government, and, in the end, to a general dissipation of efforts to develop strategic scenarios to deal with the various potential outcomes inherent in the notion of a nation-wide anti-pass campaign. At the time of Sharpeville, the gathering of intelligence and its integration into state policy was still a largely hit-and-miss operation run by people who, twenty years later, would be regarded as rank amateurs by their successors in state security circles. The problem was not that there was a plan for a massacre as the victims allege. There was no plan at all, other than the Standing Orders that governed police behaviour under normal circumstances and the vague notion that some reinforcements might be needed.

The Standing Orders, with their carefully modulated procedures for dealing with riotous crowds, simply disintegrated in the confusion and befuddlement of the morning's events. Many of the reinforcements brought in to deal with the situation were young and inexperienced personnel who had either not absorbed these Orders, were too frightened to remember them, or had never read them at all. Leadership is a crucial variable in the vortex of a massacre and the more senior police officers should have had the savvy and foresight to counter a situation fraught with the potential for disaster.

In the mid-fifties, there had been a restructuring of the police force part of which was motivated by the need to reinforce systems of command and control in the black townships based on the presumption of a high level of capability on the part of officers from captains upwards. Yet the senior officers – the Captain Therons, Major van Zyls and Lieutenant-Colonel Pienaars – did little to nothing by word or deed to explore the space for peaceful resolution of the conflict at Sharpeville. Policemen who were present at the time recall how all of these ostensibly professional senior policemen did their level best for most of the morning to reinforce the notion of the people outside as 'the enemy' – largely through the misplaced belief that this would heighten morale in the face of the gathering threat without. Even had they not demonised the crowd, even had they not consciously or inadvertently stoked racial feelings on the part of an increasingly terrified constituency of immature police with a declining belief in their capacity to defend themselves, let alone 'Western civilisation', the very first shots, as in massacres world-wide, fundamentally shifted the psychological universe of the officers, their men, and their victims.

Nothing has been done in the minutes, the days or even the years thereafter to analyse how the police felt as individuals at the 'point of delivery'. It appears that none of them suffered the extreme disorientation and personality collapse arising out of close-quarter massacre situations where the perpetrators are actually besmirched by the blood and gore of their victims. Despite what I have termed the 'intimacy' of the Sharpeville killings, Sharpeville was not, for example, the Josefow massacre where hapless Polish Jews spoke with their killers prior to the killers being spewed with their victims' remains after they had bayonetted or shot them.[36] For many of the police the low wire fence of the police station was of inestimable psychological value since it created at least some geographic distance (and depersonalisation) in the relationship between the killers and the killed. Nevertheless, many of the dynamics of close-quarter massacres with their subsequent traumatic consequences for the perpetrators, pertain to Sharpeville. Recent hearings of South Africa's Truth and Reconciliation Commission clearly revealed that many of the perpetrators of human rights atrocities under apartheid felt (and still feel) an overwhelming need to rationalise their behaviour to public opinion, their families, and no less, to themselves.

To most of the white Sharpeville police engaged in this exercise in justification, the essential issue was not the actions of the crowd but its social origins. Forty years later most of the surviving members of the SAP reluctantly conceded that they might not have fired so readily had the crowd been white. In other words the 'blackness' of the crowd becomes both the problem and the basis for exculpation. The overwhelming majority of the police had (and still have) difficulty in fully appreciating the popular emotions aroused by a mere 'reference book', and to many this was simply a cosmetic cover for black militants to overthrow the white state and eliminate its supporters at the behest of a nefarious coalition of interests including left-leaning liberals, the United Nations, and diabolical Communism. Many, on this basis, reasoned from the pass burners at the fence to universal struggles for world domination. The protestors at Sharpeville were, according to Sergeant Maas, 'on the liberty bandwagon and Sharpeville was the frontline'.

Crude race stereotyping abounded and abounds. To Constable Visser*, a resident of the nearby Vereeniging suburbs, only the thin khaki line of the police at Sharpeville stood between the raging black mob and 'civilised' white society. A peculiar sense of manhood threatened, not dissimilar to that displayed by British imperial soldiers during the course of the Indian Mutiny, is evident.[37] 'If we did not act,' he says in justification, 'the blacks would have killed us – and then gone on to slaughter our women and children'. Similar 'colonial' attitudes with their dismissive attitude to the 'natives' are evident in other statements made at the time and forty years later.

To Lieutenant-Colonel Pienaar, the prototype incarnation of apartheid police culture, the explanation for Sharpeville is to be found in the simple fact that black people lack self control and are intrinsically violent. When congregated they inevitably pose a danger to public order that can best be dealt with by short, sharp and painful treatment. This fundamental contempt for the moral condition of the 'Bantu' was the essence of his lengthy testimony before the Wessels Commission[38], and it remains a point of reference for many of his colleagues who have survived the passing of the years. Many allude (either before Wessels or our interviewers) to the accumulation of 'experience with blacks' over years of service in the SAP. In 1960 it was this 'experience' that led to the ingrained and culturally distorted presumption that the people in the veld outside the station were unstable and, without exception, distorted by a combination of rage and resentment against state authority and whites in general. The testimonies of the perpetrators bear witness to this through racial caricatures of the most malevolent type. There is, for example, Captain Theron, who diagnoses an '*ingebore haat teen die witman* [an innate hatred of whites]'. There is Sergeant van Wyk* who, decades later, still detects a collective propensity by 'Bantoes' for gross deeds of racial violence. There is Constable Fouche* who justifies the massacre by the capacity of populist symbolism – the raised fist, the cries of 'Afrika' and 'Izwe Lethu' (Our Country) and the like – to unleash hatred and undermine the driving principle of apartheid – unquestioned obedience to the white man. And, inevitably, in the long list of apologists there are the paternalists, such as Location Superintendent 'Lappies' Labuschagne who, if appalled by the killings and a decent man by all accounts, still testified before the Wessels Commission that blacks were simple, underdeveloped by the standards of 'white civilisation', perpetual adolescents, easily led astray and best punished firmly when miscreant.

These warped views reflective of the ideological context of apartheid are echoed in official police documents which refer to 'blacks in the Union who would seize on virtually any excuse to resort to violence, murder and looting' when motivated by alcohol, mass hysteria, or most dangerously, the appeals of the 'resistance movement'.[39] No one in the state, it appears, not even Pienaar and the other harder racists, anticipated punitive action on the scale of a slaughter, but virtually everyone in positions of authority or in the ranks of the SAP proved incapable of breaking free of their pre-determined *herrenvolk* universe with its ingrained assumptions of cultural superiority. The police, independent of their firepower, were heavily outnumbered – both at Sharpeville and nation wide. The huge black crowd beyond the wire exemplified the dangerously narrow 'minoritiness' upon which the apartheid state and its police was founded. It was (a very large number of) 'them' against (few of) 'us' – all encased in an explosive mixture of fear, frustration, rage and isolation. Sharpeville was no different from any other massacre in that it was made possible by the extent to which the victims were objectified, dehumanised, demeaned by their killers, consigned to a lower level of civilisation or, in some other way stripped of 'real' identity. Forty years on, one senior police officer now long-retired and a broken man, persisted in the view that 'we did not kill them because they were black' but 'because they acted like the wild animals – they were in defiance of authority'. The crowd, in this sense, had no human ties with those who killed them and could, in consequence, be placed – as Jews before Nazis – outside what one authority has graphically described as 'the circle of human responsibility and obligation'.[40]

There were other dynamics at work which allowed (and allow) the perpetrators to render their case both publicly and (perhaps more importantly) personally defensible. The treachery of camp-followers is an enduring theme in the slaughters which accompanied the dubious imperial progress in what is today deemed the Third World, and indeed, a number of interviewees went so far as to apportion blame for the entire tragedy to the contingent of black police. It was they, they insist, who had repeatedly stoked the fires of police anxiety for most of the morning by pointing to the fact that it could only end in violence. Although it is not entirely convincing, this lavish guilt-shifting is not as far-fetched as it seems. During the mid-fifties, for example, a number of international experts called into assist the SAP with its reorganisation had pinpointed the difficulty of policing communities where the police had no knowledge of the vernacular.[41] This unhealthy reliance on black interpreters for lines of communication at the grassroots was still in place in March 1960 and, in Sharpeville, was highly problematic. On several occasions in the hour or two preceding the massacre it was the black police who were sent to the fence to converse with the crowd outside, to warn them that their actions were provocative, and to gather intelligence about their intentions. This vague attempt at conflict resolution however proved fruitless. The black police feigned ignorance when asked by their white officers to pinpoint the crowd leaders and engage them in dialogue. To have done so, Constable Piet points out, 'would have been our death warrant if the crowd attacked us – and even if it did not'. Since the black police were inevitably sworn at by the community members who justifiably perceived them as 'collaborators', they also inevitably returned to their white counterparts with a dangerously subjective and largely negative conception of the crowd mood, which fed into the anxiety of the besieged white policemen. At no point, it appears, did any black policeman communicate the existence of any space for negotiation. On the contrary, 'all morning long', Sergeant Mostert* reports, 'we were told by the native police that the mob was dangerous ... there was blood in the air'. When two enterprising young boys approached the fence during the heat of mid-morning to sell Coca Cola to the police in the station, a number of 'bantu konstabels' warned that the drinks were probably poisoned. In general, the 'native' police, with their zealous desire to appease the white state and curry favour among those who fed, paid and clothed them, were fairly unambiguous about what should be done to alleviate the situation. As Constable Ben Khumalo*, who was later to become an especially vicious operative for the Vaal Security Police, laconically puts it: 'Looking back, we would probably have done the same things as the whites and shot to kill had we been so threatened.'

About a quarter of the white SAP contingent in the station elected not to shoot into the crowd – at least not with the first volley, and some, in the end, did not shoot at all. When questioned decades later many of the police attributed their hesitation simply to the confused nature of events. Others had more complicated reasons for their decision.[42] There were certainly 'hard' men among the police who had no compunction about firing on an anonymous crowd objectified by racial ideology. Pienaar and a number of his colleagues who were white supremacists by conviction clearly fit into this category. But there were also lesser men who fit into what Primo Levi has 'typified' as the 'grey zones of evil' in the dark tones of genocide, whose reaction was far more equivocal than appears to be the case in the conventional wisdom of Sharpeville with its immutable distinction between perpetrator and victim. Many people more currently involved in the horrendous business of 'ethnic cleansing' refute ideological motivation with its suggestions that they are 'prisoners' of a set of ideas to the point of being incapable of authentic individual decisions, yet still admit to their generalised 'aversion' to certain out-groups to whom they will react with extraordinary violence in a sponsored environment.[43] At Sharpeville, for example, there was Constable Els*, who did not shoot initially, but then shot belatedly because, on his own admission, he did not want his colleagues to see him as 'chicken' or 'soft on blacks'. There was also Constable Le Roux*, now a respected Vaal businessperson, who still finds himself incapable of breaking free from an arcane and stereotypical vocabulary. He did (and does) not 'really like kaffirs because you don't know how they will behave'. So he hesitated when a mass of women and children appeared in his gun sights, looked around at his immediate colleagues who were all engaged in the messy business of shooting, closed his eyes, and then eventually discharged his carbine to the full 'like we was in war'. The truism that people kill more easily in war when their acts are sanctified by the state, and kill even more comfortably in ethnic wars where their opponents can be reasoned away to sub-human status clearly applies to Sharpeville.

But there were also among that group a number of '*slapgat* [sloppy]' white constables who formed the firing squad ordered by Pienaar with considerable reluctance, and one or two who broke lines and actually fled to the physical safety of the police barracks as the first shots were fired. And there was also an, admittedly small, handful of individuals largely composed of the older reservists, who engaged in the ultimate avoidance behaviour of either firing harmlessly into the air, or not firing at all. Some

German killers pointed to the friendly relations between themselves and the Poles they eventually killed. So, in the Vaal, 'there were decent people in the crowd whom I recognised ... they had worked for my family in our business ... they went to church nearby,' says Sergeant van Rooyen, now an old and broken man. 'They had done me no harm. How ...,' he asks, plaintively (then as now in an unremitting search for exoneration) '... could I simply destroy them?'

But he did. Despite the personal ties Van Rooyen opened fire and, in doing so, became part of the unsavoury yet general company of police upon whom there were few constraints to kill. For every one or two who purportedly shot in the air (or so they said forty years later, there were dozens who fired directly and mercilessly into the packed crowd in at least two sustained bursts of fire. In the few seconds which covered the entire shooting, the great majority either acted 'mindlessly' (in the words of one now retired senior officer), or, more hideously, because they warmed to the task, as an act of personal vengeance, or, more frequently, in a warped effort to secure the esteem of their colleagues. Many of the police interviewed years later concede that they wanted to be observed in action by 'the *manne*'. Massacre was machismo, and it was at this point, some police now elliptically confess, that the shooting became a 'free-for-all'. Whatever the reasons the dimensions of the massacre as a human tragedy were now extended as the remnants of equivalence, hesitation or uncertainty were swept aside in a split-second wave of destruction rising from the lines of the police on the ground, up through the Saracens and across to the security forces poised for covering fire on the Cape Stands.

As the realisation of the first volley struck home in their consciousness, a few of the more alert officers did purportedly call in desperation for an immediate ceasefire, but, much like Spengler, who had tried unsuccessfully to prevent the initial pistol shot at the gate, they were disempowered by a whole historic process that transcended both the individual and the demands of the moment. It was in the intrinsic nature of apartheid that the shooting was 'necessary' and unstoppable and it was for this reason that the volley continued in two overlapping bursts for fifteen seconds and, in some cases, far longer than it would normally have taken to exhaust a set of cartridges. In the subsequent inquiry, the SAP was to contend that its members were as surprised by the shootings as were its victims and were, to all intents and purposes, automatons or in some other ways 'possessed' by the ominous environment. In the case of some unknowable number of police, the prisoners of events on the day and years before, this may well have been true. Yet the fact remains that most others, the equally minor agents of an invidious racial history not entirely of their creation, had the presence of mind or the innate viciousness bred in a system that dehumanised both repressor and repressed to reload their rifles, to aim, and then to fire repeatedly into a fleeing and terrified crowd which no longer presented a threat even had it momentarily done so. It was this act of repetition beyond ratiocination and all ostensible reason which led the critics of apartheid to the ultimate and not unjustifiable conclusion that Sharpeville was conclusive evidence of a system outside the boundaries of civilised existence.

Sharpeville was not the result of a depersonalised bureaucratic killing. Although universally condemned as mass murderers forty years later, the men who fired on the crowd were not for the most part habitual killers whose acts can be explained away, if not justified, by the dull and amoral principles of bureaucratic behaviour. Some of the police participants in the Cato Manor shootings which preceded Sharpeville, including their commander, were so emotionally scarred by the experience that they terminated their police careers. In the case of the Sharpeville contingent, at least forty of the white police are known to have quit the service within weeks of the massacre. As far as is known the SAP offered no official psychological debriefings or counselling, least of all to the black police who were considered 'hardened', but there is considerable evidence of some perpetrators seeking *ex post facto* spiritual guidance. 'Many of the men who were very disturbed sought forgiveness from the Reverend Harper Martins [the first chaplain of the SAP],' according to a surviving relative.[44] This is substantiated in the records of the Chaplain's Service of the SAP, ironically established a few years before 1960 to assist policemen whose 'consciousness was wracked by disquieting thoughts of murders, violent revolts and other crimes against humanity'.[45]

Several names and service numbers correspond to those of men at Sharpeville.

Many of the surviving perpetrators are clearly still appalled by their actions to this day, although they 'made sense at the time'. An unsubstantiated number of personnel from the Vaal region appear to have made private efforts to secure exoneration and personal understanding from one or two local psychologists and religious leaders either immediately after the slaughter or in the longer term. Some justified their behaviour by transferring guilt and responsibility to anonymous 'higher authorities' who 'should have trained us to handle riots', according to one policeman who was not party to the massacre but witnessed the site moments after its occurrence.[46] Despite the popular stereotype of an utterly inhumane apartheid police apparatus, shame and horror were rife in many families where participants in the massacre retreated for many years into a self-imposed taboo on discussion about the event. Some of them refer now to recurrent nightmares and periodic flashbacks to the massacre and the horrible experiences that were to follow in its immediate aftermath.

Certainly on the nights following the killings, SAP personnel who had been participants were observed to be worse the wear for liquor, including police who were engaged in the intensified round-ups of alleged 'subversives' in Sharpeville and adjacent townships. Many of those who fell into the police net still recall the alcoholic viciousness of a police force unaccustomed to soft methods of control under the best of circumstances. This was particularly evident among the black police who, especially confused, bitter and shaken, seemed, in the words of some observers, to be between the poles of extreme brutality and deep regret in the performance of their duties. Once the immediate crisis had passed with the end of the local labour boycott a few days after the massacre many of the Sunday services of the Dutch Reformed Churches in Vanderbijl and Vereeniging became sites for young policemen to cautiously come forward, to admit participation in the slaughter, and to seek solace from the local clergy.

Sergeant van Rooyen, a committed Christian, was one of these. Some of the senior municipal administrators – Superintendent Labuschagne, for example – were themselves elders in the local church community to whom they expressed regret and contrition for what had happened – albeit they blamed it on 'minority agitation'. Other more conservative Afrikaner clerics could not even concede this point, and opted to sublimate their misgivings in a bizarre mix of political rationalisation and racial mystification that would fester sub-consciously for decades to come. Meanwhile, white social gatherings in Vereeniging and Vanderbijl, contemporaries recall, were sombre for some weeks, with people consciously avoiding the topic of the massacre, particularly when municipal officials or police participants were present.

'It was only years later when any of us became truly conscious of what had happened then ... only later did it first occur to me that it had not been right.'[47] Similar sentiments were expressed by members of the German extermination units on the Russian Front.

Few of the police who recall their behaviour are, even today, conscious of its subliminal and symbolic basis.[48] Five years after democratisation, the only difference in their attitude was terminological in that the word 'blacks' had replaced 'natives'. Most interviewees still preferred to explain how the single volley was extended, and then developed into a successive volley by referring to the momentum and tense nature of the prevailing situation produced by black 'agitation' rather than to delve into long-subterranean, repressed and inevitably painful aspects of their individual and institutional personality.

There are no exact statistics of how many shots were fired: the ammunition count conducted by the SAP after the massacre suggests however that 'several hundred' rounds were fired in the fifteen-second volley. Because the police and the crowd were for the most part face to face in close proximity on a flat piece of territory, the first wave of shot emanating from the western side of the station cut into the mass of the crowd concentrated a few feet away beyond the immediate wire. This meant imminent death or injury for the vanguard of the crowd, including a high proportion of PAC activists who had become alarmed at the element of provocation inherent in the noise and fence-bending, who were close enough to see or sense the mounting fear and tension in the faces and body language of the police just across the fence, and who were desperately (if belatedly) trying to reassert a degree of crowd control. 'We did not go there to fight the police,' say witnesses. This was the message on the lips of the painfully small cadre of organisers at the exact moment when the first volley was fired directly into their ranks and at those immediately around them. The second, and even more deadly enfilade, largely directed over the heads of the people in the front to those in its centre and rear, cut down mainly bystanders some of whom, at the instant of death, were standing casually in normal conversation with their backs to the police station.

The crowd, like their killers, responded in disparate ways. A proportion along the western fence could clearly see the police loading their weapons but did not for the most part try to escape them because they believed that this was just an act of intimidation. 'I thought they were just frightening us,' as one witness to the later Commission expressed it.[49] Some of those nearest to the front were perturbed and began to try to move away from the fence, but were inhibited from doing so by those immediately behind them. In the few seconds before the firing there was some scuffling as the small backwash of people hit up against the incoming larger wave.

When the firing began this backwash became the first victims. Some members of the crowd did not hear the initial shots, others could not at first comprehend their lethal nature and, in the single instant of slaughter, stood rooted to the spot in a mixture of surprise and terror. Others immediately turned and fled, mostly down the narrow street dividing the police station from the clinic, out and around the other three sides of the station, and, more fatally, if rationally, into the wide and exposed field in the direction of the sheltering shops and library on the north side of the station. As the crowd wheeled in on itself, those in front came up hard against those in the rear, and in the ensuing confusion, people struck out at each other in their often futile attempts to get away. Many of those in the rear of the open field who failed to comprehend the nature of developments continued to move forward even as the bodies began to pile up around them.

Many of the survivors recall bizarre and sometimes macabre reactions either on their part or that of others to the moment of terror. A number speak of a single demonstrator running towards the police station after the first volley screaming for the police to desist: his pleas of 'you've shot enough' drowned by a second enfilade which killed him.[50] Surprise rather than pointless heroism was more the order of the day. The dominant emotion of many surviving victims was utter incomprehension as to what had taken place. Some of the medical personnel recount the dumbfounded expressions on the faces of many of the dead. Some of those who rendered assistance were quizzed in a mixture of broken English and Sesotho as to why the police 'have done this thing'. Because of the lightning nature of events, few felt fear and the profound sense of doom and fatalism experienced by other unfortunates who have found themselves on the brink of slaughter and genocide. There were those who ran and others who fell to the ground and 'played dead'. Some of the latter survived, others were perfect targets for the hail of random or purposive bullets. Some of the police were, it appears, as dumbfounded at the momentum and outcome of the situation as those killed or wounded – at least in the instant after the initial volley of shots. 'Kyk, hoe lê hulle dood, kêrels' (look at how they are dead, chaps) was one such reaction.[51] Many decades later, others now admit less to immediate revulsion than to feelings of 'relief', utter amazement, or even a narcotic sense of empowerment.

The echo of the last shots was followed by the descent of a crystal and almost palpable silence on the scene of carnage. Reports twenty-five years after the event mention 'the greatest stillness that could still be heard' around the now hallowed site.[52] Nor was there any crowd.[53] It appeared both to the small clutch of journalists on the edge of the field and to the police in the station that the whole enormous crowd had been conjured away. Were it not for the debris and the bodies scattered in the field and the street, the whole episode might well have been some sort of nightmare or terrible act of the imagination. There was not a moan nor a movement from the injured on the ground, nor any screams or insults from those who had fled. The white police, according to one observer, looked 'shaken': their black colleagues, simply 'sad'. In the field the dead and wounded, Joe Hlongwane (*) recalls, looked like a scattering of 'dead flies'.

After a brief pause the west gate, the centre point of the mass congregation a short while before, was cautiously opened by a visibly distraught young white policeman acting under orders from one of the senior officers. He and his colleagues began to move into the street and adjoining field – 'in awe', according to one description. Most of the white police were dazed and appeared befuddled at the consequences of their behaviour, and a few – as if to give the impossible a material shape – proceeded to delicately prod one or another body with foot or rifle barrel. Hundreds of laceless shoes, trousers, and other items of ragged clothing – the detritus of poverty and flight in massacres world-wide – were scattered across the field among the dead and wounded, intermingled with mud and blood.[54] On the perimeters, were overturned, broken and sometimes bloody folded chairs brought by the curious and the elderly who had innocently come for the day to hear the 'big baas' – the senior official who was supposed to materialise at two o'clock to make his momentous speech about the passes. Some had brought and dropped umbrellas. There were a few sticks and knobkerries abandoned by the fleeing crowd in its terror, but no other weapons. 'Even the tsotsis,' researchers were told, 'were not frightened enough to drop their guns'. The odd policeman near the station boundary began distractedly to pick up the occasional stone, weigh it in his hands as if to test its nature, and then absently mindedly cast it over the fence into the station.

Whether this act was the first step in a still germinal police conspiracy to cover up the motives and consequences of their action remains an intriguing question. Within the station itself some of the more senior and experienced officers, including Pienaar, by his own later admission, were quick to realise that they bore responsibility for a disaster which was, by any standards, of epic proportions. While nobody could yet foresee the massive global reaction – 'the enemies of South Africa would soon forget the shooting of a few kaffirs,' said one of the perpetrators callously – there were, even in the first traumatic moments after the shooting, a number of officers on site who were cynical or hard-bitten enough to understand that they would inevitably be called to account in some fashion for their actions. Despite the sympathy for the besieged police that could be curried from a white public obsessed with the notion of a 'black peril', some individuals already understood or intuited that the ruling Nationalists would have to find some sacrificial lambs in order at least to attempt to appease horrified world opinion. Questions would be asked by what was then only a partially muzzled local media, and this was likely to have reverberations for career prospects all along the chain of command and control in the police hierarchy.

At the time little importance was attributed to the 'throwing of the stones' into the grounds of the police station, which was observed by a number of wounded lying on the ground. (Some speak of policemen forming groups, kicking stones into rough piles and then intentionally hurling the projectiles over the wire fence.) Subsequently however, this act (among others), became a key component of the case built against the police and the apartheid government, both by local critics and the wider humanitarian community. It was, in their opinion, the first of a series of acts in which the police purposely tampered with evidence in such a way as to exaggerate the threat posed against them and, in the process, to exonerate their reaction.

Police vehicles carrying some of the more senior officers were quick to exit the station a few minutes after the main gate had been opened, ostensibly to summon help but, in reality, to arrange for a full cordon of the township. When the first news of the massacre was conveyed by radio from one of the Saracen personnel carriers to the district police headquarters, where it was apparently received with 'utter shock and horror' by the officers present, the Divisional Commissioner, Brigadier Els (the 'groot baas' upon whose word everyone awaited), had the presence of mind to order the 'sealing' of Sharpeville by all available police and military that could be called into the Vaal. The intention was not only to prevent the spillage of disorder and anticipated acts of revenge from the township to the adjacent white areas, but also to ensure police control over communications between the township and the wider world. While a small cadre of journalists had infiltrated Sharpeville, witnessed the enfilade, and could be expected to report on the events, further entry into the area other than by police personnel and selective sources of humanitarian assistance could be restricted. Journalists were to be informed that entry into Sharpeville was 'far too dangerous'. This was the core of the hasty conversation along the airwaves, and the rationalisation for the police vehicles now speeding – insofar as rutted township roads would allow – to the various entry points of the location. Only then, at approximately 13.49 – almost twenty minutes after the shooting – was medical assistance eventually summoned from the Chief Fire Officer of Vereeniging, responsible for ambulance services.

As telephones begin to ring between the Vaal and the new SAP headquarters, and then the highest reaches of government in Pretoria, the people of Sharpeville began to emerge from the places where they had rapidly and randomly sought shelter from the hail of fire – the houses and walls facing the station, the shops and library some hundred yards away across the veld to its north side and the various main and side streets radiating from the scene of the killings to the further reaches of the township. Outside the range of visibility the more fortunate members of the local population were confused and perplexed about what was taking place. Some had heard curious popping sounds accompanied by a sudden subsidence of the muffled crowd noises that had carried in their direction since late morning. Since the majority of those en route to the police station had already arrived at or near their destination at the precise moment that the massacre took place, most of the major arteries leading to the killing field had been relatively empty when the first volleys were released – at least until huge masses of terrified people began to swarm into the streets leading away from the slaughter. Some, believing the police to be in hot pursuit, leapt over walls and into gardens and houses in their search for sanctuary, others fled towards the boundaries of the township until they were overcome with exhaustion or the realisation that the police were not about to follow. This option was not available to the more seriously injured and wounded, most of whom collapsed in or near the vicinity of the massacre. The human tide activated by the shootings prevented the crowd clustering in a way that would have allowed it to exact retribution on the police vehicles now leaving the station. Some journalists still on their way to the police station at the fatal moment of the killings encountered the backwash crowd along with a few stones thrown in passing and in anger. For the most part however, there was no gauntlet to be run except at isolated points where a few people took the trouble to slow their flight, reach down and acquire some object to throw in pointless anger at a rapidly passing police vehicle.

In the field people began to move cautiously out into the open. There was no hostility, only a sense of utter bewilderment as victims and perpetrators congealed around the bodies scattered randomly across the terrible landscape. The slaughter was, in a sense, attributable to a communications breakdown between authorities and people. Now, in its aftermath, there were scattered verbal exchanges as participants on both sides tried to make sense of what had happened. There were also some belated signs of cooperation as a few of the police and the community members bent down to examine bodies for signs of injury or indications of life. The great majority of white police who had come out of their bastion were, however, essentially non-participant, almost as if they feared contamination by the black dead and wounded who lay scattered around them. Among the many photographs of the post-massacre scene submitted to the Commission of Inquiry, not one shows a white policeman rendering immediate assistance. Some show black police bending down here and there to lift and move inert bodies, others portray township residents standing in dread at the sight of people they know among the dead and injured. There were some displays of anger amid the gestures of despair, and audible obscenities directed at the police. But the police remained entirely passive, callously inactive among the ominous reddish puddles created by human agency combined with the effects of a sudden short but soaking downpour. They had broken the power of the crowd and now had little fear of retribution.

The rain stopped and within a half an hour the first ambulances had moved through the police road blocks at the entry points of Sharpeville and arrived at the killing field. En route, they encountered a number of dead, dying and wounded in the streets, often at a considerable distance from the massacre. Some had run from the scene of the massacre and collapsed in the roads, in the gutters, against walls and under the township's occasional trees. Others were ordinary people who had had little or nothing to do with the demonstration but, by a twist of fate, had been injured in the midst of their daily activities by stray high-velocity bullets transversing the flat terrain.

One woman was hit while drinking tea quietly in her garden. Three ministers of the church taking a quite tea on the 'stoep' (verandah) of their house some distance from the massacre site were surprised by the popping sounds they heard from the direction of the police station and then appalled when a woman staggered into the street to fall, bloody, in front of them. Innocent shoppers in a café across the field were wounded by stray bullets that came through the windows from the elevated Sten gunners on the tops of the Saracens; a woman doing her washing in the backyard of her home hundreds of metres from the station was also struck down.[55] John Mailane had his head blown off while distributing invoices for his firm on his bicycle some distance away, oblivious, it seems, to the obvious agitation around him.[56] The cycle, with its headless rider, tottered along for several dozen metres before gently bumping into a horrified old lady.[57] A substantial number of people also suffered injuries as a result of being trampled by the terrified crowd.

The small complement of medical personnel were aghast at the dimensions of the work confronting them, and approached the police, some of whose white members only now began to help move some of the dead onto pavements and other points where they could be loaded onto the gathering vehicles. Their work was done with little compassion and considerable distaste since intestines and brains were scattered all over the scene.[58] Black policemen were quickly mobilised by their suddenly more squeamish white counterparts to shovel these horrendous remnants. Some white police recall being nauseated, and one or two of the younger constables were sick on the spot. Yet, not everyone from the SAP was either appalled or contrite. Some of the wounded were taunted where they lay, or otherwise insulted in Afrikaans, as articulated racial sentiments came once more to the fore. 'Where's your land now kaffirs, where's your land,' one officer called to a group of residents huddled in shock and amazement within hearing distance of the bent wire fence of the police station[59]. '*Ja, nou gaan jy na Mayibuye-toe* [Yes, now you are going to return]' were the words of one 'European' policeman to a dying man at his feet.[60] Some corpses and the dying, initially approached with caution when the gates were first opened, were now prodded more vigorously and, in some cases, kicked aside as the newly re-empowered police fanned into the field. 'We had done what we had done ... there was nothing more we could do.' But there was. A number of contemporary witnesses swear to seeing white police moving among the bodies and, in an act of self-appointed 'humanitarianism', dispatching with a pistol bullet those whom they believed to be beyond saving. A number of ex-SAP members admit to a 'few' such cases, but insist that their presumptuous mission of mercy only pertained to the most mortally wounded – those 'on the dying side,' as one policeman put it.

The role of the black police in this gruesome business remains contentious and one of the key issues around which a web of silence has been woven to this day. Many residents of Sharpeville who were on the site of or near the massacre in its immediate aftermath, swear to large numbers of black police working their way systematically through the veld to the north of the station, stopping, prodding and then administering *coups de grâce* to crumpled and twitching bodies – either with their assegais or the sharpened steel poles normally used to extrude illegal persons and liquor stills in the course of routine police raids. Others, less dramatically, describe the police gingerly poking bodies for signs of life, but do not speak of killings. The truth appears to lie midway. Many of the black personnel had never heard the sound of mass firepower and, in its wake, simply sat befuddled as the last echoes of the massive salvo drifted away into the distance. It was white police who led the exit from the station. Many of the black police were already calculating how the tragedy would affect their relations with the local people, amongst whom some had, despite official discouragement, developed friends and acquaintances. 'How would they be with us,' one old constable asked forty years later, 'now that we had shot them?' Some of the black constables were, they say, already thinking of redeployment from the township. 'Why would we kill again,' asks the old constable, 'and make matters even more complicated?'

Such constraints were not unfortunately binding on the black contingent as a whole, particularly its 'imported' members from Johannesburg and the East Rand whose anonymity shielded them from community retribution. They had arrived that morning, they would leave that day – and, in the intervening period, many unleashed years of brutalisation on the hapless wounded. Ostensibly sent forth to collect the injured for transport to hospital, some dispatched their helpless victims with brutal zeal – in some cases in the very sight of their white colleagues – but mostly quietly and unobtrusively behind bushes and in the lees of houses where some of the injured had sought protection and now lay fallen. They seem particularly to have singled out women who had congregated in groups during the demonstration and now lay clustered and at the mercy of their killers. A five-man black contingent from Bez Valley, led by one 'Jokodo', survivors recall, was especially energetic in using their assegais on the heart, throat or genitals of women on the ground, at least until the intervention of a horrified white officer who warned them to desist 'because we are in enough trouble already'. This warning, however, came a good ten minutes after the first shaken police had emerged into the killing field from the station, leaving these perpetrators of gross atrocities ample time in which to do their dirty work. During this interval, according to survivors, 'many' of the writhing wounded were stabbed or, in some cases, simply beaten into insensibility or death with the standard police knobkerries. Others, more fortunate, were simply thrashed about the head or body with batons, sjamboks or the shovels issued to the black police to enable them to 'clear up the mess' in the station surrounds.

The 1953 Annual Report of the National Commissioner bemoans the fact that it was difficult to train 'non-white' police to the same intellectual and moral level as white policemen.[61] It was because of this ingrained belief in the organisational culture of the SAP that, with one or two individual exceptions, the white police stood passively by when they observed this obscene behaviour, and made no discernable efforts to stop it. The mechanisms of white supervision without which the state believed the police to be incapable of efficiency, could clearly be used selectively. Whether these shameful actions by the black police represented a misguided display of loyalty to their white superiors, an attempt to obliterate the sense of shame and calamity so common to the perpetrators of mass murder, or simple barbarity and human defectiveness, also remains a matter for speculation.

The first bodies to be loaded were those from the streets immediately surrounding the police station. Parties of medical personnel, assisted by the odd black policemen and some residents, defying police instructions to stay clear of the scene, were then deployed to scour the field for batches of bodies, and the wounded, not all of whom were immediately visible because of the lengthy grass clustered in patches along the perimeter. These were described as 'the dogs who are still chewing', by one police officer standing on a Saracen.[62] When the ambulances were full the police agreed, reluctantly, to transport some of the bodies in their own vehicles – but only the dead, not the wounded.

The stunned township residents were not especially active in this grisly business because the police had circulated among the onlookers to inform them that their participation and help was unwelcome. 'The crowd,' according to one witness, 'wanted to run to the assistance of the wounded who were lying there but they were chased away by the police.'[63] When questioned about the reasons for this course of action, many police readily admitted that in the short period prior to the arrival of the ambulances the senior officers had indicated that it would be 'unwise' for people to come into contact with the injured or scrutinise the extent of their injuries. This decision was based on further communications between the station and SAP divisional headquarters which saw exact public knowledge as dangerous. In the short term, evidence of the slaughter had the potential to remobilise the township crowd and might lead to further violence. The less the community saw of what had been done the better. In the longer term it was clearly in the political and institutional interests of the police – not to mention the government – to maintain a monopoly over the nature and extent of the casualties. This latter point was the gist of a series of conversations and commands that moved rapidly down the organisational chain from the Prime Minister's office, through national and regional police headquarters, to the grassroots in Sharpeville in the approximately twenty minutes preceding the arrival of medical assistance.

At the grassroots itself, many of the police now seemed to have made a remarkable recovery from their initial trauma. Some were smoking and lounging casually against their vehicles, their weaponry on the ground at their feet. There was conversation, if muted, in Afrikaans, and an occasional embarrassed chuckle. Two or three more enterprising members of the force armed with sjamboks strode between the various clutches of stunned residents to ensure acquiescence with police orders that they 'mind their own business'.[64] This produced a few minor scuffles between the SAP and distraught residents seeking family or friends among the piles of bodies. There was now a little angry screaming directed at the police from some quarters as a handful of stunned residents wandered about in semi-conscious defiance of police orders.

The Reverend Robert Maja of the Sharpeville Presbyterian Church had come to the scene when he heard the shooting while taking tea in a nearby house. Residents urged him to intervene, if only to ensure that corpses were removed in toto. This was the request of one relative of a victim who urged Maja to approach the black police moving a corpse whose brains were 'lying out' across the damp field as the body was dragged aside. Maja protested to an SAP captain and he was eventually allowed to minister to some of the wounded. The sun had now emerged once more, it was hot despite the brief shower, and many of the wounded were calling pitifully for water and other assistance. It was Maja who first noticed the high proportion of women who appeared to be suffering from stab wounds in the upper thighs and abdomen.

The geography of the massacre is fairly clear, but its exact sociology – including the final number of dead and injured – remains a bone of contention. There are however certain features in the death toll and casualty pattern, some but not all of which were revealed at the subsequent

Commission of Inquiry, that provide additional clues to the nature and dynamics of the overall tragedy.

In the first place, a high proportion of the dead and wounded – eighteen of the official sixty-nine dead, and at least fifty wounded – were women and children. This was because, if the police are to be believed, they had been consciously placed as a human shield in the line of fire in conformity with the policy of the African resistance movement 'dat Bantoe-vrouens en kinders dikwels op die voorgrond stoot word' (that Bantu women and children are often pushed into the forefront).[65]

In reality however, women had played an important, if not dominant, role in the establishment of the fledgeling PAC chapter in Sharpeville and some had been assigned the role of stewards in the planning of the 21 March demonstration. Given that at least a proportion of these organisers would have been scattered along the fence at the time that the volley decimated its front ranks, it is hardly surprising that a substantial number of the casualties would be women. Women had, in addition, recently been obliged to carry passes and this was an important lever in their mobilisation. As early as 1952 women had demonstrated against registration documents which were a precursor to 'reference books' and over the years they had become increasingly vociferous on pass issues. Men in Sharpeville were deeply insulted by this humiliation imposed on their women and it was largely (but not entirely) at their urging that a demonstration of about 300 women had taken place outside the Location Office less than two weeks before the massacre. Since the pass laws were only one in a complex of grievances including rents, raids and prohibitions on illegal beer-brewing (one of the few sources of income for females), this had flared dangerously close to violence. A legacy of antagonism was certainly established and on 21 March the women were, according to most contemporary accounts, among the most vociferous voices of protest invoking distaste and fear among the conservative young white policemen.

The particular hostility of white police to black women in the enforcement of the pass laws is legendary and in perfect accord with the many theories interconnecting racism, sex and social power.[66] During the course of the morning there were a number of instances of women *en masse* raising their skirts waist-high as a means of indicating their contempt for the forces of law and order.[67] Many of the black police were enraged by this collective display of genitalia intended to challenge their male sense of potency. Their white counterparts simply experienced confused revulsion and were confirmed in their sense of the 'otherness' of the people with whom they were dealing. On several occasions during the late morning, black police in the garrison had also heard sexual innuendos and obscenities in the vernacular coming from the ranks of female protesters – which they then compliantly translated, on request, for their white superiors. For most of Monday 'die bantoevrouens het om die mans gedans en gegia' (the Bantu women danced and ululated around the men) in a traditional form of ritual mobilisation which the police found both disturbing and distasteful.[68] Numerous witnesses report the white police shrinking away from jeering women seeking to touch them contemptuously through the fence, and the instant before the first shots was dominated by a round of particularly shrill and terrifying ululations which, one journalist surmises, was catalytic in the climate of increasing tension.[69] While the eventual shooting was random, accelerated and largely precluded selection of targets, some white police would certainly have taken a perverse satisfaction in choosing jeering women who had been a special source of their personal discomfort.

Ultimately, the relationship between the police and the women involved much more than the working out of latent sado-erotic tensions in a test-tube of mass violence. People of all persuasions had assembled for a mixture of reasons ranging from curiosity to deep social concerns. During the course of Sunday night women had not figured prominently in the demonstrations. The PAC task teams had generally forced men into their ranks as they moved from house to house and there was a strong feeling at some gatherings, such as that at the football stadium, that this was 'man's business'.[70] Yet levels of unemployment were far higher among women, and many would have had the time, opportunity and desire to break the tedium of township life by drifting along with their offspring towards the police station in anticipation of some sort of unfamiliar spectacle. There was, in any case, no special injunction on women to avoid the planned demonstration – on the contrary, the PAC plan for the day was fully inclusive – and many people, not the least women, actually took the trouble to dress their best in at atmosphere of general conviviality. Most of the umbrellas, scattered among the debris in the wake of the slaughter, were carried by women in anticipation of the searing midday sun.

The heavy presence of children, it was alleged at the later Commission, indicated that the crowd did not anticipate a fight. This is to ignore the social dynamics of township existence that cause children to appear in the most unlikely circumstances, as well as the fact that where the parents went, the children invariably followed.[71] Children, as emerged in the Soweto uprising of 1976, can also cast stones, and one or two of the Sharpeville police contingent were clearly angered (if not injured) by their doing so. Ten children died in the slaughter. Fortunately, most of the smaller children (including some of our interviewees), were consigned to the back of the crowd because of their size or parental injunction. Much the same applies to elderly people, the majority of whom were probably saved by being at the back where some had put up folding chairs and umbrellas to as to observe the occasion more comfortably.

At the epicentre after the massacre, there were no bodies within the police compound or on its fence. This is consistent with the view articulated at the inquiry that the police fired before there was any attack, but it does not rule out the possibility that an attack might have been imminent. This was the position taken by the SAP, whose officers justified their action to the Commission as pre-emptive self-defence necessitated by the overwhelming possibility of an onslaught on the garrison.

Not all the police were concentrated in the station at the point when the firing began. Apart from the sharpshooters in the Cape Stands a number of lorries were parked in the open veld to the north or in the street to the west of the station, either awaiting entry through the crowd into the station gate, or as observation posts from which to survey crowd movements. Given their exposed position, the personnel in these lorries were especially frightened and tense, so much so that when the firing from within the station began, they immediately responded in kind – and with devastating effect. A proportion of the high number of casualties from shots in the back would have been caused by fire from police sitting with their .303 rifles on the roofs of these lorries, since the majority of the crowd was facing the station which was the point of attraction when the enfilade began. Other casualties were caused when the crowd scattered in the face of fire and, in the process, turned to confront the lorries. One group surging out of the street met a hail of fire unsuccessfully designed to halt their egress into the open veld, while another, already in the veld were mown down as they fled in panic towards and alongside the parked police lorries.[72] In effect, most of the crowd was caught in a lethal pincer between the station and the lorries from which there was little or no hope of escape.

After the shootings 'bodies were scattered all over the place', according to one observer – on the pavement near the western fence, in the northern field and along its approach roads, in the streets and on traffic islands. Among the dead, Carlton Monnakgotla recalls, was a pregnant woman whose 'unborn baby [had] fallen from her stomach, and the next shot got her'.[73] A *Rand Daily Mail* journalist who arrived on the scene about twenty minutes after the shooting was forced to stop short on a road leading to the police station when his driver found it impossible to navigate around the bodies heaped in the street.

Accounts vary about the precise duration and pattern of the shooting: some especially hostile accounts refer to a period of sustained or sporadic fire lasting as much as a minute with the police firing into the crowd long after it had begun to flee (and no longer represented a danger). In a sudden reversal of their urge to terminate the siege by whatever means possible, both Prinsloo and Pienaar, to their credit, screamed for a ceasefire – and Pienaar blew forcefully on his service whistle. Yet, how much was heard, when it was heard, and whether any notice was taken in the surging momentum, remains an open question. Pienaar refers to a single volley of no more than twenty seconds before his orders took effect, while Prinsloo claims almost instant (*onmiddelik*) obedience in an ingenuous and ultimately futile attempt to uphold the image of the police as a precise and fully disciplined force acting under conditions of extreme crisis.[74] Many of the victims describe a concentrated enfilade, or even two 'massive volleys' punctuated by about ten seconds, which appeared to come from 'all sides'. Other less dramatic estimates refer to a surgical but scathing five or ten second burst brought to an end more or less at the point of crowd dispersal. Ten to fifteen seconds including the catalyst first shot by Geelbooi, plus three or four intermittent bursts of about four seconds each seems to have been the consensus reached in the inquiry – at least among the SAP witnesses – although most appear to have forgotten the short burst of fire that had emanated from the Cape Stands. Some victims were able to cover thirty metres before being mown down. Although some of them might have been at the peak of physical fitness – which is unlikely given that most of the dead were over thirty – this suggests a protracted burst of fire of at least thirty seconds' duration. A number of the wounded were shot repeatedly after lying on the ground for at least twenty seconds.[76] Even taking into account that their judgement might have been inaccurate given the circumstances, this factor contributes to the case against police contentions that they were emotionally and unthinkingly swept away at the critical instant of fire.

There is also reason to believe that in many cases the firing was not indiscriminate. Recent evidence suggests that some policemen took the opportunity to exit from the slaughter and stopped firing within the ten/fifteen second framework, but others, including the small Cape Stands contingent who were relative 'late-comers' to the slaughter, did not. On the contrary, even as some police wondered what to do next, the majority of their colleagues continued firing, or, more iniquitously, intermittently reloaded. The geography of the mortalities – the wounds, and poses assumed by the victims in their death agonies – suggests that a proportion of the dead or wounded were deliberately picked off. As some police now readily admit, a proportion of this intentional slaughter took place even *after* the crowd ceased to represent a physical threat. Among those who suffered were a number of people (frequently gangsters) whose colourful clothing guaranteed visibility among the largely drab mass; many of the grounded wounded (whose very inertia attracted fire);

women; the slowly paced; and a number of people who, in the opinion of their persecutors, were simply 'running funny'.

The intensity of the fire into the adjacent street and into the bare veld also ensured disproportionately high casualties. In the street it was hard to miss, and in the field it was hard to hide. Fortunately, because of the rapid pace of events, the absence of an order to prepare to fire, and the heat in the Saracens, the crews of the personnel carriers were for the most part perched on the external armour outside the gun turrets. This meant that they were confined to using the arms they were carrying and did not have the opportunity to employ the lethal Bren guns with which the Saracens were normally armed. It is chilling to think what the death toll might have been had heavy machine guns been drawn into the unfolding tragedy. Still, a number of the police on and above ground, were equipped with Sten guns whose rapid high-velocity fire was capable of 'raking' the crowd from the front near the station to its rear.

Pistols and .303 rifles supplemented the Stens, a few of which were loaded with explosive 'dum-dum' bullets which were capable of causing horrendous wounds and would not normally be issued to the SAP. The police went to exceptional lengths – then and now – to explain how it was impossible for their personnel on riot duty to be armed with these instruments of death and destruction, and to deny vehemently that they had been used at all.

As the crisis intensified early on the Monday morning the SAP in the Vaal, with the compliance of the South African Defence Force, had raided their military armouries for supplementary equipment. Consequently, the police who arrived in the armoured cars had the dangerous capacity to wage a minor war. This included a small but lethal quantity of explosive rounds suitable for Sten gun use, distributed to odd individuals and then casually slipped for possible use into barrels, belts, or pockets.

Senior officers and those responsible for ordinance at regional and local level in the Vaal were equally casual about ammunitions inventories, and took no particular trouble to scrutinise who was armed with what as they set off for Sharpeville. The police leadership appears not to have known that some individuals had loaded their guns with the 'dum-dums' until the bodies of some the dead were loaded into police vehicles. One of the police officers involved in this task – Captain Theron, it is said – apparently noticed the especially ghastly exit wounds of some of the deceased whose bodies had been half obliterated, and summoned Colonel Prinsloo. Detecting the use of explosive bullets, he was quick to realise that the political fallout from Sharpeville might be even worse than had been initially contemplated. Another set of hasty communications with headquarters followed and the police loading corpses in the veld were ordered to sort the dead who appeared to have been the victims of the 'dum-dums' from the other victims. Unfortunately for the police one or two of the ambulances had already departed for the Vereeniging Hospital about three kilometres away. Those that remained were quickly searched and about a dozen bodies were extracted and added to another dozen corpses in the police vehicles which were suspected of having fallen victim to explosive cartridges.

At the Vereeniging Hospital, the cargo of the arriving ambulances which had escaped police examination at the Sharpeville site was carefully, if unobtrusively scrutinised by members of the security police who had been instructed to meet the incoming casualties. A nurse who was present distinctly recalls a number of plain-clothed policemen requesting stretcher bearers to lay their human cargo on the ground for inspection. When she questioned this she was told that the purpose of the unusual procedure was to see whom among the dead had been 'extraordinarily damaged'. A number of the incoming dead who appeared to fall into this category were summarily removed and loaded into a nearby lorry, despite the protests of the medical personnel. In the end an estimated two dozen corpses were extracted, either at the killing field or from the ambulances at the hospital. Urban legend has it that they were 'disappeared' that night along with leaden weights directly into the Sharpeville Dam. (Indeed, rumour has it that the spirits of the massacre victims still exist in this expansive body of water: few of Sharpeville's inhabitants will drink from it.)

In reality this selective group of dead were taken much further afield. Constable Dirk Theron* distinctly recalls being summoned near midnight to the Vanderbijlpark police station from his home. In the yard was a civilian truck loaded with 'more than a dozen shapeless sacks' designated, he was told in whispers, for 'special disposal'. Accompanied by the ubiquitous Bantoe-Konstabel 'Jokodo' and several other black policemen, Theron proceeded 'across the river' (the Vaal) to some destination in the vicinity of Parys. (Theron refused to be more specific, nor would he speculate on the nature of and secrecy surrounding his strange consignment which, he admits, left 'a sticky residue' on the floor of the truck.)

Meanwhile, back at the Vereeniging Hospital where a number of doctors had begun during the afternoon to question what one now deems the 'remarkable' character of some wounds on the dead and injured, the police had begun a damage control exercise of some proportions. Some of the more inquisitive medical staff were told bluntly by senior officers such as Major van Zyl that it would not be 'in the national interest' to make 'exaggerated' disclosures. The police approach proved successful at the Commission of Inquiry when forensic experts, the state and representatives of the dependents concurred, not without strong if private reservations in some cases, that none of the casualties appeared to have been caused by any projectile other than a 'normal' bullet.

The fact that roughly seventy percent of the dead and wounded were ostensibly shot in the back was less easily disguised and formed the basis of the view expressed by Kentridge and his team at the inquiry that when the shooting started the crowd was not in the process of lurching forward *en masse* to attack the station as the police alleged. On the other hand, it does not necessarily mean *prima facie*, as some analysts have concluded, that the police (acting as a body) took a delight in shooting people who were in the process of running for their lives away from the station.

The 'shot-in-the-back' thesis that forms part of the Sharpeville martyrology fails to take account of the important distinction between the dead and the wounded. Almost all the dead were shot in the front. The seventy percent injured from the rear were wounded. While this does not justify police behaviour it clearly suggests that most people in this unfortunate category were injured in the later stages of what some sociologists term the 'massacre delivery' – that is towards the end of the period of fire. This is borne out by the dispersal of the casualties immediately after the killings. Most of the dead were, unsurprisingly, near the station. Further into the veld and beyond the dead give way to the wounded shot from the rear and this is consistent with the notion of people running from the station several seconds into the shooting period.

A good proportion of the first volley of an estimated 700 rounds actually appears to have missed or to have caused leg injuries, not, as the SAP alleged *ex post facto,* because of the desire of a well-drilled police force to minimise injuries, but either because of extraordinarily poor marksmanship by panicked policemen or, perhaps more importantly, because some individuals, motivated by the sheer horror of shooting into a nearby and tangible crowd containing a fair proportion of women and children, subconsciously shrank from doing so. This, the official police history notes almost ruefully, 'allowed the crowd in front of the gate some time to get away'.[76]

These constraints did not operate on the police positioned on the Saracens who were relatively disconnected from the crowd by height and distance. Most of the back injuries appear to have been caused in the second stage of the volley which was largely (but not entirely) dominated by the relatively sustained firing of the 'Saracen group' who were, in the end, best equipped, strategically, psychologically and technologically, to take up the vanguard position in the massacre. Relative to their colleagues on the ground who tended to cease firing when the 'enemy' in front evaporated, those at a higher elevation had a more extended view of a group whose human characteristics disappeared in direct proportion to their physical distance.

The exact number of casualties remains unclear. In addition to the fact that roughly two dozen victims of explosive bullets 'disappeared', it is very difficult to pin down these figures. The usual figure of sixty-nine dead quoted in the official reports and the media of the time is obviously too low if one takes into account those killed with the 'dum-dums', and this is inferred in the correspondence of Location Superintendent

Labuschagne who overtly refers to 'a much higher figure'.[77] There are also some strange inconsistencies between the references in the now dilapidated Official Native Register of the Sharpeville municipal authorities to those 'killed by gunshot wounds' and the weather-beaten inscriptions on the tombstones of the dead of 21 March in the equally decayed and nearby cemetery. Fifty-six names appear on the Register, and it is a mark of the poverty of the community that only eleven of this group enjoyed the commemorative luxury of a tombstone, the rest were buried in unmarked graves. Yet there are a further twenty-one tombstones whose names do not correspond with those in the Register and, to add to the confusion – the cynical would allude to the 'cover-up' – there is a third official police list of the dead, whose entries are out of kilter with both the cemetery list and the tombstones. (See Appendix 2a). This last list has the merit of being the only one to include a 'Geelbooi' among the deceased.

On the other hand, the official statistics deal with 'immediate' casualties on the Monday and take no account of that unfortunate proportion of the wounded who passed away in succeeding days, weeks or months as a direct result of their wounds. There is, for example, Irene Modiko, who endured twenty years of excruciating pain before being consigned to her grave. But even if one does not take into account these extreme cases, the Register after 21 March is peppered with the names of gunshot victims whose surviving friends and relatives, many wounded themselves, recount their death throes.

Not everybody was buried in Sharpeville. Some of the recent migrants to the township were returned to their places of origin in the rural areas, while other families felt 'shamed' that their dead should be put permanently (and in many cases anonymously) among the victims of a mass murder. Some bereaved families feared that they would suffer police reprisals if their deceased were *not* buried anonymously far from the site of the killings, others preferred to bury their dead with tribal rites and rituals rather than under standard Christian auspices. None of these figures is included in the official sixty-nine, and all suggest a death toll far in excess of that number.

Given the massive scale of the enfilade it is difficult to believe that so few died – unless, of course, the police, were extraordinarily poor shots. Then, too, there is the question of the undesignated graves in the Sharpeville Native Cemetery itself. Clearly, many of the families of the dead could not afford even a modest marble testament to the deceased. In many cases a simple wooden cross had to suffice and was later swept away by time, weather or, in some cases, human hand. There are countless stories in Sharpeville of police trucks arriving at the dead of night in the cemetery with shapeless bags, of the clatter of spades, and of freshly turned earth revealed when morning came. Most of this may be urban legend encouraged by people seeking to extract maximum sentiment and/ or political capital over the years. What is known for a fact is that the cemetery was persistently desecrated at night for years after 1960 by white vigilantes, hooligans and their police associates who would arrive drunk in the area on Fridays shouting 'Amandla', 'Afrika', or various obscenities intended to malign the dead. The soil of many graves was also frequently disturbed although there were no actual attempts to disinter bodies. Veronica Makhela, whose fourteen-year-old son David was one of the youngest victims, recounts how her wooden cross was constantly uprooted, stolen or daubed with the words 'kaffirhond' or 'Sobukwe' for months after March 1960. In the end she simply desisted from placing any token of remembrance on the place where she believes David to be buried. As to who or what exactly lies beneath these mounds one can only speculate. What is more certain is the fact that the number of mortalities would have been substantially higher had it not been for the medical staff at Baragwanath, the huge hospital south-west of Johannesburg, to which overflow casualties from Vereeniging were quickly transferred. Six emergency operating theatres were quickly designated for the massive influx, under the general control of a surgeon-in-charge for Sharpeville, Dr Paul Keen. He and his team, working under enormous pressure, were among the few people to emerge from the whole tragedy with an unreserved degree of distinction.

The number of wounded is even more difficult to assess. One of the few journalists present at the scene, Humphrey Tyler, refers to 178, which conforms roughly to the figures of the South African Institute of Race Relations at the time.[78] The report of the Location Superintendent however quotes a higher figure and, with the mythologisation of the incident, the official figures have in some instances been inflated as high as 400. About 185 to 190 is a common estimate although it remains impossible to pin down the exact arithmetic and account for the discrepancies simply because many of the injured were *not* among the 'honderde van beseerde Bantoes' (hundreds of injured Bantu) who were reportedly admitted to the wards in the first half hour after the massacre and, when these overflowed, into the courtyard of Vereeniging Hospital. Some of these people, as well as later arrivals, were transferred to Baragwanath when it became clear at an early stage that the local facility could not cope. Rather than undergo such a move however, some of the more lightly wounded, simply discharged themselves despite medical advice and before the official casualty count.

The police added to the confusion early in the afternoon when they began to comb the wards in search of everyone with gunshot wounds of any description.[79] Anyone who displayed any injuries of this type, even the half-lucid, was callously cross-examined about the motives and leadership of the protest, and their names were noted. Despite protests from hospital staff, a number were prised from their beds and taken into immediate custody in their bloodied hospital gowns. They included Petrus Mokhele, one of several victims of crime, who had been in the hospital for days before the massacre, and who said he was arrested 'because we could not answer what were had been doing that Monday'. Given the nature of race relations and attitudes towards the police, these actions inevitably aroused suspicions among the conscious injured that they were to be charged *en masse* under the laws governing public violence. Some who were physically capable of rising from their beds left the hospital undetected by either the police or medical personnel. Since the news of what was happening was quickly transmitted back to Sharpeville itself, many people still lying injured in township houses decided against going to any medical installation where the police might be on the lookout for Sharpeville residents. This was, of course, not an option for the more seriously wounded, who required immediate treatment. Nonetheless, a number of hospitals throughout the Witwatersrand and even in the nearby northern Free State reported the appearance of significantly higher than normal numbers of casualties with gunshot wounds for days after the massacre. In most cases, these were written off as the results of violent township life and were not added into Sharpeville statistics.

At Baragwanath some of the more acute of the medical personnel on duty to receive the Vaal casualties suspected from the nature of some wounds that 'normal' bullets had not been used. One politically sensitive senior doctor conveyed this information to Anglican clerics visiting the wounded, including Ambrose Reeves, the Bishop of Johannesburg (and subsequently, the author of one of the better accounts of the massacre). Inquiries to the police concerning the type of ammunition used seem to have been 'lost' in the prevailing confusion – not surprisingly, given their sensitive nature and the prevailing circumstances. Reeves never received his answer.[80] The sudden onslaught of wounded who were transferred and then interned in Baragwanath also affected the accuracy of the statistics on admissions – it seems that 138 wounded arrived from Sharpeville on 21 March but, as hospital administrators were to admit later, a number of cases, appear to have vanished or have been mysteriously unaccounted for. Like their colleagues in the Vaal, the police – and in particular the Special Branch – took an enthusiastic interest in who was among the dead and wounded, so much so that a number of administrative staff at the hospital complained that their presence was either intimidating or obstructive. Hospital administrators now concede that 'mistakes' could quite conceivably have been made about numbers and identities.

The police were more thorough, albeit belatedly. Within hours of the massacre it was clear to some of the hospitalised victims that the police were trying to pinpoint certain 'subversive' persons among their number. A Captain Van den Bergh of the Special Branch had been dispatched to Baragwanath along with a team of black and white security personnel and, shortly after their arrival, bloody victims of the shooting were being dragged from their beds in a repeat performance of what had happened at Vereeniging Hospital and with scant respect for the normal legal procedures governing the identification of suspects. Some of those who were left insist to this day that many people were simply spirited away by the police, never to be seen again (but this remains insinuation rather than hard fact based on provable evidence). For the most part, the arrested wounded were dragged from the wards, shackled, irrespective of their condition, and carried off to Boksburg Prison where they were stripped, hosed down, and redressed in their bloody clothes which they were forced to wear for months on end as an example to other prisoners of the price of 'agitation'.

Data on the dead and wounded provided by Drs Keen, Jack Friedman (then Senior District Surgeon of Johannesburg), Dr Steyn (his counterpart in Vanderbijl), and Dr Swanepoel (Superintendent of the Vereeniging Hospital) is relatively unequivocal and provides further confirmatory evidence of the dynamics of the massacre. In the opinion of the team at Baragwanath, about fifty of the wounded had multiple injuries caused by bullets that had entered directly from the rear, while fourteen out of fifteen victims of ricochet wounds had also been shot from behind. This challenges the SAP version of the shooting presented to the Commission of Inquiry which argues, *inter alia*, that many of the injuries and mortalities were caused inadvertently by ricochets or the fragmentation of stray bullets. Many wounds were unclassifiable, essentially because victims were struck as they were falling, but as a general estimate approximately two-thirds of all wounds can be taken as having originated behind the victims. Similar conclusions, which accord roughly with contemporary observations, that 'only fifteen percent of the wounds were inflicted from the front', are reached in the post-mortems conducted by Drs Friedman, Steyn and Swanepoel (except that a higher proportion of the dead, relative to the wounded, may have been killed from behind).[81] There were many wounds to the perineum consistent with a person crawling away from the line of fire – if he or she had not already been hit in the head or the spinal cord. The mobility of heads and limbs precludes evidence about the origin of wounds to these areas of the body, but all three doctors found that a very high proportion of wounds were in the mid-body – the stomach, buttocks and bladder in particular. This suggests that no particular caution was exercised in line with the rules of engagement or Standing Orders then in operation to guide police behaviour in crisis conditions to minimise casualties. Much frontal wounding was indicative of immobile persons stooping, kneeling, or already prone, either because they were already injured, had stumbled, or were more or less rooted in terror to a specific spot. Dr Friedman indicated the ragged nature of tissue at the entry point of many wounds, suggesting high-velocity split bullets of an 'abnormal' nature, but could not conclusively determine use of the dreaded 'dum dums' as the cause of these horrible mutilations. Under pressure from Advocate Claassen (acting for the state at the Commission), he attributed the gross exit injuries to bullet striking bone. He could not, he added, comment further since wounds caused by bullets of an explosive type were outside the realms of his professional experience as a pathologist at work in civil society, and required examination by an expert in military medicine. This line of questioning was abandoned, and no such expert was ever summoned or consulted. The SAP, it appears, had 'misplaced' its records on the quantity and type of ammunition issued to those on duty in Sharpeville and, perhaps as important, the ammunition returned to police armouries thereafter. In the circumstances the whole issue of autopsies was postponed *sine die*.

---- ✦ ----

AFTERNOON

Not that the SAP was entirely disorganised. By early afternoon, in Sharpeville itself, they had recovered sufficiently from the trauma of the shootings to form search parties within the *cordon sanitaire* that had quickly been thrown around the township. The arrests that followed and were to continue for a number of days were partially random, partially targeted. In the initial hours after the massacre most of the police simply combed the streets and vented their anger on often hapless people who were treated 'as if they [the SAP] were the victims', according to Saul Moise, an unfortunate who fell foul of the patrols, was beaten senseless for no apparent reason, thrown into prison and then released three weeks later without charges. The black police, particularly those who had been in the Sharpeville station, appeared particularly frustrated and enraged. Sharpeville residents recall that many were blind drunk so that much of the violence they visited upon the community with their sticks and truncheons was entirely senseless.

Accustomed to police molestation in the normal course of producing their hated 'dompasse', township residents now had to contend with a situation where any visible sign of a physical injury – a limp or a bloody shirt – was taken as *prima facie* evidence of 'opstokery' (subversion). A young (now old) man who had gone to Vereeniging on the Monday morning in search of a dentist returned in the afternoon and was arrested because his swollen face was presumed to be an injury related to the shootings. When he protested, his dental pain was substantially increased by an onslaught of police fists and batons. Despite orders that SAP members should avoid provocative actions which could stoke the crisis, many houses filled with mourners and traumatised people uncertain as to whether their family and friends lay among the dead and wounded were subject to police harassment, at the base of which lay the unstated message that the less said about the massacre by the people of Sharpeville the better. This would seriously compromise the upcoming Commission of Inquiry. More fundamentally, it would create a culture of silence around the events of 21 March that endures into the present.

The mass detentions were not however an entirely incoherent rampage by the white guardians of law and order. Most of the white police reserved their binges for the evenings following the killings. During the day they were, for the most part, stone cold sober and armed with a clear idea of who should be incarcerated. Within two hours of the slaughter, the uniform police had been briefed by their security counterparts in Vereeniging, Vanderbijl and Sharpeville itself as to who had been pinpointed as known 'trouble-makers' in the area by police intelligence in the past three months. These approximately 100 people, obviously including the entire PAC executive, now became the primary targets on a list provided to the street patrols.

The question has been raised as to why these 'subversives' who had come to the attention of Spengler and his associates weeks, if not months before 21 March, had not been prophylactically apprehended at least once it had become clear during the preceding weekend that trouble was brewing. Arguably, this might have inhibited the demonstrations and even avoided the catastrophe that followed. Unfortunately, this was not part of the perspective of the state, whose representatives, as I have noted, remained remarkably quiescent throughout the prior Saturday and Sunday for all kinds of reasons, one of which was a certain over-caution on the part of people like Spengler who feared that pre-emptive action might worsen an already bad situation. Alternatively, the authorities might well have recognised a serious crisis, but preferred that the activists first compromise themselves, whatever the social and human costs. A retired police commissioner insistent on absolute anonymity hinted as much when he said that 'we [the SAP] knew that there would be trouble, but wanted the radicals [the Africanists] to fully expose themselves before we cast the net'. This clearly adds some grist to the mill of the argument still prevalent in Pan Africanist and other militant circles – albeit in the face of much of the evidence – that the whole massacre, from start to finish, was engineered by the police and/or the Nationalist government.

In either event, the police now moved rapidly to eliminate the individuals they believed to be at the root of the disturbances. The people of Sharpeville, appalled by developments and in a state of collective shock, did not, in the main, volunteer their help, but many, when faced with police intimidation, were quick to finger the designated 'subversives' as a matter of self-protection. There were also a number of unfortunate cases where residents enthusiastically helped the police to track down people who were not on the dreaded list, but with whom there were personal scores to settle. In the end, several hundred people were arrested, including seventy-six on the 'most wanted' list who were quickly charged with various crimes against the state before being dispatched to await trial in the bleak stone yards of Boksburg Prison.

They included ten people whom the Special Branch considered ringleaders of the mass action, as well as a large number of innocents and simple bystanders whose identities had become intermingled with those of the genuine activists, either through incompetence or because of the malicious desire of informants to ingratiate themselves with their political masters. Security police documentation at the time refers to many people caught in the dragnet whose wounds and inclusion on the list suggested crimes against the state. Roy Mokwa, who was wounded in the leg and arrested at the Outpatient section of Vereeniging Hospital, was detained on the multiple grounds that 'he had no reference book', 'had absented himself from work', and to top the list of heinous offences, 'had shouted "Afrika" and gave signs'. Many people, like David Sithole, shot in the legs and in excruciating pain, were carried off in police vans despite the admission in police dockets that they 'had not been seen doing anything specific'.

The ease with which the local PAC executive was identified, picked-up and incarcerated has led to allegations that one, if not more of their number were police agents. Whether this is so or not, the executive was decimated within hours of the shooting, as was the 'reserve' executive of Stefaans Lepee, which was supposed to continue functioning and develop a new core to supplant PAC members picked off by the authorities in the wake of the demonstration. None of the eight functioning members was among the ranks of the wounded, leading to allegations from political opponents that the PAC leaders were careful to stay out of the front line of fire. These allegations echo in the ongoing debate over the memory of Sharpeville to this very day. In reality however a number of members of the executive were already in police custody when the fatal killings took place. They included Tsolo and More who, following their arrest at the station gate moments before the slaughter, were subject to a vicious beating by what they describe as 'half demented' police in the Sharpeville cells in the immediate wake of the fusillade.

Johannes Monyake, described as one of the 'main inciters' in newly revealed SAP documentation (along with Thaddea Ntoampe, Tsolo and More), surrendered himself for arrest to Wessels in line with the political agenda behind the demonstration and with the words *'ek dra nie 'n donnerse pas nie* [I will not carry a damned pass]'. Teketsi, towards whom even the mild-mannered Spengler had developed a deep antipathy, was detained by municipal police led by notorious 'Bantoe-Sersant' Ben Pitso in a pre-emptive sweep even before midday on the Monday. The burnt pass in his possession, defaced with the words 'from today I will not carry a pass' and his signature, confirmed the police view that he was not only a 'main inciter' but 'a violent insurrectionist'. The remaining members of the executive – Lepee, Ramodibe and Hophny Marabe – were accorded the less prestigious status of 'main meeters who worked the crowd emotionally', bundled into police vans, and taken off to Boksburg Prison.

To all intents and purposes, the Vaal PAC now disappeared, and for many months Sharpeville and its abutting communities were rendered politically leaderless. In the township itself, the days following the massacre were extraordinarily painful for everyone because most of the inhabitants had been touched by the killings in some way or another. Given the size of the community, the numbers at the scene, the casualties, the tight family networks, and the crowded conditions of township existence, there was virtually no-one who did not lose a relative, a friend or an acquaintance. The community reeled in the collective state of shock induced by a physical or social disaster of epic proportions. Rather than generate the massive physical violence which the state and its security organs half anticipated, the massacre produced a general state of numbness in which people were largely incapable of normal, let alone political, behaviour.

Households that had experienced casualties were wracked with despair as funeral preparations were made, and throughout the township there was an air of incomprehension, particularly on the part of people who had been in the forefront of the crowd but who had miraculously escaped with their lives or minor injuries. Like most survivors of genocide or more-contemporary 'ethnic cleansing' many of those who lived felt deep feelings of guilt and depression. Disorientation was especially intense in households whose inhabitants could not locate their friends and family at Vereeniging or Baragwanath Hospitals or through local police channels which appeared (with good reason) to be avoiding questions about what had happened to people whose movements and fate could not be accounted for. Many people were, in any case, too intimidated by events to approach or press the police for information. Symptoms of post-traumatic stress disorder (which were to endure for decades among some individuals) are clearly evident in contemporary descriptions of the collective psychological climate in the immediate aftermath of the massacre. The debilitation, anxiety and demoralisation associated with this syndrome tended to diminish popular anger against the police or state authorities so that the activists who had not quickly fled the Vaal and now sought to capitalise on the situation to remobilise popular protest faced a brick wall of collective apathy – even prior to the later State of Emergency with its statutory restrictions on political protest.

All of this was understandably lost on the white population of Vereeniging and Vanderbijl whose gut reaction was to prepare against a black invasion from the townships. From the first disturbances on Sunday night, heavily armed whites had materialised at local police stations to offer assistance in protecting their segregated areas from black invasion. The police, fearful of a racial rampage, politely declined these dubious offers of help unless the volunteers could indicate their membership of the local commando. Should they do so, they were assigned to back up the regular police in road blocks leading from the townships into Vereeniging and Vanderbijl which were established during the course of the evening. Some men nevertheless decided to take the law into their own hands, and there were a number of reports throughout Sunday night and Monday morning of blacks who had inadvertently strayed into the 'white' areas being viciously assaulted by random groups of vigilantes, ostensibly acting under the authority of the local commando. Needless to say, no charges were ever laid or substantiated. Images of a racial war with black mobs swarming into the affluent white areas to wreak vengeance and havoc largely wiped out any initial feelings of compassion even after the massacre.

Many domestics working in nearby Bedworth Park were summarily dismissed by their white 'madams' as if they personally carried the plague of protest into polite white homes. When Segametsi Makhanya reported for work on the day after the massacre, his employer expressed her disappointment that the police had not killed more 'natives'.[82] Since the massacre had led to a largely spontaneous and immediate withdrawal of black labour from local industry, commerce or domestic work throughout the region, an ominous and hostile silence descended for several days. At the massive Iscor steelworks and other industries in Vanderbijl, production ground to a standstill: at the nearby Vekor works only a handful of the 800 black employees reported for work on the days after 21 March. At Dorman Long, another major metalworks, not one of a workforce of thousands appeared in the workplace.

During the days of the immediate aftermath heavily armed whites continued to form self-protection units to patrol the suburban streets in private vehicles, despite official police reservations. The authorities nevertheless did not prohibit activity of this type: no white member of the public was disarmed or, to the best of my knowledge, asked to produce a firearm licence. The police were nevertheless under considerable public pressure to apprehend the black 'troublemakers' to whom whites attributed the massacre, and had to be seen to be stepping up security in Sharpeville and its adjacent townships. This warranted joint operations with the SADF who moved into the Vaal in force, as well as the relatively quick and brutal implementation of the cordon-and-search operations discussed above. Meanwhile, white society took the initiative and, according the local media, 'het ingespring en baie van die nie-blanke takke self verrig' (jumped in and undertook many of the non-white tasks). What this meant, behind the bonhomie, was that whites performed the menial work normally 'reserved' for the black underclasses in a situation which was seen, in most cases, as frightening, unnecessary and altogether inconvenient.

The stayaway was however only temporary. The shock of Sharpeville had temporarily thrown off balance the resistance movement at regional level where there were no powerful labour or party structures to maintain momentum. Within a few days, despite what one inhabitant later described as the 'atmosphere of dread and disaster' in Sharpeville, Vaal workers were driven by necessity to return to work or face the prospect of losing their jobs in a sharply competitive labour market. Once black workers began to drift back into town the virtually paranoid sense of siege that had seized the white inhabitants of Vereeniging, Vanderbijl and other small communities began to dissipate, and at least some whites in both local government and civil society began to take a more balanced view of what had happened.

Fear of a race war did not however convert into sympathy in most circles. When the Sharpeville Advisory Board questioned the Vereeniging Town Council about the massacre within a few days of its occurrence, its questions were casually dismissed with the standard argument prevalent among whites then and now that the police had acted in self-defence because 'the natives had been throwing stones'. When questioned on why children and the old were among the casualties, Sam Kolisang, Sharpeville's unofficial mayor for many years, remembers, 'there was no answer'.[83] For the most part, now that the feared race war had been averted, the major concern of the Council was its public image, particularly the effects of the fallout from the massacre on a town with a 'model' location. Municipal officials (and the local police) lived in fear of official rebuke from the Department of Native Administration or the senior SAP establishment for months after 21 March, while the elected councillors noted a distinct drop in tourism to the Vaal River, a previously popular destination for jaded Johannesburgers. It was this need for pre-emotive action, as much as any humanitarian concerns, which quickly motivated the mayor to suggest the establishment of a local fund for the victims, drawn on the municipal budget, and working in tandem with the various Sharpeville churches who had quickly sprung to the aid of the victims and their families under the energetic coordination of the Reverend Mahabane. Not unsurprisingly this proposal was strongly opposed by councillors from the local National Party who were of the opinion that the people of Sharpeville had given succour to 'agitators' and had only themselves to blame for their tragedy. A fund backed by municipal finance 'in keeping with the small requirements of the natives' and open to contributions from the general public was however put in place.[84]

The rain that had fallen on that Monday afternoon had, according to urban legend, washed the blood from the place of the slaughter, down Seeiso street and into the Sharpeville Dam, whose waters remain polluted by the martyrs of March to this day. On Wednesday 30 March, nine days after the shooting, it was raining again as the first thirty-four bodies of the victims were laid to rest. Bereaved men and women wept openly as dark clouds and cold wind enshrouded Sharpeville Square. In the late morning gloom hymns were sung by a crowd of about 3 000 at the beginning of a service conducted by Reverends Mahabane, Voyi and Robert Maja – the minister who had been allowed to give water to the dying and wounded on the days of the killings. Reverend Voyi from the Anglican Church initiated the congregation with an assurance that 'the whole world is with us at this hour', and then proceeded to quote phrases on human suffering and predestination extracted from the Book of Job. A hymn and prayer followed before the funeral procession moved towards the cemetery singing 'Abide with Me'. On arrival Reverend Maja and Reverend Ngwenya presided over the committal and burial. All thirty-four coffins – paid for by the Vereeniging Council at £15 each – were then lowered into their graves simultaneously. Few carried the individual silver nameplates that had been promised by a Council in a state of initial benevolence immediately following the massacre.

There were no political harangues or invocations, primarily because one of the conditions laid down by the authorities for the funeral was that it should only be addressed by religious leaders, but also because of the more deep-seated fear on the part of the state that the dignity of the mourners would once again be manipulated for malignant purposes by the ubiquitous 'agitators'. Most of these dangerous elements in both the PAC and ANC were however already in hiding or on the run as the police moved to track down and arrest anyone even vaguely suspected of having instigated the protest. PAC cadres who had managed to avoid arrest made for the Lesotho border in most cases, leaving behind an underground skeleton executive which would continue for a while to attempt to mobilise what was, by any standards, a deeply depressed community. Local relations with the ANC went from poor to worse as the latter's local leaders were swept into the police net despite their lack of involvement in the previous week's demonstration. In essence the position of the ANC was ambiguous. On the one hand there was anger at the PAC whose actions and lack of preparation had laid hundreds of innocent lives on the line. On the other, there was also recognition that the political consequences of Sharpeville opened up enormous possibilities for building political capital, particularly through internationalisation of the anti-apartheid struggle. Some elements in the Vaal ANC thus distanced themselves from their PAC counterparts, even while their colleagues moved tactically closer.

The SAP was seriously embarrassed by what had happened and, in the week between the shootings and the funeral, various of its senior members from the Vaal and Witwatersrand more generally were called in by the National Party leadership to give an account of their behaviour. Contrition, of course, only went so far – the primary concern of the state and its security agents was to manage the political fallout from the whole messy business rather than to genuinely probe its origins. Atonement and assignation of blame was not really on the government's agenda – and could not conceivably be, given its illegitimacy, its increased reliance on the police and armed forces for its very survival, and the massive global backlash in the immediate aftermath of 21 March. As contemporary critics recall, this tended to shut off the possibilities for any real dialogue which would inevitably lead to structural criticism of the entire apartheid system.

In the Vaal itself, the SAP and their allies in the local authority were taking every precaution against a repetition of the violence, and this meant, quite simply, stifling any incipient signs of popular protest at its outset.

All media were prevented from covering the funeral by road blocks placed at the main entrances to Sharpeville, although some enterprising black journalists, posing as mourners, managed to give the wider world a taste of the occasion. The Vereeniging Council had offered to provide hearses, but the offer was turned down by what remained of the community leaders once it became known that this philanthropic gesture had originated in regional police headquarters. The bodies of the dead were therefore brought to Sharpeville in police lorries but then transferred to five privately-acquired local lorries for further transportation. Meanwhile, at the massacre site itself, heavily armed squads of police clustered round a single parked Saracen. There was, in the end, no violence, if only because of popular grief and exhaustion.

A second funeral for thirty-five more victims was held a few days later, on 2 April, and this also went off peacefully before a crowd of about 3 500 people. 'Abide with Me' was sung once again in melodious Sesotho while the funeral oration by Reverend Maja dwelt on the transitory nature of human existence. The graveside speeches were made by Reverend Voyi and Reverend Tima of the Dutch Reformed Church, the committal by Reverend SS Khama. All 'Europeans' were banned from the service. The police were stationed on a small hill about a kilometre away and observed the proceedings through high-powered binoculars.[85]

In the witch hunt for agitators the police had interfered with the medical treatment of the wounded immediately after the massacre. In the days that followed the security police succeeded in exploiting the fears of white staff at Vereeniging and Baragwanath of an imminent racial bloodbath and had set up a network of informants. Several doctors now admit that they were persuaded as a matter of patriotism to 'keep an eye' on the progress of the Sharpeville casualties, all of whom were designated by the SAP as 'dangerous subversives'. Parked police lorries whose purpose was immediately to arrest the discharged at the gates of both hospitals were a common sight for almost two months after the massacre. Isaac Moteung, one of many innocent bystanders who were wounded, still recalls with anger how a month later he was offered a lift to Sharpeville in a police truck – and then promptly dispatched as 'a PAC member' to Boksburg Prison where 'everyone was pushed into a corner and they used a high-pressure hose to spray us clean'. He remained there in his bloody rags for a year.[86]

Apartheid would not let its victims rest. The reason why there are only fifty-six names on the official Native Cemetery Register is that the municipal authorities at first refused to allow the burial there of non-residents. After protests by the community concerning the extraordinary nature of the funerals, the authorities eventually agreed to a special dispensation under which the 'foreigners' could be buried, but not at the normal burial cost of 12/6d. When this was also rejected by the inter-denominational African Ministers Association responsible for funeral arrangements, the petty-bureaucrats at the Location Office finally relented – the non-residents could be buried for 12/6 (about R1.25) each, but at that price their names could not be officially recorded. They were 'illegals', the perpetually anonymous, interred but not allowed to remain in Sharpeville. In an equally gracious gesture, the Minister of Bantu Administration and Development, Daan de Wet Nel, bent the regulations to allow the Vereeniging Council to carry the funeral expenses – but only with monies drawn on the local 'native revenue account'.[87]

There were other dead and other less publicised funerals of victims at several cemeteries along the East Rand, and as far afield as Lesotho. These also went unrecorded as Sharpeville casualties because the immediate families feared police attention. In Boksburg, for example, an unusually high number of people who died of gunshot wounds were buried during the period between the two Sharpeville funerals. Officially the victims of 'normal' township violence, some of these people were additional casualties of the massacre – or so it is alleged by a number of survivors and relatives who still live Vaal region. Several of the Sharpeville wounded who feared arrest at the local hospital and then entered the PAC underground network leading to Lesotho, subsequently died across the border and are buried in the Maseru cemetery. In Sharpeville itself, some of the older residents who lived through the massacre and the terrible days that followed recall visits by police lorries and burial parties at work for several weeks after 21 March, either in the cemetery or in other open spaces. The local authorities and the SAP, it is alleged, covered many graves with seed as a means of concealment. Most of the few luxuriant trees in the township today are attributed to the presence of human fertiliser at their roots.

DID SHARPEVILLE HAVE TO HAPPEN?

Much of the above is, of course, urban legend woven into the general martyrology of Sharpeville and can never be corroborated. What is not martyrology is the fact that Sharpeville was not the only police installation besieged by demonstrators organised by the PAC on 21 March to protest against the pass laws. The PAC campaign was nation wide and even though many of its efforts failed, the organisation succeeded, probably far beyond its expectations, in bringing out its constituency in the Vaal. By early Monday morning, the police station in 'white' Vanderbijl was confronted by a substantial demonstration by an estimated 2 500 protestors, and a few hours later Evaton police station, a few miles away from Sharpeville, was surrounded by an an even larger crowd of 15 000. It was events at Evaton, curiously enough, that attracted the heavy security police presence, including that of Colonel Willem Prinsloo, the authority's grey behind Spengler, who had given so much special attention to Sharpeville in preceding months.[88] Yet in none of these cases was there a slaughter like that which eventually took place at Sharpeville. Was this because of the mood of the demonstrators or that of the police? Was it because of the nature of the PAC campaign in certain places, the character of police leadership, major communications breakdowns peculiar to Sharpeville, the structural violence of the South African system incarnate in a single place, or all of these variables in some intricate and combustible combination? Was the slaughter perhaps the result of a singular quirk of fate compounded by the pace of a particular social moment? Had the 'groot baas' arrived on time to address the expectant crowd, would the tragedy have been averted? As it was, the 'baas', Witwatersrand Divisional Commissioner, Brigadier Els, arrived on the outskirts of the township at exactly the moment the police opened fire: he had, in a cruel twist of history, been delayed by a flat tire on the road through De Deur. Ultimately, the key question remains – was the tragedy at Sharpeville, in whole or part, inevitable or avoidable?

Sharpeville was neither the first nor the last of the violent clashes that peppered 20th century South African history as the entrenched power of a racial minority was challenged over the course of the years. Prior to the official advent of apartheid with the National Party's accession to power in 1948, there were a number of incidents reflecting the institutionalisation of minority control – the Bulhoek massacre for example.

After Sharpeville, from the seventies to the edge of democratisation in the nineties there were other slaughters which typified the rising political temperature with popular resistance coming up hard against a progressively decomposing apartheid – in Soweto during the course of the 1976 uprising, and, with the mass mobilisation of the mid-1980's, in the Vaal once again at Boipatong. While what we would today label 'ethnic cleansing' is not unfamiliar to the Southern African sub-continent in this century – the decimation of the Herero in neighbouring Namibia is a case in point[89] – conscious genocide as opposed to physical separation of the races at the cost of enormous human suffering was never part of the grand plan of apartheid.

Among the grand planners, and even their lesser counterparts, there was never an exterminationist tendency despite the brutal nature of segregationist policy, so that, in the end, the various massacres that took place between 1948 and the early nineties were spontaneous rather than procedural. While the recent hearings of the Truth Commission indicate that the state far too often tolerated, condoned or sometimes even explicitly encouraged its security forces to act with a vigour that made the gross violation of human rights largely inevitable, large-scale slaughter of the black population was not standard operating procedure. To use the provocative phrase of Christopher Browning, 'atrocity by policy', involving the methodical execution of political or military opponents as an act of state calculation, was not the case in Soweto 1976.[90] Nor had it been the case in Sharpeville sixteen years earlier. Brute enforcers of the apartheid state its security agents certainly were – the list of outrages committed in defence of racial segregation is very substantial – but massacres were not usually part of the military or police repertoire.

If Sharpeville was not a case of premeditated state slaughter, was it then simply caused by a tragic breakdown in discipline and the chain of command among the perpetrators, as determined by the Commission of Inquiry in its logically neat and legal examination of police behaviour? More broadly, emotionally and at the opposite end of the political spectrum, was Sharpeville the defining act that exposed the moral reality of apartheid in all its harsh and ugly nakedness, the inevitable culmination of rising and unquenchable popular resistance to the imposition of a racially-driven authoritarian state as described in the 'struggle literature' of the anti-apartheid years and still sanctified in post-democratic popular consciousness? Perhaps so. Yet these popular explanations so tantalising in their simplicity do not do justice to the events of March 1960. They have a far wider socio-political significance which touches on far more universal and infinitely complex issues such as the general mechanics of the authoritarian state, crowd behaviour, the social psychology of oppression and violence, the impulses and forces motivating political behaviour, and, in the last instance, the mutation of men into killers.

It is both fashionable and easy to attribute state behaviour on 21 March to frenzy, bitterness and frustration arising from a basic racism serviced in its turn by a legitimating ideology of segregation, but the explanatory route out of Sharpeville is far more complex than prejudice of an order and depth which allowed the agents of the state to kill with relative impunity or little emotional disturbance. The 'race wars' of the 20th Century, in Europe and Africa, and the persistent atrocities committed by the American military in the Pacific (and later at the infamous massacre at My Lai) are testimony to the fact that the normal conventions governing human decency in cases of violent conflict decompose quickly under the combined impact of brutalising warfare and deeply negative but embedded racial stereotyping.[91] Part of the explanation for the massacre at Sharpeville rests in an implicit and undeclared state of war between white and black arising out of colonial conquests by an isolated white minority situated at the nether end of a colloquially 'dark continent'.

This is not to say that the people in the Vaal were consciously dwelling on the racial conquests of the past in the tense circumstances of 21 March, but the events of the day were a microcosmic projection – a bloody culmination in a certain sense – of the historic racial struggles over geography, and nowhere was the sense of siege and occupation more intensely felt than in the confines of the Sharpeville Police Station. Much of the historical psychology of South Africa is crudely reducible to the anxiety of its rulers in the face of ongoing struggle with a largely unknowable mass enemy with a presumed potential for limitless violence at the slightest provocation. This formed the mental backdrop for the police at Sharpeville, their colleagues in the municipal administration and, indeed, the entire white population of the Vaal, not only in 1960 but in the following decades which were to witness an intensification of apartheid in all its cumulative brutality at both the ideological and institutional level. The natural consequence twenty years later was the purported 'total onslaught' on South Africa, fuelled by a lethal garrison psychology that created space for a now virtually paranoid ruling class to lash out both indiscriminately, pro-actively, and with enormous destructive consequences in protection of accumulated interests and privilege – not only within the territorial parameters of apartheid but in the ravaged wider regions of the sub-continent.

As I have intimated, the Standing Orders to the SAP could not possibly have stood in the circumstances which prevailed at Sharpeville. The preceding year (1959) had not been a good year for the SAP and, at its conclusion, the Commissioner of Police had warned against 'agitation by radical organisations and persons ... having a detrimental influence on good [race] relations'.[92] After Cato Manor, there had been numerous resignations from the SAP and a reduction in the numbers of white applicants for police service – both of which were to be accentuated after Sharpeville. By March 1960 there was already an element of churning demoralisation in police ranks so that it took only two shots in the early morning, some intermittent firing later, waved sticks, shouts, piercing whistles and, ultimately, the two critical shots of Geelbooi at the height of the crisis, to bring the official rules of engagement down.

In the behaviour of the state on that fateful Monday lay the germs of even more terrible things to come. At the same time, the complex evidence suggests that most of the police and white township administrators at Sharpeville were not akin to the pool of moral and political eunuchs on the exterminationist edge of Second World War European fascism, whose recruitment led to the genocidal excesses of the period.[93] Admittedly, most of the Sharpeville perpetrators were contaminated by the morally inverted world of apartheid and, for many, if not most, the eventual killings actually made sense within the politico-cultural framework of the time – as would be the case in future atrocities committed by the apartheid system. Yet, with the exception of a 'hard core' of security personnel to whom the very notion of a protesting 'native' represented a complete perversion of the social universe as they then saw it (or now say they saw it), most of the police who shot and killed at Sharpeville were not simply the products of blind racial hatred. If the police were cruel, to paraphrase, Zygmunt Bauman, it was because apartheid policing attracted mostly cruel people.[94] They were, in John Steiner's terms, the 'sleepers' who could live ostensibly suburban lives, but who harboured, beneath the 'tough' bonhomie of 'beer-and-braai' an enormous capacity to inflict sanctified violence at the slightest provocation against ideologically targeted outgroups.[95]

For many, Sharpeville was the catalyst for these contained subterranean impulses with their enormous capacity for destruction. Without exculpation of what was done by those to whom history has assigned the status of callous slaughterers, the massacre was, in the end, the macro-consequence of a concatenation of personal, cultural and situational forces which formed the bedrock of apartheid and were, to use the dramatic word of contemporary historian Daniel Goldhagen, 'unshackled' by the extraordinary demands of a particular historic moment.

Sharpeville was, to put it simply, the result of leadership failure, and it was largely on this relatively simple explanation that the Commission focused in its overall analysis of what had transpired. The police had violated, circumvented, or otherwise ignored the Standing Orders dealing with a potentially riotous situation and much of the culpability lay with their officers who had neither warned the crowd to disperse within a specific time, fired over their heads if the order had been ignored, or, finally, at their feet as an indication of their seriousness of intent. All this is indisputable forty years later, barring various shifts in emphasis and detail that are likely to be debated in perpetuity – or at least as long as Sharpeville remains in the public memory. Equally indisputable however is that extreme political behaviour by crowds, the very disarticulation of the crowd into the characteristically incoherent 'mob', is very much a product of those who lead and who, by their predominance, set both the strategic and moral example for large collectives of people. The extraordinary charismatic appeal of a Gandhi played a significant role in the emphasis on passive resistance in the Indian anti-colonial struggle and, more recently, in the extraordinary projection of reconciliative values by a single Mandela into the potentially violent politics of transition that accompanied South Africa across the abyss of history into a functioning democracy.

Sharpeville, unfortunately, lacked such leadership. On the side of the perpetrators, Pienaar and his senior officers incarnate the fatal combination of racial stereotyping and social distancing whereby the Other becomes dehumanised, and thereby killable without much tumult of conscience. Among the victims, the key organisers, with the exception of Nyakane Tsolo and one or two others, were 'circulating' outside the terrain of the killing in order to avoid detection and arrest – and, in one or two cases, to steer clear of the personal consequences of a clearly deteriorating situation. There can be no doubt that Sobukwe sought to build the PAC into an orderly and disciplined force and, in this regard, was 'a man in his own class' among the many able and dedicated men who joined the nascent PAC.[96] Nonetheless, in the crucial hour or two around 13.30 in Sharpeville, the field was left open for poorly trained community leaders and marshals in the much-vaunted PAC 'task teams' whose primary purpose was to stir up the mob, and who were then either unable or unwilling to steer the crowd away from what was clearly fast becoming a cataclysmic situation.

Sharpeville at its simplest may also typify the horrific consequences inherent in breakdowns of human and institutional communication under conditions of political miscomprehension. The Vereeniging Council was probably no more or less enlightened than its counterparts when measured against the local security and administrative organs of the central state. As the women's anti-pass demonstrations before the location superintendency had indicated, its senior officials were reluctant to enter into conversations with 'kaffirs' or 'kaffirmeide', least of all on matters of public policy determined at the higher levels of a rigid bureaucratic hierarchy. At the end of 1959 letters of complaint sent to the superintendent by residents concerned with deteriorating living conditions were ignored as a matter of policy, presumably because blacks were not considered to have worthwhile opinions.[97] The regional SAP and the municipal police were probably no worse in their brutal enforcement of apartheid laws than those elsewhere, and there are instances of more 'progressive' councillors suggesting a lighter hand in the late months of 1959 and the early weeks of the following year. Still, the Vereeniging Council, according to a previous study, 'was so caught up in its image … as the best administered and equipped in the Union that it refused to accept that its residents … could have had any grievances at all'.[98] Because most of its conservative members were, like the township officials, secure in their belief that the leaders of the 'kaffirs' could not conceivably have anything worthwhile to say on public matters, the Council consistently ignored the representations and advice of the township's Advisory Board, some of whose own members certainly had knowledge of popular grievances in the months leading up to March 1960.

The Board, of course had its own agenda. Generally it tended to downplay the intensity of those grievances whose existence, Board members feared, would cast doubt on their own capability. This would, in its estimation, fuel popular forces such as the local ANC and PAC who saw these toothless government-appointed institutions as apartheid collaborators and who took every opportunity to undermine their shaky legitimacy. So, the members of the Board said little, while the Non-European Affairs Committee heard less in a municipal environment where the Council remained self-satisfied in its ultimately tragic self-delusion that it had developed a 'model' black location, an island, as it were, within the whole framework of an inherently repressive system of race relations. For most of the fifties (and certainly from 1959 on) it might well have listened more carefully to the mounting sounds of protest if the Advisory Board had been more energetic, honest and civic-minded. Even in the months or days before the massacre this might have enabled it to take some course to avert a situation with the innate potential for public violence.

Most apartheid atrocities were, in the end, 'desktop' violations of human rights. They were not unlike those committed in far more serious cases of 20th Century proto-genocide, where dull administrative apparatchicks performed what they perceived as routine tasks without any real understanding, identity or even concern to comprehend the fit between their banal behaviour and the grand schemes for social engineering designed by genuinely macro-evil men. Many of the little men of apartheid had no real sense, although they might have had a suspicion, of the drastic human consequences of what they did. To understand this is essential to an understanding of the background to an event like the Sharpeville massacre. Although apartheid was 'philanthropic' in that it foresaw possibilities for 'uplifting' the 'lesser peoples', and at no time shared the exterminationist ethic of its Nazi bedfellow, it shared with its far more lethal German counterpart the fundamental antipathy to those 'lesser peoples' deciding upon their eventual historic destination. Hence the reluctance of either the Sharpeville or Vereeniging authorities to communicate or to detect what was happening in the township and then take steps to avert a mounting catastrophe.

This is however only one among the many ingredients in the recipe for the eventual massacre. The 'gap' between ruler and ruled represents only one aspect of a greater severance (or skewing) of communication that was compounded all down the line, from the intra-bureaucratic struggles within the police, through the various social interests in the Sharpeville community itself, right into that critical nexus where the culture of apartheid connected explosively with that of the township. The state in its various manifestations was incapable of comprehending the world of those it governed. Years of oppression and segregation had led to the situation where the power-holders and the disempowered inhabited two largely separated worlds, so that even if the Council, the police or the Department of Native Administration had had the capacity to recognise what was happening in Sharpeville (which they patently did not), they would probably have remained incapable of responding in an appropriate manner. Ultimately Sharpeville arose out of a cultural ravine in which those who protested could not be heard because those in power felt no real obligation to listen.

None of the actors in the Sharpeville drama emerges entirely pristine, notwithstanding one's natural tendency to sympathise with the victims. Although they were pawns on a much wider historical chessboard, some of the more mobilised were conscious participants in a political action against an authoritarian state which contained, from its very outset, the possibility of degeneration into some form of violence.

It is as condescending to the memory of those who died or were injured to display the crowd as a happy gathering of innocents as it is historically inaccurate to paint a more heroic picture of a gathering that had been constructed for the specific and justifiable purpose of asserting its fundamental civil rights. The crowd that gathered at the police station and its abutting streets on that fateful morning was a disparate group with many different motivations, agendas and not without, one might add, a number of unsavoury elements. Crowds of this nature are notoriously difficult to control or steer and the task of doing so was way beyond the organisational capacity of a fledgeling and tactically inexperienced PAC that had successfully whipped up the group with little comprehension of where it would go, or what it would do. There is little evidence to suggest that the demonstration would have been better managed had it been a joint venture between the ANC and PAC. It is questionable who, in March 1960, was more lacking in local organisational capacity, and more effectively destabilised by the covert operations of the security police, their Sharpeville informants, and their agents provocateurs. Ironically, it was partly because the authorities had been so successful in undermining coherent political expression that widespread popular antagonism took forms outside the supervisory realm of the two main political parties. As it was, a shaky and nascent PAC was left to act alone in its first national campaign where enthusiasm, anger or political immaturity (or all of these variables acting in combination) effectively cancelled out any thought and planning about what to do should matters go horribly wrong.

While popular anger against apartheid could compensate for the lack of mobilisation skills on the part of PAC organisers, there was no substitute for weakness in the areas of crowd control and negotiation in the vortex of violence. By exploiting the volatile issue of the pass laws the PAC had created a community mass movement and the result was 'people summoned by anger: in a "township on the move"'.[99] The desperate attempts of the beleaguered police to find a vestige of leadership with which to talk as the clock ticked to 13.30 is insufficient excuse for the eventual 'decision' to open fire. Yet, if spade be called spade, that 'decision' was partially a result of the fact that the PAC's primitive organisational structure had miserably failed to coordinate and steer the crowd in a manner commensurate with the national leadership's commitment to positive non-violence. The repressive circumstances under which the PAC was established necessitated a 'double executive', half-public, half-covert, but altogether uncoordinated in its ability to douse the popular flames once they were set alight. The much-vaunted 'task-teams', with their mix of sincere and dubious youth, were equally confused, static or incapacitated as the situation moved into confrontation mode. Ultimately, the official PAC leadership was simply swept aside, not by state repression, but by the mass pressed threateningly forward against the state at the fragile wire boundary of the police station. Recognition of 'the Other' as a means of conflict resolution is a two-way street, and if the 'mob' was incomprehensible to the apartheid state personified in Spengler or Pienaar, the motivations and behaviour of the popular leadership, the Tsolos and the Mores in their wild political rhetoric, was way beyond the cognitive boundaries of the police crowded within the perimeter of their station. In the end both the PAC and the state lacked the capacity to match stones, Stens and slogans with the vastly different political realities and messages that lay below different cultural signifiers in the environment of that fateful Monday. Claims to 'non-violence' in these conditions, however sincere, were more a hope than a guarantee.

Violence breeds its own lethal momentum, and when the key role-players were neither willing nor able to concede mutual validity, a physical clash was all but inevitable. Having said this however, one cannot explain Sharpeville without including the role of conscious intention. There is little concrete evidence to support the proponents of 'conspiracy' theories who believe, in a nebula of variations, that the apartheid government, the police, the local state (or some combination of all), sought from the outset to slaughter the Sharpeville population as an act of demonstration or retribution. There are surviving victims who speak of ambulances being parked on the Sharpeville borders an hour before the killings in anticipation of what was supposedly planned to follow. There are vivid but ludicrous descriptions of police and military 'death squads' roaming the streets through Sunday and Monday slaughtering the local residents at will. And there are more subtle theories which refer to carefully calculated provocation by the security police, the purpose of which was to legitimate the police opening fire behind the cosmetic mask of 'self-defence'. Through the succeeding years all of this has been filtered into what Hobsbawm might have termed the 'invented tradition' of Sharpeville. Yet, all history contains invariance, the human memory is marvellous but infinitely malleable and, in the end, there is nothing substantial to support any of these theories. Admittedly there was anger, rage and confusion in the ranks of the state where certain individuals, like Prinsloo and Pienaar, sailed dangerously close to 'final solutions' involving mass violence, but, in the end, Sharpeville vastly superseded a simple neo-genocide in its infinitely complex institutional and human connections.

Conspiracies, like massacres, are two-way streets. In the Commission of Inquiry and in testimonies by police and state officials forty years later, there is a view that the massacre was an outright PAC construction, that the aim of the nascent organisation was to provoke the authorities to violence and the killing of innocents and then to reap political capital in its claims to hegemony in the black liberation movement.[100] If this were the case – if the agenda of the PAC was to taunt the police to the point of slaughter for '*propaganda doeleindes*' (purposes) – then it certainly succeeded – albeit by strategic error and organisational incompetence. Here again, there are echoes to support the murky yet general theory. The nation-wide demonstrations of March 1960 were not spontaneous eruptions, but preplanned acts of mass resistance calculated over a period of several months. There were people on the fringe of the PAC, in Sharpeville and elsewhere, who, in their wilder moments, believed the anti-pass campaign could be the leading-edge of a wider onslaught against apartheid and whose resolve to adhere to the principles of non-violence were severely tested in the clashes between police and people on the days immediately preceding the massacre and on the fateful Monday. There was also intimidation of local residents whose support for the campaign was weak, although this intimidation was not of the dimensions suggested by the official police theory that a small band of agitators had managed to steer an entire community into the gun sights of the authorities. But once again none of this actually supports the argument still cited in police circles decades later that the whole gruesome business was little more than premeditated, gross and extraordinarily dangerous exercise in political one-upmanship.[101]

In the last analysis, both the crowd and its antagonists had a conscious, if different, purpose: the crowd had gathered as a collective to protest the passes, and the police had been deployed to uphold order. In principle these purposes need not have been dialectically opposed but they became so, at least in part because events quickly and dangerously built upon each other. In some instances there was a logical progression – from conflict within the police, through inadequate contingency planning for crowd control, to the release of withering firepower upon a group whose presence *en masse*, according to the dominant ideological system, connoted demonic violence. In other cases, events – both before and during the massacre – interconnected with a frightening and largely inexplicable coincidence in the random collision of political atoms. Spengler's struggles at the gate, Pienaar's indecisiveness, the sudden silence that set the context for the shot by Geelbooi, his presence – indeed, his very existence.

It is this element of incoherence which makes the massacre – along with assassinations, genocides, revolutions and other manifestations of extreme political violence – the most terrifying among the events which social scientists confront in attempting to explain the political universe. The incarnation of these events in a John Wilkes Booth, a Hitler, a Lenin or a Geelbooi – a particularity in the long river of history – compounds the fear and distaste with which people approach these issues. The massacre (and its bloody relatives) are nevertheless critical indications about the body politic. Much like tumours and other physical malignancies they represent reasonably measurable criteria which provide us with organic information about the current state of health of a corporeal entity and its probable longevity.

Sharpeville is crucial to South African history in the last century not because it enjoys the dubious distinction of being the biggest, most violent or sustained physical clash in the country's sad history of race relations – it does not – but because it represents an end, a beginning, a social commentary and an evaluation. Prior to 21 March 1960, the over-whelming majority of South Africans opposed to apartheid – indeed, most people of global repute – still believed that the country's deeply entrenched racial problems were tractable and could be resolved by the application of good civic sense lavished with a dose of mutual goodwill. Sharpeville rudely shattered this illusion and set South Africa on a long path of violence that may still not have ended.

More importantly however, the Sharpeville massacre indicated that apartheid, then in its incipient form, was simply not sustainable – except at the unacceptable human cost of irreparably damaging relations between the races. Again, we are wiser well after the event and in historic retrospect. No one at Sharpeville on the day of the massacre could fully have foreseen the consequences, particularly the chain of events which would, down the years, both physically and psychologically damage the perpetrators, the victims and their heirs.

PART III

TOWARDS DEMOCRACY: SHARPEVILLE 1960-1999

Sharpeville buries its dead

AFTERMATH

Massacres, political thinkers concur, are not, as political devices go, especially productive. On the contrary, as Machiavelli, Kautilya and the others in the more bloody-minded traditions of state strategy have readily conceded, while generalised killing may have the short term advantage of satiating passions and eliminating opposition (or discouraging those who support it), state terror eventually has the consequence of limiting political options. In the more contemporary world, no-one has been especially enthusiastic to treat with states or governments like Nazi Germany, Serbia or others of a genocidal ilk who follow (or appear to follow) policies of systematic human annihilation. This is most true of the surviving victims themselves, be they individuals or persecuted out groups to whom the experience of institutionalised state slaughter is an iconic tool for political mobilisation. At the very least, as history persistently indicates, massacres are the handmaidens of political vengeance.

South Africa in the wake of Sharpeville is no exception to the fact that state-sponsored killings, mistaken or otherwise, harden both the political and military battlelines. As the shockwaves of the killings echoed quickly round the world, erstwhile supporters of the country (if not the ruling Nationalists) who had believed that apartheid could be negotiated away were reduced to a minority in the wider market of global opinion. In the wake of the massacre distaste for apartheid turned to horror, and even among countries and statesmen who had previously envisaged the dismantling of apartheid through a combination of international opprobrium and the passive resistance of local African nationalism, there was now serious doubt as to whether the racial system in South Africa could be dismantled without massively intensified pressure both at home and abroad. At major international forums the first moves were taken to isolate the country that were later to culminate in political, economic, military and cultural sanctions. In relatively respectable circles the possibility of opposing the force of apartheid with coercion was now openly discussed. In such a climate, South Africa's historic friends and allies in the more moderate international circles were placed on the defensive.[1]

Many of these views were reflected in a change wrought by Sharpeville in the political climate in South Africa itself. Though public calls for revenge by the black opposition were stifled by the almost immediate State of Emergency and residual commitments to the traditions of passive resistance, the notion of a peaceful negotiated settlement was now severely tested. The ANC's reaction to Sharpeville was, in some senses, equivocal. On the one hand, it politically and morally identified with the victims, as symbolised by the decision of its President, Albert Luthuli, to burn his passbook and urge others to follow. Yet, there was a keen awareness that the events at Sharpeville were a major source of political capital for the PAC, to whom the tide of public sympathy appeared to have turned. The political struggles that ensued as the PAC sought to protect its investment in Sharpeville against ANC hijacking are not part of this narrative, except insofar as the massacre inevitably undermined the notion of dismantling apartheid through non-violent forms of political protest.

In the end, Sharpeville drove both the contestants to accept the logic of the armed struggle in a commitment that was to shape the anti-apartheid resistance movement for decades to come. Within the black community the massacre was seen as a tragic signal that the National Party would stop at nothing in its implementation of its grand plans for racial segregation. And much the same reaction was encountered in selective segments of white liberal circles, many of whose members now moved decisively towards the left in mapping out a programme to oppose apartheid. This inevitably cleaved the liberal community from the mass of South African whites who, much like their counterparts in the Vaal, tended to see Sharpeville as evidence of the incipient violence and danger posed by African nationalism to minority interests. Since the government either shared this view or calculated that the emerging siege mentality could be turned to party political purposes, it now began to build the foundations of the garrison state that was to characterise South Africa for the next thirty years. In doing so, it deepened both racial divisions and those that had previously existed between South Africa and its shrinking circle of supporters in the world community.

All massacres share one consequence: they unify the victims and they unify the perpetrators. When the latter are Europeans, as the colonial experience of the 19th Century proved repeatedly, the massacre crystallises a sense of superiority over the native peoples[2], and this was much the case in South Africa in the days, months, and years that followed the catastrophe of 21 March 1960. Mounting international hostility and internal disturbances in the immediate aftermath contributed directly to the increasingly paranoid perceptions of whites that they were now on the brink of an externally inspired revolutionary-type war between the races, and this, in its own right, legitimated the progressive use of force in defending apartheid. On the same day as the massacre a similar major protest initiated by the PAC against the pass laws took place at Langa township on the Cape Flats and quickly spilled into nearby Nyanga and other areas of the Western and Eastern Cape. On 1 April the symbolism of 'Cato Manor' materialised once more when thousands of its inhabitants marched on the Durban City Hall. This latter march took place despite the fact that on 29 March a State of Emergency had been proclaimed, which was to last for five months – with strong support both from a white minority which saw itself on the brink of physical obliteration, and the more illiberal segments of the international community who, in line with Nationalist propaganda, deemed Sharpeville the thin edge of the wedge of 'Communist' efforts to subvert the Southern African sub-continent.

Since the terms of the Emergency placed particular emphasis on contravention of the pass laws and the dissemination of 'Communist' ideology, the seventy-six key subversives produced by the police immediately after the massacre suffered accordingly. Although some escaped eventual trial on the basis of weak evidence and legal technicalities, virtually all spent lengthy terms awaiting trial in prison as defence lawyers wrangled with the authorities. While Colonel Pienaar became the recipient of a mass of local and international hate-mail which typified him as the 'butcher of Sharpeville',[3] the 'Sharpeville subversives' were singled out for particularly vicious treatment at various state prisons in a process that was to scar many for life, both physically and emotionally. In an eventual trial of eight persons, seven were convicted on charges of public violence, one, David Ramodibe, was discharged, and all the guilty were sentenced to prison terms. Nyakane Tsolo was able to flee to Lesotho while on bail (and then went on to play a key role in the organisation of APLA, the PAC's new armed wing).

Those who were not tried were released into a nightmarish life of unremitting police harassment. Sharpeville had tainted them as 'Communists' and 'subversives' who warranted regular night visits, house arrests, bannings and constant re-detentions on dubious grounds. Many were forced into eventual exile, poverty, and in some cases, insanity. Immediately after 21 March, most important black leaders nationwide, be they ANC or PAC, had been detained under the same legislation that had largely undermined the Defiance Campaign some eight years before – the Riotous Assemblies Act, the Public Safety Act of 1953 (which legitimated the Emergency), the amorphous Suppression of Communism Act and the 1953 Criminal Law Amendment Act which specifically targeted public unrest and rioting. All of this was to facilitate a decades-long climate in which the state could move actively against all its critics, black or white, militant or moderate – indeed, anyone or any organisation who appeared to oppose in even the mildest of forms the grand design of apartheid.

In the short term, there was an urgent requirement to bring clarity to what had happened at Sharpeville, both for the purposes of future government policy and in an attempt at least to appease segments of international opinion and various political and economic interests still potentially supportive of the country. The decision to establish a Commission of Inquiry was taken almost immediately after the shootings with the activation of the lines of communication between the site of the massacre and the upper realms of central government. After discussions between Dr Hendrik Verwoerd, the Prime Minister, his Minister of Justice,

F C Erasmus, and other senior officials, an emergency Cabinet meeting was convened to decide on short and medium-term strategy to meet a situation which was, by any definition, a national crisis. Prior to the meeting there were hasty telephonic discussions to initiate immediate damage control procedures. These involved the Ministry of Bantu Administration and Development and senior police and military officials in Pretoria and in the Vaal itself. It was in the course of these discussions, which took place within an hour of the shootings, that the decision was taken to cordon off Sharpeville and limit public and media access. Thereafter the Minister met with his senior colleagues to devise ways and means to deal with the crisis.

The records of this and a number of subsequent Cabinet meetings are scant, but the decision to establish a Commission of Inquiry was almost certainly taken early on. It was clearly vital that the state be seen to be in full control of the situation and its aftermath – both in order to inhibit the wave of panic now sweeping the country and to head off any sympathy demonstrations and protests that could reasonably be expected in the wake of public reaction.

The white minority, international investors, and the black community had to be convinced that the state could act both decisively and effectively to take the situation in hand – and these issues, with security concerns at the centre, appear to have dominated the first deliberations. It was however also important that the mailed fist be encased in a velvet glove. Quite apart from the fact that in any other 'democratic' country it would be normal bureaucratic procedure to investigate the circumstances leading to an event like Sharpeville, it was important, both internally and externally, that some sort of inquiry be initiated. While the state had its own sources of information in its various security organs, any assessment of the massacre had to be made public if South Africa were to remain distinguishable from other authoritarian systems. Some senior officials in the state also suspected in the immediate wake of the massacre that what had taken place represented a breakdown in the communications system supportive of normal governance and, regardless of the tendency of some of their colleagues to write the event off as circumstantial, a simple 'mistake', or a 'black conspiracy', were determined that there be some sort of investigation of either an internal or public nature.

Since the SAP would inevitably shoulder the blame this was not an especially popular view in senior police circles, many of whose members either genuinely believed in conspiracy theories or saw the whole situation as a veritable 'night-of-long-knives' to be used by other interests in the state bureaucracy to settle scores with the police. Among these were the military who were scathing in their criticism of the role of police intelligence, the logistics, the strategic planning, and the whole police reaction to the Sharpeville crisis which, in their view, represented a perfect exercise in institutional mismanagement. Still, even the hard-liners in the police recognised that some sort of public investigation was politically necessary, and might even be tailored, under carefully circumscribed circumstances, to exonerate the SAP.

A public investigation was also dictated by a number of other considerations linked to political support-building among various constituencies in the domestic and foreign arena. While any commission of inquiry carried the risk of wholesale condemnation of the government and the whole apartheid system, such an exercise could also be turned to advantage in mobilising support for the ruling party. A pliant (or partially pliant) commission which confirmed the vicious intent of the Sharpeville mob and presented police responses as a natural, if over-reactive, case of self defence could connect very positively with the prevailing persecution mentality among white South Africans in the aftermath of the massacre – including many who would not, other than in these exceptional circumstances, lend their support to the Nationalist government. This was the view of a number of people close to Verwoerd who, looking on the 'bright side' of Sharpeville, saw it as a unique opportunity to build political capital and undercut the support base of the opposition United Party. Ultimately, a sympathetic commission – indeed any commission – was essential to smoothing the panic and fears of a vast array of international interests with stakes in a post-Sharpeville South Africa.

From the moment the shootings at Sharpeville were revealed to the world, human rights groups throughout South Africa, as part of their general anti-apartheid agenda, had launched a concerted campaign for the establishment of a public investigation into the tragedy. Like the ANC, members of such organisations as the Liberal Party and the Anglican Church realised that Sharpeville was a powerful lever for mobilising intensified pressure on the Nationalist government, both locally and, perhaps more importantly, in the foreign arena. Not that cynical calculations alone informed their agenda. Both Liberals and Anglicans were outraged by the official line that the victims had only themselves to blame for the tragedy that had befallen them and were quick on the scene to offer practical humanitarian assistance to the families of the dead and wounded.

Ambrose Reeves, viewed by the police as the 'radical leftist ecclesiastic' Bishop of Johannesburg, had been the driving force of the anti-apartheid Bishops Committee as early as 1958, and he now quickly emerged at the centre of a substantial local network which was determined, not unjustifiably, to exploit the massacre to the embarrassment of the government.[4] The Nationalists, on their part, were reluctant to offer a public apology for what had taken place, partially because contrition, they correctly calculated, would be politically manipulated by their opponents on the one hand, and taken as sign of political weakness by their supporters on the other. Sentimental as opposed to party support for the NP had actually increased as paranoia spread among the white minority in the immediate aftermath of the shootings, and in the circumstances the state saw no particular value in public displays of sympathy for the victims. This added fuel to the fire as far as the ANC and the liberal white opposition was concerned. While the former moved to upgrade popular resistance and protest, the latter moved towards the goal of a full, official and open public inquiry within which the exact circumstances of the massacre could be fully explored.

Within days of the tragedy, after consultation with some of the dependents of the victims, both living and dead, Reeves and like-minded people in the white liberal community moved towards this objective. In the course of doing so, communication was initiated with those elements of the ANC and PAC who represented the public face of these organisations and who had not yet gone to ground. From these discussions Reeves and his associates received a mandate to lobby for a public commission of inquiry, although both the ANC and the scatterlings of the PAC declined to be publicly associated with such a 'moderate' initiative in the face of rising demands from their own constituencies that they reassess the strategic value of continued passive resistance. Armed with this explicit support the Reeves group proceeded to recruit the very best legal team who could represent the civil rights of the deceased, the wounded and the survivors.

Government, as I have noted, had a double and difficult agenda. On the one hand the ultra-Right in the National Party such as the Minister of Bantu Administration and Development, De Wet Nel, were pressing for a firm hand in the form of no public apology and a state of emergency. Others in the ruling party however, including Dr Verwoerd, were disposed to a softer approach, at least in part because they were accountable to a wider global constituency of which South Africa was, at this point, desperately trying to maintain its membership. This would require bending to demands for an investigation – at least insofar as it was possible to hold an inquiry that would not condemn the security apparatus of the state unduly.

The result was a carrot-and-stick strategy with mass arrests and the State of Emergency as the stick. The SAP, as I have noted, had taken various covert measures to limit its liability and, in the circumstances, government believed that it could offer a commission as a carrot. Once this decision was taken, every effort was made to ensure the appointment from the ranks of the judiciary of a Commissioner who was tame but not suspiciously compliant. Such a judge, it was decided from the outset, must be capable of meeting the challenge posed by the intellectual and legal heavyweights whom Reeves and sympathisers were already in the process of recruiting.

Mr Justice PJ Wessels of the Natal Division of the Supreme Court was, in most respects, the man for the mission. Most senior members of the judiciary had already compromised themselves through collaboration with the apartheid state in the implementation of its legal grand design but Wessels had displayed a reasonable degree of independence in the face of the principle that the sovereignty of Parliament (where the Nationalists predominated) reigned supreme over the judicial branch of government. Wessels was however not considered, at least by government, an especially powerful personality who would pursue his own legal agenda at all costs.

The Wessels Commission of Inquiry into the disturbances at Sharpeville began on 12 April 1960. Its brief included examination of all the disturbances which had taken place in the Vaal on and around 21 March, since these were seen as intrinsically related to the shootings at Sharpeville. The legal team acting on behalf of the Bishop of Johannesburg, some victims and their dependents was composed of a formidable group of lawyers, (many of whom were later to become prominent both in South Africa and internationally. They included Mr AI 'Issy' Maisels QC and Sydney (now Sir Sydney) Kentridge (who would later catapult to global attention during hearings into the death of Black Consciousness leader, Steve Biko). Mr Rex Welsh and Mr Harold Hanson supplemented the team, along with Mr Chris Plewman, Mr HC Nicholas and Mr Michael Parkington. Kentridge began by cross-examining Sergeant JT Grobler, the policeman normally in charge of the Sharpeville Police Station who described graphically 'crowds armed with *kerries* and other weapons stoning the police in the Sharpeville location and surrounding them on the morning of 21 March this year'.

The exact proceedings of the Commission do not warrant detailed description here. Much of what emerged has been covered in earlier chapters. Its findings – that the crowd was hostile, that the police did nothing to inflame the crowd and acted in self defence on the basis of a possible skewed judgement following many hours of violence, that there was no actual attack, but might have been had the police not acted swiftly, are also of secondary importance, because substantial discrepancies exist between the evidence led before the Commission and that which has emerged in the forty years since its deliberations.

Generally speaking, much of the evidence heard by the Commission was sociologically weak and/or suffered from a number of lacunae whose nature has only been exposed with the passage of time. A great deal of the information on the critical question of the mood and intentions of the crowd was, in retrospect, fairly homogenised and simplistic as was the evidence led on police behaviour where many of the crucial underlying motives were left largely unexplored. The exact circumstances surrounding the actual shooting were never fully delved into, while the Commission, to its very end, avoided, circumvented, or lightly touched upon many of the important technical and brutal aspects of the killings – such as the type of ammunition used by the SAPS and the actions of the black police whom the SAP, in their official history of the events of the sixties, admit 'occasionally acted without self-restraint and in an undisciplined manner'.[5]

Many of these omissions could be put down to considerations of time rather than to conscious calculation. Like the Diemont Commission which considered the simultaneous disturbances at Langa, the Wessels Commission was obliged to produce a publicly palatable set of conclusions in a very short time. Still, its overall findings, read four decades later, are so densely unintelligible, so ridden with double-talk, qualifications, and refutable logic as to defy both legal reasoning and ordinary comprehension. On the important issue of the duration of the shooting, for example, Mr Justice Wessels found 'that some time elapsed before the shooting actually ceased' because 'not all the police began shooting at the same time'![6] Excessive space in his final assessment was devoted to the imminent danger facing the police, but very little was said, least of all admonitory, about why they had acted without orders. While the police were praised for assisting the wounded, nothing was said about their reluctance to do so, and the general circumstances in which their help was extended. Then there was an extraordinary incidence of evasive and mind-boggling double negatives. The learned judge decided 'that I could neither find that there had not been an attack at the gate, nor [he added] that there had in point of fact been an attack'.[7]

In his final summation attributing responsibility for the massacre, Justice Wessels was far harder on the police than the state had anticipated. The state and its security services were nevertheless not entirely unhappy with the pronouncements of the Commission which 'proved' (as they saw it) that allegations levelled against the SAP by Bishop Reeves and others were 'blatant lies and fabrications'. Reeves's book on Sharpeville was condemned as 'conspicuously prejudiced' or, in more polite moments, 'irrelevant' in the light of the Commission's findings. 'Even black members of the public,' it was noted with evident satisfaction in police circles, 'declined to purchase it'.[8] Ultimately the work of the Commission makes no sense unless it is seen in the context of the constraints within which it was operating.

Apartheid justice was based on a legal system which, in the words of one author, 'systematically favoured the state ... devised rules that turned suspects into convicts ... and moulded the rule of law to serve the role of the legal system in enforcing economic, political and racial oppression'.[9] Whether this was indubitably the case or not is beyond the scope of this study. Nonetheless, the Commission was a by-product of a set of political arrangements based on minority domination in all spheres of South African existence whose spirit and logic inevitably wove its insidious way into its workings. While the police were technically under observation for an act of gross public violence, this took place within the context of a system with an inbuilt presumption that black protest was unacceptable if not demonic. The notion that the police had not erred – or if they had they had done so under extreme provocation – was central to white psychology. The state, and even the more liberal mass media, had done nothing in the period after the massacre to damp down irrational minority urges and encourage a more balanced climate of opinion; indeed, both had, for their own institutional reasons, directly stirred up the escalating climate of white terror. This inevitably empowered the police and the state functionaries who could confidently walk into the white legal system virtually assured of little more than a sharp slap on the wrist. It also disempowered the defence, the survivors, and the black witnesses.

The state and its functionaries were all too willing to come forward and 'clear their names' but many important black witnesses were petrified of testifying about what they had done or seen for fear of retribution from the police, the PAC, or even their friends, neighbours and families and many who would have been vital could not be persuaded to hold forth in public through fear of a judicial system which they saw to be loaded against them. In the end the team acting on behalf of the victims could only a garner a few bit players, the black marginals to the massacre, who were willing to face the rigours of public interrogation.

A tiny handful of people survived both the passing of time and the Commission. Some did so because they were able to play the role imposed on them by the circumstances in which they found themselves 'playing the simpleton or feigning ignorance' as the price of maintaining personal and physical authenticity in an intimidating environment.[10] Andrew Mathonsi* clearly remembers being told by his friends to 'play the fool' as a survival mode once he had taken the momentous decision to testify. Petrus Mokoena* however speaks of how he was personally approached by Bishop Reeves to give evidence, despite the grave misgivings of his family. Thereafter followed the 'humiliation' of appearing in a legal process ostensibly created to assist him and his community. Forty years later he recalls the contemptuous and self confident smirking of police officers (in the gallery and in the witness box), the ominous atmosphere in the 'non-white' lavatories which he was forced to share with a number of 'bantoe konstabels' who had been at Sharpeville, the arrogant hectoring of the lawyers appearing for the state, 'as if I had done the killings', and the complex questions in Afrikaans that he could not understand. The police assumed as a matter of racial arrogance that the black witnesses would discredit themselves – as many indeed did with the entire weight of the social apparatus loaded against them. Ultimately, the responses of Petrus and the other black witnesses were reduced to a monosyllabic 'ja' or 'nee baas' – as intended by the logic of an investigation system that assumed the ingrained stupidity of all the 'non-white' witnesses.

The political culture that infused the proceedings interconnects with the political agendas of the major role players in the Commission. The state had presumed that a quick commission would carry a double advantage. It would send a message to the world about the deep concern of the South African government and, perhaps more importantly, it would undercut the case of the victims by forcing their lawyers to draw on witnesses who, if they could be persuaded to testify at all, would do so while they were still in a state of shock. The State of Emergency proclaimed even before the opening of the Commission capped this strategy – so much so that Reeves, his supporters, the victims and the legal team actually argued (at least in private) for the postponement of the public hearing until the dust had settled.

The problem of persuading witnesses to testify was aggravated by the police arrests within hours of the massacre which signalled that it would be unwise for anyone to come forward and condemn police behaviour, least of all under the spotlight of the Commission. The older members of the security police who have survived the ravages of time remember with some pride that 'we did not even have to use "kragdadigheid" [force, for which read torture] to get our case across'. This was partly because the moral degeneracy of apartheid had not reached the depths of later years when the physical abuse of political detainees was a virtually institutionalised and regular occurrence. It was sufficient for police operatives to circulate rumours throughout the Vaal among the bereaved families and friends of victims that those who testified would be remanded in custody as a 'precautionary measure', and that there would be no bail for anyone who 'lied' before the inquiry.

Judge Wessels's frequent assurances that nobody would be criminalised for what they said before the Commission were not powerful enough to counter these dubious messages, given physical expression, as they were, by dozens of arrests for public violence even as the Commission went though its deliberations. One result was a widespread public perception that the black residents who eventually appeared before the Commission had either been raked up by the state or by the PAC, to represent their particular interests.

In retrospect it appears that the PAC had a hand in this discrediting dynamic. Although many of its Vaal leaders were in prison or hiding by the time of the Commission's first sessions, those who remained had come to appreciate the political value of the Commission – if it could be convinced by a 'popular' account of events which would throw mud in the eye of the apartheid state. Part of the intimidation which took place in Sharpeville once it became known that a commission was on track had to do with the police dissuading people from coming forward, but part, the PAC part, had also to do with persuading people to testify once they had been schooled in a 'popular' line. In the event, the tussles that took place between black witnesses on either side were between two constituencies, each of whom conformed, in their different ways, to extraneously-determined political agendas.

None of this is to say that the entire small body of black witnesses were 'stooges' adhering to either a police or a PAC version of what had transpired. Neither the SAP nor the PAC had the educative capacity to ensure that 'their' witnesses conformed in every respect, and, in the great mass of evidence led before the Commission there are various points where the dividing line between witnesses for the two sides is fairly ambiguous, though the police witnesses, with rare exceptions, stood firmly behind the state-perpetuated view that the massacre was a matter of self-defence or some sort of mismanagement in a situation rendered impossible by uncompromising agitation. At many points the brilliance of Kentridge or Maisels cut like a knife through butter in dissecting police evidence, particularly that presented by SAP personnel who were still somewhat disoriented, or, in some cases, plain stupid.

Notwithstanding the institutional injunctions of their superiors conveyed in a series of briefings between the state's legal team, senior police leaders and the Sharpeville contingent prior to the opening of the Commission, many of the individual policemen could not withstand the rigours of high-pressure cross-examination. There were inconsistencies of evidence which the other side exploited with surgical precision, and many of the police leaving the Commission now recall doing so in a state of uncertainty and sheer exhaustion. Yet, for the most part, the SAP witnesses did not incriminate each other as would future generations before the Truth and Reconciliation Commission more than thirty-five years later, if only because they were, in the end, still part of a viable state structure which could guarantee jobs, careers, and a supportive network of professional and social identities. Unlike their later colleagues who were the product of a failed pattern of power relations, the SAP before Wessels could afford to smirk because of the still potent and rationalising ideologies within which they could encapsulate their actions. Ultimately, they would lie because they could not see beyond the narrow universe of apartheid, and should they lie, they would not be punished by the apartheid system.

And lie they did, as became plain with each interrogation by the lawyers for the community. Virtually every police witness was forced to concede that there had been no order to shoot. But none would admit to being the first to do so. Even though victims near the fence recall some sort of scream or other verbalisation in which the word 'skiet' (shoot) was heard in some form or another, this was ostensibly inaudible to every one of the police contingent. The police witnesses also brashly denied that any shots had emanated from the tops of the Saracens, because, they insisted, all the police were ground-based at the exact moment of the shootings. This position, which neatly coincided with the SAP case that they shot because of their assumption of an imminent and overwhelming danger that could not be evaluated by observation from ground-level, was dashed to smithereens when photographs were produced which clearly show police firing from atop the armoured carriers.[11] Photographs taken by the small group of journalists on the scene immediately after the massacre also show the police carrying sjamboks, despite persistent denials by police witnesses that their personnel either had or used whips of this type during the day and the night preceding the fateful demonstrations.

Police witnesses had no compunction whatsoever in fabricating and concealing evidence with an audacity that astounded the lawyers. Given their ability to seal the site of the killings almost instantaneously, the police had a monopoly over the forensic evidence which was, by today's standards, extremely primitive to begin with. Notwithstanding the excellence of the experts called by the lawyers for the community on such matters as the use of explosive bullets, it was the perpetrators who had had immediate access to the scene in a way which was to allow them hegemony over what was concealed and what was discovered – even by their own experts. Detective-Sergeant Fourie*, whose job it was to collect forensics along with his Vereeniging CID team, was warned off the site

of the killings by the security police when he appeared in Sharpeville late
in the afternoon of the fateful Monday. He was told, or so he recalls, that
'it was more important to find the subversives and make them confess
than all this scientific *krap*'. Contemporary police archives even today
contain piles of unanalysed forensic evidence (bullets extracted from the
dead and wounded) – neatly packaged in dusty brown paper envelopes
and closed with red sealing wax – which were either unknown or
unavailable to the Commission. The representatives of the victims and
their families were unable to cut through the bureaucratic barriers
purposely erected to inhibit access to vital forensic information – as befits
a system tainted by its subservience to the state. The legal team for the
community, its surviving members recall, was also under 'immense
pressure' from the public and the police some of whom, presaging the
later and more lethal years of total strategy, were not above issuing veiled
threats intended to intimidate them.

It was only the sheer brilliance of people like Kentridge and Maisels
that allowed them occasionally to overcome these impossible constraints.
In the end however, the wilful and blatant public attempts to skirt the
truth did not embarrass the state and its agents to the extent that the
critics had hoped – precisely because there were so few critics within
South Africa outside of the black community. The great majority of white
opinion inclined towards an excessively generous view of police behaviour
during both the massacre and the subsequent Commission. The pursuit
of justice was small stuff when the stakes were set by basic interests,
social privilege and access to state power. In the circumstances, the police
had over-reacted, panicked, misjudged, and might even be entitled to a
certain economy of truth when their actions were seen against the wider
backdrop of their role in protecting 'white civilisation'. On the part of
the black majority and the dependents of the victims very little was
anticipated from another creature of a white legal system that had worked
hand in glove with state oppression for longer than most cared to
remember.

The Commission was also damaged by the fact that it was nothing
more than a routine inquiry into an unfortunate set of politically

embarrassing circumstances. Whatever the public relations spinoff – for the state, the SAP or South Africa more globally – there was never any intention, at least on the part of the state, to bring functionaries to book or, as was to happen after democratisation, to trade amnesty for full disclosure. In the circumstances it took place in what was in some respects a political vacuum. Despite their individual and collective legal brilliance, the legal team representing the community could never quite escape the sense of demoralisation arising from the knowledge that the findings of the Commission, no matter how injurious to the state, would not shake apartheid. The police drew strength from the fact that they knew they were untouchable in the context of the times and, while the black witnesses were cowed and intimidated, they were self-assured and, in most cases, bluntly unyielding even under intense cross-examination. To many who survive today the Commission, called to investigate a major human rights violation, was little more than a gross inconvenience – ' a complete waste of time,' according to one of their number, 'when we should have been on the job of real policing'.

By its closing stages it was clear that the Commission was a mixed blessing for all the stakeholders. Although it did a fairly thorough job it did not, and could not, fulfil the expectations of the more vehement critics of apartheid and its multi-volumed findings played an important role in adding fuel to the fire of criticism of South Africa both foreign and domestic. Much depended on what different parties read into the findings. Viewed through the ideological spectacles of the South African government and its apartheid supporters, they appeared to exonerate the state. But seen from a more humanitarian perspective, the self-same pronouncements could also be interpreted as a general condemnation of the police and the system of social relations that their behaviour upheld. In the end the fundamentally ambiguous conditions in which the Commission functioned were echoed in its report. If nothing else, the Commission gave rise to the inherent duality which has surrounded the events at Sharpeville ever since.

It was also not the brief of the Wessels Commission to deal with the massive sociopsychological consequences of the massacre for the community. Unlike the Truth and Reconciliation Commission many decades later, its work took place within an environment of intensified apartheid whose unstated purpose was to demoralise the black population into submissive units in the grand scene of racial segregation. Although the events at Sharpeville played an important role in the transformation of passive resistance into armed struggle, in Sharpeville itself the impact of the killings was such that for many years the flame of freedom was to flicker very uncertainly. Towards the end of 1960 the media, in bizarre celebration, reported the birth of a number of 'Sharpeville babies'. These were the children of pregnant women, who had been wounded in March and then confined in hospital for lengthy periods. There was Puseloto Mahelo who son was born 'healthy and happy' despite his mother's wounds, and there was 'Cannon' Mnguni, named after the guns and born retarded, no doubt because of his mother's trauma.[12] Politically speaking however, the sixties were not a period of rebirth for Sharpeville. On the contrary, they were a decade of political silence during which the people who had witnessed the massacre, the victims, the survivors and their offspring, wrestled with a mixture of sadness and anger to come to terms with what had transpired. The SAP, in whose mind Sharpeville was a special place of political resistance, did not let up. Their brutal raids continued – with the survivors as their target.[13]

Much of the following decade was a period of collective depression for the entire community. Many of the older residents recount an almost palpable sense of disaster which seemed to pervade the whole atmosphere, seeping into the most intimate and private of social relations. Sharpeville may well have become famous and prominent on the international stage, but at home, in the small houses surrounding the massacre site, the streets were stained with blood – physically, for several weeks, and metaphorically for the years thereafter. Individual and collective psychoses of various sorts were widespread in an environment where many families had been broken by death, the loss of a breadwinner, or the harsh demands made on a poor household by the burdens of caring for a disabled member. Many of the elderly shrivelled into themselves in a manner that would remain largely undisturbed for the remainder of their lives, while many of the younger people turned to deviant forms of social behaviour. The tightly-knit cultural networks that had made Sharpeville a centre of excellence in sport and music during the fifties died away as many talented people left the community for greener pastures. In the long-standing struggle for superiority between Sharpeville and Soweto, be it in soccer, boxing, art or criminality, the latter shifted to prominence as the former simply faded away.

The enormous sense of loss and disorientation was compounded by the apartheid state to whom the very existence of Sharpeville represented a threat of global political proportions. Although ruthless action nationally and regionally after the massacre had stifled the possibility of further political protest (at least in the short term), the internationalisation of the shootings had led to the emergence of a martyrology which threatened the national interest. Though the findings of the Commission did not undermine the state, which remained resilient if mildly damaged, it was important from the perspective of the government that the memory of Sharpeville disappear as quickly as possible. This involved a two-pronged approach. In the short term it was important to reinforce state propaganda that the people of Sharpeville were anything but the naïve and innocent community with which humanitarians world wide had begun to identify. In the longer term, it was important to wipe Sharpeville off the political map by eliminating it physically.

The groundwork for the first project had already been laid during the emergency Cabinet meetings held within hours of the shooting and by the rapid movement of the police into the streets and hospitals to detain anyone who appeared to have any links whatsoever to the originating demonstrations and arraign several dozen of them on charges of public violence. Unfortunately for the state, most of the more significant members of the local PAC and ANC structures had successfully gone to ground with the declaration of the State of Emergency so that the majority of those who appeared before the courts were insignificant and (for the most part) patently innocent individuals against whom it was difficult to secure convictions. Confronted with a similar problem to that which faced the Commission – of eliciting witnesses – the prosecution experienced considerable difficulty in making its case. In the end, to the consternation of the state, the few individuals sentenced to short terms of imprisonment on charges of public violence failed to portray Sharpeville to a wider outside audience as an intrinsically violent community.

In the circumstances, the physical eradication of Sharpeville became a priority. Vastly underestimating the power of remembrance, and naïve in their view that out of sight was out of mind, the national and regional authorities began to campaign for the dismantling of the community and the forced removal of its inhabitants. Even prior to the massacre, the principle of concentrating the black people of the Vaal into one super-location amenable to better control and extraction of labour had been discussed in terms of national legislation. The massacre and the security concerns generated thereafter fuelled this policy, and within weeks of the killings arrangements were beginning to be made for the elimination of the township and the redistribution of its residents into the wider pool of anonymous 'Bantu' in the region. The area today called Sebokeng had been designated as the site for this removal prior to 1960 and it was to this new concentration point that the people of Sharpeville were to be taken and then, hopefully, forgotten.

For a variety of reasons not excluding the financial costs and political opprobrium associated with this policy, the destruction of Sharpeville did not take place. There were some last-ditch attempts by the municipality to at least obliterate the public visibility of the massacre by Africanising the name of the township. Kotisephelo ('place of rest') was one name suggested to the Vereeniging Council which garnered some support, but the suggestion was laid quietly aside as the ironies struck home so the community continued to endure as 'Sharpeville'. For fifteen years or so after the massacre immigrants from rural areas to the Vaal region were systematically steered by the influx control regulations towards Sebokeng or Evaton, and this had the effect of limiting population growth to the reproductive capacity of the people who had been in the area since 1960. Even with the declining capacity of these laws to channel the movements of 'illegals' by the mid-seventies, many migrants forced from the land into the Vaal townships chose to avoid

Sharpeville because of the not unfounded belief that it was subject to intense surveillance by the authorities as a result of its turbulent history. Given the greater level of diversification which came with the growth of Sebokeng, Evaton and even nearby Bophelong, employment and other economic opportunities were relatively better in these larger townships and their size, to some extent, made close scrutiny by the police and local officials most difficult.

In the first decade after the massacre, when the continued physical survival of Sharpeville was under consideration, it made no sense to promote socio-economic development there. The enthusiasm of the Vereeniging Council for its 'model' black township appears to have died along with the victims of the slaughter, and for many years thereafter, there was little sustained effort by the local state to upgrade the environment apart from a brief spurt of administrative and developmental activity in the first few months after March 1960. Then, no doubt motivated by the need to head off further disturbances if nothing else, the local authorities introduced a number of minor policy reforms which, in their interpretation, had fuelled some of the conditions which had caused it.

It was not until plans for the transfer of Sharpeville to Sebokeng had been effectively laid to rest that any further efforts of any substance were made to alleviate social conditions in Sharpeville. By the late sixties the Vereeniging Council had come to the belated conclusion that it had a place of international significance which was, for many observers, a reference point against which to measure its administrative performance. While apartheid tourism was not on the cards – nor, for that matter was any developmental agenda that violated the cardinal postulates of grand apartheid at the time – there was, in more enlightened municipal circles, a restorative vision in terms of which Sharpeville would be returned once again to its former glory. By the early seventies a number of Vereeniging councillors and officials harked back to the Sharpeville prototype of a 'model Bantu township', and to the extent that this was endorsed by central government personnel in the township itself, there was a spate of developmental activity over a period of a decade. This resulted in some significant improvement in physical conditions which had the added advantage of taking the political edge off a community that was beginning to shake off the aftershock of its devastating experience.

By the end of the seventies a number of developments were also beginning to fuel the various forces that were to take apartheid into its terminal phase – although this was not necessarily evident at the time. At national level, the 1976 disturbances in Soweto had revitalised the forces of popular resistance as thousands of young people went into political exile and then joined the ranks of the liberation armies of either the ANC or the PAC. With the development of the United Democratic Front (UDF) as the internal wing of the ANC, the state was increasingly under pressure to broaden its constituency beyond the white minority – and sought to do so with the creation of a new Constitution which extended limited political rights to South African Indians and Coloureds in the central government sphere through the new Tricameral Parliament. The more difficult task of building legitimacy among the African population remained unresolved given their exclusion from this body. Nor did the new Constitution satisfy the global community where international sanctions against the Republic gained momentum. Within the armed forces a reappraisal of the sustainability of apartheid was initiated as part of a wider dialogue within the state about how to maintain the system within the framework of white domination.

Most of these developments were deflected down to local level and, in places such as Sharpeville, where apparent serenity had reigned for the decade and a half after 1960, both the ANC and PAC had been covertly active in remobilising the community. In the beginning they came up against the fear and exhaustion that followed the massacre, as well as the tight security arrangements designated for the Vaal after 'the troubles'.

These included the rigid implementation of the mounting corpus of security legislation – bannings, arrests, detention without trial, torture – indeed, the entire armoury of a police state determined to stamp out all but the most limited forms of political opposition. The campaign served its purpose in producing resentful compliance, and few could resist the powerful mixture of coercion and positive sanctions that formed the basis of the state's policy of counter-revolutionary 'total strategy' as South Africa moved into the late-seventies. Nonetheless, a flicker of resistance remained, particularly among the youth, after the 1976 Soweto uprising.[14] Some of the sons and daughters of the massacre generation joined their counterparts from Soweto and other townships in exile across the borders. Given the historic connection between the Vaal and Lesotho, this almost always meant heading for Maseru into the ranks of the PAC and its armed wing, APLA. Others, activists who remained behind, waited for the turn of events to create islands of opportunity in the sea of political repression.

The space for regenerated popular action began to emerge in the early eighties when many of the forces that had been mounting in the run up to the demonstrations of 21 March emerged once more to fuel discontent. These included a sudden decline in social conditions, the emergence of a new generation of young people both willing and able to bear the costs of confrontation with the state and, perhaps above all, the collapse of local government institutions despite state attempts to upgrade segregated black municipalities to legal and administrative equality with their white counterparts.[15] The Soweto uprising had initially been a protest against inferior Bantu Education and, from the early eighties, the Sharpeville schools, along with some of the Catholic and Anglican churches, became designated sites of struggle for the production of leadership, the development of community organisations, and the articulation of strategy for deployment against apartheid. The post-massacre generation had by now come of age and moved towards the mobilisation of the local population. Closer links were forged between students and workers in the area while within most Sharpeville schools the older and more conservative teachers were politically emasculated in favour of militant student bodies such as the Congress of South African Students (COSAS) and Azanian National Youth Unity (AZANYU), variously affiliated with the ANC, the PAC or the Azanian People's Organisation (AZAPO), all of whom reached back to evoke the massacre in the process of popular support-building.[16] Sharpeville was not in the vanguard of black communities in confrontation with the state: its internal balance of obedience to revolt (insofar as is measurable) was not distinguishably different from that of similarly repressed, depressed, or otherwise disadvantaged areas of the Republic.[17] Its population was not distinguishably less willing to absorb the social costs of mounting unemployment and decreased standards of living that negatively impacted on black townships nationwide with the birth of the eighties. Nor is there any reason to believe that popular tolerance of the cost and inferior standard of housing was any more intensely felt in Sharpeville than in other communities whose rents and rates boycotts had begun to reach their boiling apogee by the mid-eighties. What Sharpeville had however – what distinguished it from even the most volatile townships of the Eastern Cape – was a martyrology. It was this – seeded in the schools, germinated in the community, nurtured by economic, political and educational grievance, and watered by memory, that ultimately thrust Sharpeville to the spearhead of the growing number of communities in protest against a dying political system.

The rapid and mass dissemination of 'struggle' ideology that catapulted people from quiescence to resistance took place, in Sharpeville as elsewhere, at the very time that the state-sponsored Community Councils were rendered incapable, unwilling or simply too corrupted by enmeshment with the patron-client networks spawned by apartheid to respond.[18] The Community Councils had been the response of the state to the 1976 uprising. Their creation as representative structures was intended to replace the redundant mass of decades-old advisory boards and Urban Bantu Councils which had fallen into disrepute through inactivity and compliance with the apartheid regime. It was intended that they would take on some of the executive powers of the local Administrative Boards which functioned in tandem with black municipal structures in the townships and, through the management of housing policy designed to meet the desperate needs of local communities, co-opt at least a section of the township population.[19] This was the theory. In practice the new municipal organisations were no less incompetent and no more receptive to grassroots social demands than their predecessors. The Lekoa Town Council, embracing Sharpeville, Boipatong, Evaton and Sebokeng, was not armed with enough financial muscle to back its mandate. Its source of revenue was the old native revenue accounts which its members, like their predecessors, milked with enthusiasm. Since the state was reluctant to create new forms of financial support the inevitable result was that by 1982 the whole community council system in the Vaal, as well as in many other areas such as the Eastern Cape, had all but decomposed – to the point of immobilisation or, in many cases, total collapse.

In a desperate attempt to revitalise them, the government decided in 1992 to further upgrade all these institutions to euphemistically named Black Local Authorities (BLAs) with increased powers and responsibilities to work with a Department of Bantu Administration and Development that had, over the years progressively reinvented itself into an ostensibly more benign Department of Cooperation and Development.

Unfortunately for the state, the whole system of black municipal administrations had been so fundamentally compromised and illegitimated by this point that even had these new black municipal institutions been armed with appropriate administrative and financial means to carry out their brief under a new banner, they would have remained generally unacceptable to the majority of township inhabitants. The die was cast, and the 1983 elections for the new BLAs in the Vaal failed to activate a population now sceptical of cosmetic political appearances. The inevitable result was that for much of the next eighteen months the region, along with many other township areas facing the false promises of black self-rule at local level, experienced a dangerous melange of intermittent labour stayaways and rent and consumer boycotts sustained, in most cases, by popular protests against rising rents and service charges levied by the unpopular new local authorities desperate for funds. In a manner reminiscent of 1976, adolescents (and even pre-adolescents) were prominent in the vanguard of protest as the struggle was taken from the streets into the schools under the banner of 'liberation before education'.

In the Vaal itself matters came to a head in September 1984 in a series of disturbances which flowed from the rent boycott centred on

Sharpeville, diffused into the volatile nearby townships, and were, unlike those of 1960, unequivocally violent. During the last weeks of August Sharpeville embarked upon a total and indefinite rent boycott when the Regional Council spurned a delegation of Vaal residents urging alleviation of their social conditions. With mobs surrounding the offices of the Sharpeville Administration Board the Vereeniging Town Council eventually agreed to lower rentals in line with national tendencies, but this failed to placate the crowds who demanded the resignation of the entire local council in accordance with the intentions of the activists to render the community both 'liberated' and ungovernable.[20] On 3 September, South Africa's 'bloodiest day since the 1976 Soweto riots'[21], the regional morning bus service was brought to a halt in a grim prelude to the carnage that was to follow. Dozens of people were hacked to death and burnt alive in an orgy of violence that surprised even the most hardened members of the SAP's reaction units and riots squads. As rampaging mobs led by activist youths released years of pent-up anger and frustration on apartheid 'collaborators', the uniform police, backed up by counter-insurgency units called in from further afield, desperately tried to avert mounting disorder and the spread of the demonstrations into nearby 'white' Bedworth Park. This initially involved the use of the 'soft' means of riot control that might have averted the disaster of 1960, but then when these failed, the live bullets began to fly. While the security forces moved into the volatile schools, to stem what one senior police officer later described as 'the most violent riots in my entire career'[22], the gathering crowds zeroed in on members of the Community Council and other township officials whose ill-gotten gains were burnt in a purgative orgy of fire and destruction that eventually consumed the chairman of the Lekoa Town Council, the much-despised Esau Mahlatsi, and the Mayor of Sharpeville and two other councillors, all of whom were either hacked or stoned to death.[23]

Twenty-five of the thirty-five councillors of the Lekoa-Vaal municipal authority, of which Sharpeville was a member, had their houses destroyed or damaged. An estimated R30m to R50m of state and private property allegedly owned by local councillors was torched or damaged in a conflagration that testified to the changing character and intensity of anti-apartheid protest in the two-and-a-half decades since 1960.[24]

The decision by the authorities to establish political links with the conservative, socially marginalised and politically erratic Zulu inhabitants of the local hostels in the process of restoring control stoked an already atrocious situation. The result was mass destruction and death of a magnitude unprecedented in the experience either of Sharpeville or of the abutting townships. Thirty-one people died on the first day of the 'insurrection', a further sixty in the first month, and another sixty as violence puttered on in ebbs and flows until the end of 1984[25]. Much of this developed a tragic momentum that went beyond politics per se: behind the makeshift barricades of burning tyres and concrete blocks erected to impede the police, many innocent people who were not proven 'collaborators' lost their lives and property in a vortex of indiscriminate and liquor-fuelled violence that quickly turned to looting and random arson whose physical testimony remains to this day. Yet world opinion was inclined to pardon this moral lapse, this blot on the historical landscape of a community with so ravaged a past. For the most part, the 1984 popular uprising was glamourised and celebrated and its excesses simply airbrushed out with the notion that what took place was a natural culmination of events set in train so many years before.[26] As in 1960, the mass mobilisation of the mid-eighties saw the intensification of international pressure on apartheid even as the South African state moved to higher levels of 'total strategy' in implementing its counter-revolutionary agenda on a nation-wide basis.[27]

The Vaal disturbances stemmed in the immediate instance from an explosive mixture of socio-economic and political resentments that were not dissimilar to those that had existed in the region more than twenty-five years before. To many however, the 1984 violence had a closer relationship to the events of that March Monday in 1960. Enos Mahlangu*, one of the massacre survivors, recalls that many of the older generation saw a direct link between 1960 and 1984. Looking back on those dangerous September days, 'all of us knew it would come to this ... that our suffering would be carried through by the next generation'.

Having said that, however, not everyone enthusiastically and un-ambiguously endorsed the agenda of the 'comrades' with their emphasis on rendering the community eminently ungovernable as a precursor to dismantling apartheid. There is a tradition of analysis of political development in Sharpeville which echoes a wider tendency to crudely consign everyone who did not vigorously participate in the unrest of the mid-eighties to the ranks of 'vigilantes' who opposed the popular will by rendering support to the state security forces and retrograde social elements in the defence of vested interests.[28] South Africa, not unlike contemporary France, has still to come to terms with the tricky ethical and practical problems of whom amongst its historically disadvantaged did (or did not) 'collaborate'. Yet, as in 1960, there were different conceptions of political participation, dissimilar reserves of personal and collective courage and, in the end, many carefully nuanced political agendas within the overall framework of antipathy to apartheid. There were many reasonable, civically minded people and otherwise decent members of the Vaal black population – be it in Evaton, Sebokeng or Sharpeville – who reached back to the reigning principles of resistance that had preceded the massacre twenty-five years earlier, and who were aghast at the recurrence of the mutually reinforcing brutality between people and police in 1984.

While they shared the concerns about deteriorating social conditions and the long-standing racial restrictions imposed by apartheid on the community, many could not fully condone the choice of unmitigated armed struggle in preference to a resolution of South Africa's outstanding conflicts through a negotiated settlement with the minimum of violence. Few of the angry young men on the burning streets were sufficiently sensitive to debate the complex ethics of revolutionary warfare, but some – indubitably older and more experienced – recognised the situation of 'dual power' that had clearly begun to emerge during the last half dozen years of apartheid. They saw (or say they saw) that the state could not eradicate its opponents, yet they could not, in turn, overthrow the state. The state might (as it did in 1984) detain a thousand people in the Vaal, it might teargas and baton-charge people at political funerals, or it might suborn Inkatha Freedom Party (IFP) vigilantes to dispense rough justice that would culminate in the horrendous Boipatong massacre ten years later. But, in the end, it was locked into a stalemate where it could not eliminate popular dissidence except at the expense of enormous structural damage to the long-term political economy. Still, much of this was lost at the community grassroots where peer pressure was strong and the militants could draw strength and inspiration from the equality of violence embracing both protestors and police. The 'comrades' had also partially institutionalised their efforts at mobilisation and popular government through the creation of multi-purpose community-wide street committees modelled along similar networks created in other townships at the instigation of the UDF. The aim of these bodies was to symbolise an alternative government arising from an emerging power symbiosis between state and people. At a more practical level, the street committees were to act as an early warning system against police intrusion in the township, and, not least of all, to enforce political compliance.

Many of these issues of passive versus active resistance, freedom of expression in conditions of civil unrest, the relations between fence-sitters, collaborators and militants, were brought into sharp focus in the case of the so-called 'Sharpeville Six' – five men and a woman whose arrest, trial and death sentence for the murder of local Councillor Dlamini, who had unwisely chosen to fire into the inflamed mob on the first day of the uprising, called into question many of the delicate issues of individual and collective participation in the struggle against apartheid. Since the conviction of 'the Six' was rooted in the dubious principle of 'common purpose' which was condemned as reprehensible throughout the international community, their behaviour during the disturbances, including such key issues as whether they had organised, led or instigated the mobs to kill and burn (which they claimed they did not), was essentially irrelevant. Ultimately, in a judgement which further cemented the link between the memory of Sharpeville and the ongoing international struggle for human rights, they were found guilt by virtue of their mere presence at a site where gross criminal acts were committed. Perhaps more importantly in Sharpeville itself, the effect of the judgement was to politically reinforce the message of the activists that no-one could remain neutral, aloof or otherwise uninvolved in the ongoing struggle. The outcome of the case against 'the Six' was to raise political consciousness in Sharpeville to even greater heights. After the conclusion of the case the enforced silence woven around public expressions of reservations about the legitimacy of popular warfare was redoubled. Henceforth, the political militants in the township occupied the commanding heights of the ongoing campaign to administer a final *coup de grâce* to a tottering apartheid.

Fortunately the fate of the condemned was entwined with the twilight days of the system. The violence of the mid-eighties clearly indicated the political limits of state policy to entrench white rule through a mixture of adjustments in the labour market, cosmetic reforms to black local government and the promotion of a compliant black bourgeoisie.[29] Sharpeville ranked high on the nation-wide list of townships rendered 'ungovernable' as the death-knell tolled for apartheid. The end was designated by the decision of the state in February 1990 to lift political restrictions on the banned ANC, PAC and SACP, and in the climate of impending democratisation 'the Six' were eventually pardoned.

Democratisation also witnessed the creation of the Truth and Reconciliation Commission which devoted a small proportion of its hearings to the Sharpeville massacre. By this time, though, most of the protagonists, both guilty and innocent, had disappeared from the historic stage and Sharpeville did not figure significantly within the huge panorama of state-initiated atrocities which became the investigative terrain of the Commission. Despite its stature and significance in 20th Century South African history, Sharpeville receives short shrift in the gargantuan findings of the Commission on the crimes against human rights committed under apartheid.

POSTSCRIPT

A short time before the massacre, the British Prime Minister, Harold Macmillan, had, in his address to the South African Parliament in Cape Town, spoken of the 'wind of change' sweeping the African continent. The speech had not gone down well with Afrikaner Nationalists, ever sensitive to slights from their former colonial master. Macmillan was labelled condescending and was considered to be interfering with South African sovereignty. If winds of change were indeed blowing, Sharpeville was a tornado for everybody concerned – for the South African state, for its black opposition and, not least, for an international community some of whose members had been forced by South Africa's membership of the British Commonwealth and the community of nations to stifle their criticism of apartheid. While apartheid might have been a blot on the nation prior to Sharpeville, South Africa still enjoyed a fairly high level of international good standing.

The massacre was, however, not a 'stand-alone' event. On the contrary, it was, in many respects, a grisly manifestation of what had been taking place for years behind the more polite face of racial segregation. Langa, the teeming Cape Town township, erupted simultaneously and, to the horror of the South African government, an estimated 30 000 anti-apartheid demonstrators appeared before the gates of Parliament.

As these 'winds of change' diffused, Sharpeville became the essential reference point for world attitudes towards the South African system. Though nobody could conceivably justify the tragedy, in the so-called 'developed' nations of the industrialised West – the United States, Britain and Europe – Sharpeville did not at first evoke a deeply emotional reaction among elder statesmen who were either sensitive to or sought political shelter behind the provisions of the United Nations Charter which guaranteed states the virtually unfettered right to determine their domestic affairs. President Eisenhower was one of these. Many of them, with memories of Jan Smuts and South Africa's participation in the war effort against Hitler, could not be persuaded to believe that Sharpeville was the thin edge of the wedge of a regime determined to protect itself by genocide if necessary.

Yet even in the most polite and pragmatic of circles, the nature of what had taken place at Sharpeville shook established concepts of what white South Africa and its Afrikaner rulers were about. The international press rapidly fuelled the constituencies to which the Western leaders were responsible, and under their pressure no leader of any stature could avoid commenting. In the end, the sheer horror of what had taken place, as portrayed through the media, called for condemnation of some sort from virtually every leader of every major democratic system.

For the leaders of the less 'developed' world, particularly the African and Afro-Asian states, determined to forge a political bloc out of the iniquities of colonialism and neo-imperialism, Sharpeville provided a political meeting point around which the members of the so-called Bandung Group of 1956 could muster. Although some of the elder statesmen of the West could cynically dismiss these expressions of abomination as histrionics designed to serve narrow political purposes, these outcries were the start of what was to become a global movement to isolate South Africa – within a matter of months from the Commonwealth and, with the passing of the years, from the political, economic, military and cultural mainstream of the world community. Sharpeville may well have been the beginning of the end of apartheid.

What then of Sharpeville today? Relative to enormous urban concentrations such as Soweto or Sebokeng, it remains a small township – a mere 'stain on the map' – compacted by the memory of a collective disaster.[30] While the passing of the years has seen a degree of immigration that has fuelled social diversity, Sharpeville has, since 1960, never attracted many of the masses of people moving from South Africa's rural areas to its cities. Among those South Africans who have heard of the place, be they itinerant travellers, passers-by or black migrant workers, the name still conjures up visions of a place of violence best avoided. Most of the people in Sharpeville today were born there,[31] and, forty years later, remain variously united in common remembrance among the debris of the past and last month's uncollected litter.

I have touched on some aspects of Sharpeville's bleak physical environment which is, in most respects, little different from that of other historically disadvantaged black communities. Like its counterparts, Sharpeville has partially benefited to some extent from the Reconstruction and Development Programme of the new democratic government, but perhaps less so than other areas of the Vaal region because of its PAC associations (or so the stalwarts of the PAC suggest). Almost ten years after the transition and amid plans for a national memorial that it is hoped will revitalise this profoundly important historical site, the social decay inherited from apartheid remains in grim evidence.

In 1960 there were few substantial structures other than the already aged one-story stucco houses behind which people desperately sought shelter from the killing fire from the police station on that hot Monday. Today, there are still very few double-story buildings among the sea of squat, old and now even more dilapidated houses. While few new people have arrived, many have left, and in their search for upwardly-mobile and personal betterment have gravitated away from the economically-deteriorating Vaal region to the ostensibly more opportune township areas of the Central Witwatersrand nearer to Johannesburg.

Sharpeville, its inhabitants sometimes say, has a spirit derived from its sad history, which sets it apart from the vast, anonymous and deadly artificial townships of the Vaal. Sharpeville is not Sebokeng with its urban geography of pastel box-type houses and zones which attest both to apartheid planning and, more latterly, the RDP. In some respects the very shabbiness of Sharpeville with its decayed old houses predating the RDP by decades, lends it a far more human quality – albeit a humanity infused with a spirit of sadness. To some extent this has been reinforced over the decades by inter-generational transfer: there is virtually no-one, barring the toddlers, who cannot accurately identify the date of Black Monday (as some still call it). 'We try to forget and reconcile,' says Segametsi Mahkhanya who witnessed the killings and saw the police 'putting knives and stones into the hand of dead people', but, he adds, 'it isn't going well'.[32] Although the vicissitudes of time have rendered the young less knowledgeable about the exact dynamics of the massacre, there is still an almost palpable sense, embracing all the ages, that Sharpeville is special, in the vanguard of the anti-apartheid struggle – if only by selective accident.[33] Behind this lies the multiple and cascading facets of a community that has experienced disaster, be it by natural or social catastrophe. The collective fear that cocooned the people and forced them back in on themselves in the traumatised immediate aftermath of the massacre has been healed to a large extent by the passing of the years. The police repression of the early sixties in which Sharpeville was singled out for special treatment is no longer. Curiously enough, some survivors suggest, the state persecution visited upon those who even dared to speak of the massacre in the thirty years that followed it may even have had a therapeutic effect.[34]

Still, Sharpeville remains what Pierre Nora has aptly described as a 'laboratory of remembrance' within which the long-term symptoms of mass stress disorder are still evident among those to whom this day remains a defining point in their existential history.[35] For them the 'sociology of atrocity', explored in all its intricate facets by many leading intellectuals such as Halbwachs, is infinitely more than an academic curiosity or mere intellectual abstraction.[36] Survivors of what is still simply referred to by some as 'the tragedy' still gather weekly to provide important testimony and mutual support. Many of their increasingly elderly and depleted numbers, bearing both the physical and emotional scars of that fateful Monday, still speak of the enduring sense of menace, the nightmares and the feelings of anger against those who 'collaborated' then and afterwards with the apartheid state. Even though that state has been swept deservedly into what Trotsky once described as 'the rubbish heap of history' and despite the ravine of time separating then and now they cannot forget the loss of friends and family.[37] The night vigils still occasionally take place as they did in the worst days after the slaughter, when 'people would sit down for an entire night and speak about the lost one, honour his or her memory, sing hymns and pray till dawn.'[38]

The perpetrators do not engage in similar commemorative practices if only because, as historic losers, they wish to forget the moral depravity of friends, family and colleagues who supported the apartheid order. This does not mean that March 1960 is not equally seared on their sub-conscious in their more private moments: they, like their victims, do not live apart from what one scholar has termed 'the afterlife of political events'.[39] Among the simulated memories and stylised remorse there is often genuine regret and emotion. 'It [Sharpeville] never entirely leaves me,' says a man who was a young constable, a senior police officer and then a successful businessman. He has collected many documents relating to what was for him, a defining moment. The yellow and fragile papers ensconced in dusty cardboard boxes behind the lawnmower and other accoutrements of normal suburban existence in his Vereeniging garage, are of no consequence to the grandchildren who play beside the swimming pool on the lush green lawns a five-minute drive and forty years from the scene of the slaughter..

The PAC in Sharpeville is a political and historic remnant which may, in time, once more resurrect to meet the call of the 'masses', but has, at this point, been depleted, in people, ideological substance and the rewards of power by successive defections to the ruling ANC. Much of its residual strength lies in its cultural but politically-loaded appeal to 'Afrika', and much of this turns on its role, however ambiguous, in what some analysts have termed the 'mobilising myths' of Sharpeville that lie behind political power.[40]

Internationally too, the memory and historic identity of Sharpeville as a small but defining moment in the history of human relations remains strong and vital. Although many of the great atrocities of the past century – the holocausts, genocides, mass murders and ethnic cleansing – vastly supersede in their sheer horrific scale what happened at Sharpeville, the name Sharpeville has a universalism and poignancy of its own that continue to reverberate in the consciousness of most knowledgeable people.

Sharpeville has come full circle since the decision to demolish Topville township and the sadly successive events that characterise its history –

the massacre, the uprising of the eighties, and the more personal agonies suffered by the 'Sharpeville Six' in their quest for justice. It was in recognition of the fact that Sharpeville in many ways typifies the pathway of South Africa from racial oligarchy to open democracy that the country's first democratic Constitution was signed into being by President Mandela at the George Thabe Stadium in 1996, just a few hundred metres from the site of the massacre. His words on that austere occasion were both suggestive and instructive in a way which reinforces the dramatic and enduring symbolism of Sharpeville as a martyred township.

Unfortunately, little of this is reflected at the massacre site itself where only a small and ugly knee-high stone dedicated to the victims bears witness. Laid by Mandela in the course of his visit, it is directly opposite the Mafube Bottle Store which forms part of the small complex of dilapidated shops where terrified victims of the slaughter desperately sought shelter on a terrible day in March 1960.

At the nearby Sharpeville cemetery there is equally little to commemorate a place that signifies, in its own particular way, the victimisation of people under apartheid. The politically useful rhetoric about Sharpeville has been indispensable in keeping the memory alive, but precious little has been done to concretise the massacre in commemorative terms. A major national museum is on the drawing boards, but this will have to surmount the politically thorny problem of who 'owns' the memory of Sharpeville. It is far easier to memorialise the deaths of soldiers than civilians or to testimonialise the past to suit the agendas of the those with power in the present. Until then, most of the graves in the existing cemetery will remain in decay, with stones that have tumbled into the overgrown grass. Those that remain defiantly erect have mostly lost their inscriptions to the ravages of time and weather. At the local municipal offices, a largely burnt-out shell in testimony to the violent history of the area, the tattered Natives Cemetery Register is worked through by the occasional tourist en route to the graveyard or the notorious police station further westwards along Seeiso Street and up the hill. The pages are worn thin and scarred by the innumerable thumb prints of friends, relatives of the deceased, administrative *apparatchicks*, the morbid, and the simply curious. At the entry point, March 1960, are several pages of now largely illegible names carefully inscribed in once dark blue ink by some long-forgotten apartheid functionary. Unlike the numberless names of those who died of disease, old age or the other normal causes which take their toll on humanity, there is one single collective entry, italicised over several pages. These people, we are told – sadly and anonymously – 'perished by gunshot wound'. Such is the landscape of memory.

NOTES

INTRODUCTION

1 Most massacres have this dramatic characteristic. See Mark Levene and Penny Roberts (eds), *The Massacre in History* (New York: Berghahn Books, 1999), p 26.

2 Quoted from Ambrose Reeves's, classic study, *Shooting at Sharpeville: The Agony of South Africa* (London: Victor Gollancz, 1960), p 154.

3 See Benjamin Pogrund, *How Can Man Die Better: The Life of Robert Sobukwe* (Johannesburg: Jonathan Ball Publishers, 1990), p 37.

4 Andrew Ward, *Our Bones Are Scattered: The Cawnpore Massacre and the Indian Mutiny of 1857* (New York: Heny Holt & Co, 1996), p xvii.

5 Primo Levi, *The Drowned and the Saved*. Introduction by Paul Bailey (London: Abacus Books, 1989), p vi.

6 Ibid, p 10.

7 Ward, ibid.

8 See Sarah Farmer, *Martyred Village: Commemorating the 1944 Massacre at Oradour-sur-Glane* (Berkeley: University of California Press, 1999). This is one of a number of classic and more recent studies on which I have drawn which deal with the complex issue of recapturing social memory, and in particular the memorialisation of historic atrocity. See, in addition, Maurice Halbwacht's seminal work, *Les Cadres sociaux de la memoire* (Paris: Libraire Felix Alcan, 1925); Lawrence Langer, *Holocaust Testimonies:The Ruins of Memory* (New Haven: Yale University Press, 1991); Henry Rousso, *The Vichy Syndrome: History and Memory in France Since 1944* (Cambridge: Harvard University Press, 1991); James E Young, *Writing and Rewriting the Holocaust: Narrative and the Consequences of Interpretation* (Bloomington: Indiana University Press, 1988).

PART ONE

1   Matthew Chaskalson. The Road to Sharpeville: A History of Vereeniging's African Township in the Fifties. Seminar Paper, African Studies Institute, University of the Witwatersrand, Johannesburg, 1986, p 10. See also Tom Lodge, *Black Politics in South Africa Since 1945* (Johannesburg: Ravan Press, 1983), pp 205-206.

2   See T Shakinovsky. The Local State in Crisis: The Shaping of the Black Working Class, Vereeniging, 1939-49. Honours Dissertation, Department of History, University of the Witwatersrand, 1984, pp 36-8.

3   Ian Jeffrey. Cultural Trends and Community Formation in a South African Township: Sharpeville, 1943-85. Master's Dissertation, Department of Anthropology, University of the Witwatersrand, Johannesburg, 1991, p 53. Nt 37.

4   Ibid, nt 38.

5   Chaskalson, p 10; Lodge, p 206.

6   Chaskalson, p13.

7   Jeffrey, p 154.

8   Chaskalson, p 13.

9   Jeffrey, vi.

10   Ibid, p 154.

11   Chaskalson, p 13.

12   Ibid, p 12. See also *Vereeniging News* (Vereeniging), 19 January 1954.

13   Jeffrey, p 155.

14   Chaskalson, p 20.

15   Jeffrey, p 164.

16   Ibid, p 155.

17   Ibid, p 164.

18   Ibid.

19   Ibid, p 159.

20   Ibid.

21   See Petrus Tom, *My Life Struggle* (Johannesburg: Ravan Press, 1985).

22   Jeffery, p 159.

23   Ibid, p 164.

24   Ibid.

25   Ibid, p 158.

26   Ibid, p 131.

27   Benjamin Pogrund, *How Can Man Die Better: The Life of Robert Sobukwe* (Johannesburg: Jonathan Ball Publishers, 1990), p 2.

28   Jeffrey, p 165.

29   Pogrund, p 95.

30   See Sobukwe's speech at the 'Completers' Social', 21 October 1949, quoted in Pogrund, p 36.

PART TWO

1   Hannah Arendt, *Eichmann in Jerusalem: A Report on the Banality of Evil* (New York: Penguin Books, Penguin 20th Century Classics, Revised edition, 1994).

2   Joseph Mahlomola Ngoaketsi, An Introduction to the History of Sharpeville, 1942-96. Honours Dissertation, Potchefstroom University, Vaal Triangle Campus, 1998, p 23.

3   Marius de Witt Dippenaar, *The History of the South African Police, 1913-88* (Pretoria: Promedia Publications, 1988), p 240.

4   Matthew Chaskalson, The Road to Sharpeville: A History of Vereeniging's African Townships in the Fifties. Seminar Paper, African Studies Institute, University of the Witwatersrand, 1986, p 28.

5   Dippenaar, ibid.

6   Ngoaketsi, p 23; Chaskalson, p 28; Dippenaar, p 240.

7   Ian Jeffrey, Cultural Trends and Community Formation in a South African Township: Sharpeville, 1943-85. Master's Dissertation, Department of Anthropology, University of the Witwatersrand, 1991, p 158.

8   Dippenaar, p 240.

9   Ibid, p 241.

10   Ambrose Reeves, *Shooting at Sharpeville: The Agony of South Africa* (London: Victor Gollancz, 1960), p 23.

11   See, for example, Philip Frankel, The Politics of the Passes: Control and

Change in South Africa. *Journal of Modern African Studies* 17(2), June 1979.

12   The local government officials were, in general, far more worried than any other element of the local state, including the police. There was, in fact, a strong suspicion that the police lacked the necessary vigilance or capacity to contain mass black violence should it occur.

13   On this point see Michael Ignatieff, *Blood and Belonging: Journeys into the New Nationalism* (London: Chatto & Windus, 1994), pp 22-42.

14   Jasper van der Bliek, The Sharpeville Scars, Mimeo, 2000. Interviews: Frederick Batkani and Albert Mbongo.

15   Official Deposition: Major Willem Abraham van Zyl. Pretoria: South African Police Services Museum.

16   Van der Bliek. Interview: George Mayuba.

17   Ibid. Interview: Carlton Monnakgotla.

18   Dippenaar, p 277.

19   Ibid, p 243.

20   Official Deposition: Colonel Willem Carl Ernst Prinsloo. Pretoria: South African Police Services Museum.

21   M A Labuschagne. Sharpeville. Mimeo, nd.

22   Reeves, p 234.

23   On these issues and others on crowd psychology see, *inter alia*, George Rude, *The Crowd in the French Revolution* (Oxford: Oxford University Press, 1959) and, particularly, Elias Canetti, *Crowds and Power* (Harmondsworth: Penguin Books, 1973).

24   Testimony to the Commission of Inquiry. JV van Wyk, Non-European Affairs Department, Vereeniging Municipality.

25   Corroborated by Nyakane Tsolo. Interview, Rotterdam, April 2000.

26   Dippenaar, p 272.

27   Ibid, pp 274-75.

28   Van der Bliek.

29   Dippenaar, p 277.

30   Van der Bliek.

31   Ibid.

32   Testimony to the Commission of Inquiry. Colonel Willem Prinsloo, South African Police.
33   Reeves, p156.
34   Dippenaar, p 278.
35   Mark Levene & Penny Roberts (eds), *The Massacre in History* (New York: Berghahn Books, 1999), p 13.
36   Christopher Browning, *Ordinary Men: Reserve Battalion 101 and the Final Solution in Poland* (New York: Harper Perennial, 1993), p 68.
37   Andrew Ward, *Our Bones Are Scattered: The Cawnpore Massacre and the Indian Mutiny of 1857* (New York: Henry Holt & Co 1996), p 438.
38   Testimony to the Commission of Inquiry: Colonel G D Pienaar, South African Police.
39   Dippenaar, p 252.
40   Browning, p 73.
41   Dippenaar, p 271.
42   For a highly effective and detailed summary of this debate see Browning.
43   Browning, p 151
44   Interview with (anonymous) surviving relative of the Reverend Harper Martins, Vereeniging, October 2000.
45   Dippenaar, p 244.
46   This particular individual, later a senior SAP officer and then a National Party Member of Parliament, was one of our respondents who insisted on absolute anonymity. Even a pseuronym was not considered adequate protection.
47   Browning, p 78.
48   Ibid, p 72.
49   Reeves, p 156.
50   Van der Bliek.
51   Reeves, p 134.
52   The *Star* (Johannesburg) 20 March 1965.
53   Humphrey Tyler, *Life in the Time of Sharpeville* (Cape Town: Kwela Books, 1995), p 18.
54   Ngoaketsi, 31.
55   Reeves, p 64.

56   Ibid, p 65.

57   Interview with Samuel Dhlamini, Sharpeville, September 2000.

58   Reeves, p 113.

59   Van der Bliek.

60   Reeves, p 152.

61   Dippenaar, p 249.

62   Reeves, p 134.

63   Ibid, p 141.

64   Ibid, p 151.

65   June Goodwin and Ben Schiff, *Heart of Whiteness: Afrikaners Face Black Rule in South Africa* (New York: Scribner, 1995).

66   On some of the subtle interconnections between gender, race and the exercise of political power, see, *inter alia*, Calvin Henton, *Sex and Racism* (London: Andre Deutsch, 1969).

67   Labuschagne, ibid.

68   Official Deposition: Major Willem Abraham van Zyl. (Pretoria: South African Police Services Museum).

69   Tyler, p 19.

70   Van der Bliek.

71   Interview with Oscar Musibi, Sebokeng, April 2000.

72   Testimony to the Commission of Inquiry: Constable W C Els, South African Police.

73   Van der Bliek.

74   Official Deposition: Colonel Willem Prinsloo (Pretoria: South African Police Services Museum).

75   *Rand Daily Mail* (Johannesburg), 17 May 1960.

76   Dippenaar, p 283.

77   Labuschagne.

78   Tyler, p 20.

79   Peter Parker and Joyce Parker-Mokhesi, *In the Shadow of Sharpeville: Apartheid and Criminal Justice* (New York: New York University Press, 1998), p 13, Fn12.

80   Reeves, p 70.

81   Ibid, p 64.

82   Van der Bliek, ibid.

83   Ibid.

84   *Rand Daily Mail* (Johannesburg), 26 May 1960.

85   Ibid, 3 April 1960.

86   Van der Bliek.

87   *Sunday Times* (Johannesburg), 29 March 1960.

88   Official Deposition: Colonel Willem Prinsloo.

89   See, for example, Tilman Dedering, A Certain Rigorous Treatment of All Parts of the Nation: The Annihilation of the Herero in German South West Africa. In Mark Levene and Penny Roberts (eds), *The Massacre in History* (New York: Berghahn Books, 1999), pp 205-223.

90   Browning, p 161.

91   John Dower, *War Without Mercy: Race and Power in the Pacific War* (New York: Pantheon Books, 1987). On My Lai in particular, Robert Jay Lifton, *Home From the Wat: Vietnam Veterans – Neither Victims Nor Executioners* (New York: Beacon Press, 1985).

92   Dippenaar, p 273.

93   Browning, p 150.

94   Zygmunt Baumann, *Modernity and the Holocaust* (Ithaca: Cornell University Press, 1994).

95   John Steiner, *Power, Politics and Social Change in National Socialist Germany* (New York: Walter de Gruyter, 1975).

96   Pogrund, p 91.

97   Jeffery, p 158.

98   Chaskalson, p 16.

99   Parker & Parker-Mokhesi, p10.

100   Official Deposition: Major Willem Abraham Van Zyl (Pretoria: South African Police Services Museum). See also Dippenaar, p 276.

101   Ibid, p 275.

PART THREE

1   For a detailed discussion of these and other issues in the wake of the massacre, see Tom Lodge, *Sharpeville 1960: The Massacre and its*

Aftermath (Oxford: Oxford University Press, forthcoming 2002).

2   Andrew Ward, *Our Bones Are Scattered: The Cawnpore Massacre and the Indian Mutiny of 1857* (New York: Heny Holt & Co, 1996), p xviii

3   Marius de Witt Dippenaar, *The History of the South African Police, 1913-88* (Pretoria: Promedia Publications, 1988), p 282.

4   Ibid, p 272.

5   Ibid p 283.

6   Ibid.

7   Ibid.

8   Ibid, p 284.

9   Peter Parker and Joyce Parker-Mokhesi, *In the Shadow of Sharpeville: Apartheid and Criminal Justice* (New York: New York University Press, 1998), p 3.

10   Ibid, p 5.

11   Ambrose Reeves, *Shooting at Sharpeville: The Agony of South Africa* (London: Victor Gollancz, 1960), p 96.

12   Jasper van der Bliek, The Sharpeville Scars. Mimeo, 2000.

13   Ibid.

14   Joseph Mahlomola Ngoaketsi, An Introduction to the History of Sharpeville, 1942-96.   Honours Dissertation, Potchefstroom University, Vaal Triangle Campus, 1998, p 33.

15   Ibid.

16   Ibid, p 19.

17   Barrington Moore, *Injustice: The Social Bases of Obedience and Revolt* (London: Macmillan, 1978).

18   See *The Star* (Johannesburg), 20 March 1965.

19   For a detailed discussion of these issues see, *inter alia*, Jeremy Grest, The Crisis of Local Government in South Africa and Jeremy Seekings, Political Mobilisation in the Black Townships of the Transvaal. In Philip Frankel, Noam Pines and Mark Swilling (eds), *State, Resistance and Change in South Africa* (London: Croom Helm, 1988).

20   Ibid.

21   *The Star*, 4 September 1984.

22   Parker and Parker-Mokhesi, p 12. See also *Rand Daily Mail* (Johannesburg), 8 November 1984.

23   Parker and Parker-Mokhesi.

24   *The Star*, 22 September 1984.

25   *The Star*, 21 September 1984.

26   See, for example, Johannes Rantete, *The Third Day of September: An Eye-Witness Account of the Sebokeng Rebellion of 1984* (Johannesburg: Ravan Press, 1984).

27   For the emergence and practice of 'total strategy' see, *inter alia*, Philip Frankel, Race and Counter-Revolution: South Africa's 'Total Strategy', *Journal of Commonwealth and Comparative Politics*, XVIII (2), November 1980.

28   For example, Ngoaketsi.

29   See, *inter alia*, Jeremy Seekings, Political Mobilisation in the Black Townships of the Transvaal. In Frankel, Pines and Swilling.

30   Jasper van der Bliek, The Sharpeville Scars. Mimeo, 2000.

31   Emendo, Sharpeville Local First Socio-Economic Survey (Midrand, 1999).

32   Van der Bliek.

33   Philip Frankel, Business Development and Economic Revitalisation in Sharpeville: Conclusions of an Analysis into SMMEs in the Sharpeville Area. Unpublished study for the Australian Agency for International Development, 2000.

34   Van der Bliek.

35   Sarah Farmer, *Martyred Village: Commemorating the 1944 Massacre at Oradour-sur-Glane* (Berkeley: University of California Press, 1999), p xii. Also see Maurice Halbwachs, *Les Cadres sociaux de la memoire* (Paris: Libraire Felix Alcan, 1925).

36   Halbwachs, ibid.

37   Farmer, p xiv.

38   Van der Bliek.

39   Farmer, p xiv.

40   Farmer, p 6.

APPENDIX 1

THE POLICE AT SHARPEVILLE

The following is a list of SAP uniform personnel and Sharpeville Municipal Police who are known to have been in, or in the immediate vicinity of, the Sharpeville Police Station on Monday 21 March 1960 at 13.35 – the time of the massacre. From all accounts there were others whose names are now unknown.

The list includes six additional members of the Criminal Investigation Branch (the CID) of the Vereeniging SAP as well as several members of the Special Branch (security police) especially deployed from Pretoria or Johannesburg, who were central role players and whose names appear in the text – Brigadier Els, Colonel Spengler, Colonel Prinsloo and Lieutenant-Colonel Pienaar.

FROM SHARPEVILLE (UNIFORMED SAP)

Name	Armament	Fired
Sergeant J Grobler	.38 Pistol	No
Constable H Beyl	.38 Pistol	6 Rounds
Constable W Steenkamp	.38 Pistol;	6 Rounds x 38;
	.303 Rifle	9 Rounds x 303
Bantu Detective Sidwell	.25 Pistol	No information
Bantu Detective David	.25 Pistol	No information
Bantu Detective Mokabela	.25 Pistol	No information
Bantu Detective Matthew	.25 Pistol	No information
Bantu Sergeant S Mdikane	–	Not applicable

Bantu Deputy-Sgt H Mnqayi	–		Not applicable
Bantu Constable D Mokabela	–		Not applicable
–	N. Njumbuxa	–	Not applicable
–	J. Mabusa	–	Not applicable
–	O. Mashisane	–	Not applicable
–	J Musi	–	Not applicable
–	J Leromo	Assegai	Not applicable
–	G Mhlongo	Knobkerrie	Not applicable
–	S Mosolo	–	Not applicable
–	M President	–	Not applicable
–	P Makhosa	–	Not applicable
–	J Motsapi	Assegai	Not applicable
–	S Goniwe	Knobkerrie	Not applicable
–	R Mapheleba	–	Not applicable
–	D Kutoane	–	Not applicable
–	E Pasha	–	Not applicable
–	N Chabalala	Knobkerrie	Not applicable
–	A Nomwesu	Assegai	Not applicable
–	D Maruping	–	Not applicable
–	L Gqaba	–	Not applicable
–	D Makubela	Knobkerrie	Not applicable

SHARPEVILLE (MUNICIPAL POLICE)

Name	Armament	Fired
Inspector Lessing	.25 Pistol	No information
Inspector Ellis	.25 Pistol	No information
Mr Miller	–	No information
Mr Vorster	–	No information
Bantu Sergeant Ben Pitso	.25 Pistol	No information

VEREENIGING

Name	Armament	Fired
Chief Constable J Kruger	.38 Pistol	6 Rounds
Chief Constable J Heyl	.38 Pistol	No
Sergeant B Terblanche	.38 Pistol;	4 Rounds x 38;
	.303 Rifle	2 Rounds x 303
Deputy Sergeant J Kotze	.38 Pistol	No
Constable F Bredenkamp	.38 Pistol; .303 Rifle	No
– T de Koker	.38 Pistol; .303 Rifle	2 Rounds x 303
– H Scheepers	.38 Pistol; Sten Gun	3 Rounds
– J van Aswegen	.38 Pistol; .303 Rifle	14 Rounds x 303
– E Fouche	.38 Pistol	10 Rounds
– J Grove	.38 Pistol	12 Rounds
– E Pennekan	.38 Pistol; .303 Rifle	6 Rounds x 303
– J Karsten	.38 Pistol; .303 Rifle	1 Round x 38;
		3 Rounds x 303
– J Tredoux	.38 Pistol; .303 Rifle	No
– J Le Roux	.38 Pistol	6 Rounds
– J Coetzee	.38 Pistol; .303 Rifle	1 Round x 303
– A Kallis	.38 Pistol; .303 Rifle	8 Rounds x 303
– D Benadie	.38 Pistol; .303 Rifle	No
– P Faurie	.38 Pistol; .303 Rifle	No
– J van Rensburg	.38 Pistol; Sten Gun	12 Rounds x Sten
– J Potgieter	.38 Pistol; .303 Rifle	3 Rounds x 38;
		7 Rounds x 303
– C Els	.38 Pistol; .303 Rifle	6 Rounds x 38;
		4 Rounds x 303
Bantu Dep-Sgt. M Moleko	Knobkerrie	Not applicable
Bantu Constable M Kaizer	–	Not applicable
– L Tlelase	Knobkerrie	Not applicable
– E Ngwenya	–	Not applicable
– D Mtokomo	–	Not applicable

–	E Nkomo	Knobkerrie	Not applicable
–	F Mbowane	–	Not applicable
–	P Myando	Knobkerrie	Not applicable
–	J Leepo	–	Not applicable
–	A Sombane	–	Not applicable
–	P Mathunda	–	Not applicable
–	A Neluvhani	Knobkerrie	Not applicable
–	J Paka	Assegai; Knobkerrie	Not applicable
–	J Modise	Baton	Not applicable
–	A Dipha	Assegai; Knobkerrie	Not applicable
–	M Thobetane	–	Not applicable
–	A Magoro	–	Not applicable
–	J Machologi	–	Not applicable
–	L Nkhabu	–	Not applicable
–	J Leotlela	–	Not applicable
–	A Mkize	–	Not applicable
–	B Mnomyia	–	Not applicable
–	J Gumede	–	Not applicable
–	G Bixi	–	Not applicable
–	W Nsibande	–	Not applicable
–	L Monahetsa	–	Not applicable
–	S Ntshoering	–	Not applicable
–	F Molijane	–	Not applicable
–	F Melomakulu	–	Not applicable
–	M Ramagaga	–	Not applicable
–	L Motsoahae	–	Not applicable
–	P Ngakana	–	Not applicable
–	T Maepho	–	Not applicable
–	J Molusi	–	Not applicable
–	K Khoarane	–	Not applicable
–	Z Mogorosi	–	Not applicable
–	I Thekiso	–	Not applicable
–	J Kabi	–	Not applicable
–	P Moloi	–	Not applicable

VANDERBIJLPARK

Name	Armament	Fired
Sergeant N Lemmer	.38 Pistol	No
Sergeant C Gregory	.38 Pistol; Sten Gun	No
Deputy-Sgt W. van Tonder	.38 Pistol	No
Constable R du Plooy	.38 Pistol	No
– J Olivier	.303 Rifle	7 Rounds
– H vd Westhuizen	.38 Pistol	No
– A Botes	.38 Pistol	No
– A van Staden	.38 Pistol	No
– F Bester	.38 Pistol	No
– J Farrell	.38 Pistol	No
– W Mostert	.38 Pistol	No
Bantu Dep-Sgt M Moleko	Knobkerrie	Not applicable
Bantu Constable 'Elliott'	–	Not applicable

JOHANNESBURG CENTRAL

Name	Armament	Fired
Chief Constable S Malan	.38 Pistol	No
Sergeant W Marais	.303 Rifle	No
Constable L Pelser	.38 Pistol	No
– B Kemp	.38 Pistol; .303 Rifle	No
– G Nel	.303 Rifle	7 Rounds
– C Meyer	.303 Rifle	3 Rounds
– J Smit	.38 Pistol; .303 Rifle	6 Rounds
– D Collins	.303 Rifle	14 Rounds
– Prinsloo	.303 Rifle	8 Rounds
– F Peach	.38 Pistol; .303 Rifle	4 Rounds
– F Stapelberg	.38 Pistol; .303 Rifle	6 Rounds

– J Meyer	.38 Pistol; .303 Rifle	15 Rounds
– G Volschenk	.38 Pistol; .303 Rifle	16 Rounds
– P Saaiiman	.38 Pistol	15 Rounds
– White	No information	No information
– Spies	No information	No information
– Lourens	No information	No information
– Hanekom	No information	No information

BEZUIDENHOUT VALLEY

Name	Armament	Fired
Sergeant J Cornelissen	.303 Rifle	No information
Constable Smith	.303 Rifle	No information
– Ackerman	.303 Rifle	No information
– Du Preez	.303 Rifle	No information
Bantu Constable 'William'	Assegai; Knobkerrie	Not applicable
– 'Phineas'	–	Not applicable
– 'Herman'	–	Not applicable
– 'Elias'	–	Not applicable
– 'Jokodo'	–	Not applicable

JEPPE

Name	Armament	Fired
Captain F Coetzee	.38 Pistol	No information
Chief Constable D Genis	.38 Pistol	No information
Sergeant J Botha	Sten Gun	No information
Constable Booyens	.38 Pistol	No information
– Botha	.303 Rifle	No information
– . Steyl	.303 Rifle	No information
– Bonthuys	.303 Rifle	No information

| – | Cornelissen | Sten Gun | No information |
| – | Jacobs | .303 Rifle | No information |

JOHANNESBURG RADIO (KASERNE)

Name	Armament	Fired
Lieutenant M Barnard	.38 Pistol	No information
Sergeant J Horn	Saracen Personnel	No
Constable S Arnold	Saracen Personnel	No
– A Struwig	.38 Pistol	6 Rounds
– S de Kock	.38 Pistol; .303 Rifle	No
– L Szente	.38 Pistol; Sten Gun	No
– P Mynhardt	.38 Pistol	16 Rounds
– J du Plessis	.38 Pistol; Sten Gun	6 Rounds x 38; 65 Rounds Sten
– C Janssen	.38 Pistol; Sten Gun	35 Rounds Sten
– P Steyn	.38 Pistol; Sten Gun	6 Rounds x 38; 70 Rounds Sten
– LC van Wyk	.38 Pistol; Sten Gun	6 Rounds x 38; 68 Rounds Sten
– J van Zyl	.38 Pistol; Sten Gun	6 Rounds x 38; 75 Rounds Sten
– S van Niekerk	.38 Pistol; Sten Gun	9 Rounds x 38; 45 Rounds Sten
– J Pretorius	.38 Pistol	12 Rounds

HOSPITAL HILL

Name	Armament	Fired
Lieutenant J Claasen	.38 Pistol	No
Chief Constable H Hallatt	.303 Rifle	10 Rounds

Deputy-Sergeant R Pretorius	.303 Rifle	No
Constable P van der Merwe	.303 Rifle	No
– N Theunissen	.303 Rifle	8 Rounds
– D Michau	.303 Rifle	12 Rounds
– A Swanepooel	.303 Rifle	9 Rounds
– W Makkink	.303 Rifle	5 Rounds
– J Serfontein	.303 Rifle	No
– G Booysen.	.303 Rifle	15 Rounds
– AG van Wyk	.303 Rifle	6 Rounds
– AJ van Wyk	.303 Rifle	9 Rouns
– B Botes	.303 Rifle	10 Rounds

BRAMLEY

Name	Armament	Fired
Deputy-Sergeant van den Berg	Saracen Personnel	No
Constable Geyser	.38 Pistol	No
– Bosch	Sten Gun	63 Rounds

PARKVIEW

Name	Armament	Fired
Sergeant A Hugo	.303 Rifle	No
Deputy-Sergeant C Smit	.303 Rifle	10 Rounds
Constable F Swanepoel	.303 Rifle	No
– J du Preez	.303 Rifle	3 Rounds
Bantu Constable A Mphadza	Assegai; Knobkerrie	Not applicable
– P Matau	Assegai; Knobkerrie	Not applicable

ROSEBANK

Name	Armament	Fired
Deputy-Sergeant K le Roux	.303 Rifle	No
Constable J Diemieniet	.303 Rifle	8 Rounds
– J de Kock	.303 Rifle	5 Rounds
– B Theron	.303 Rifle	5 Rounds
Bantu Constable T Matimela	Assegai; Knobkerrie	Not applicable
– P Kola	Assegai; Knobkerrie	Not applicable

NORWOOD

Name	Armament	Fired
Deputy Sgt E. Engelbrecht	.303 Rifle	8 Rounds
Constable D. Hattingh	.303 Rifle	15 Rounds
– R. Barnard	.303 Rifle	10 Rounds
– C. De Jager	.303 Rifle	14 Rounds
– C. Hattingh	.303 Rifle	No

FERNDALE

Name	Armament	Fired
Constable P Botha	.303 Rifle	3 Rounds
– Jerasmus	.303 Rifle	11 Rounds
– H de Kocker	.303 Rifle	5 Rounds
– L Erasmus	.303 Rifle	5 Rounds
– M Fourie	.303 Rifle	10 Rounds
Bantu Constable E Mahlinza	Assegai; Knobkerrie	Not applicable
– P Radebe	–	Not applicable
– J. Moatsi	–	Not applicable
– I. Noakana	–	Not applicable

YEOVILLE

Name	Armament	Fired
Constable A Robberts	Sten Gun	No

CRAIGHALL

Name	Armament	Fired
Bantu Constable F Poswayo	Assegai; Knobkerrie	Not Applicable
– M Malaka	–	Not Applicable
– M Mbuse	–	Not Applicable
– A Motlana	–	Not Applicable
– S Mhlongo	–	Not Applicable
– B Giliwe	–	Not Applicable

NEWLANDS

Name	Armament	Fired
Lieutenant-Col AJ Holmes	.38 Pistol	No
Sergeant J Kok	Saracen Personnel	No
Dep-Sgt A van der Merwe	Sten Gun	45 Rounds
Constable F Sneygans	Sten Gun	65 Rounds
– J Steynberg	Sten Gun	88 Rounds
– M Le Roux	.38 Pistol	No
– F van Niekerk	.38 Pistol	Np
– G van der Mescht	.303 Rifle	No
– J vd Westhuizen	.38 Pistol	No
– P Meyer	.38 Pistol	15 Rounds
Bantu Constable R Matsana	Assegai; Knobkerrie	Not applicable
– J Mbombela	–	Not applicable

–	S Maroane	–	Not applicable
–	D Nabe	–	Not applicable
–	K Mokone	–	Not applicable
–	B Thobejane	–	Not applicable
–	D Ledwaba	–	Not applicable
–	J Radebe	–	Not applicable
–	D Mogotse	–	Not applicable
–	A Mogale	–	Not applicable
–	A Nothobone	–	Not applicable
–	L Lamola	–	Not applicable
–	W Mosheshe	–	Not applicable
–	G Ngaei	–	Not applicable
–	T Bopape	–	Not applicable
–	M Ramosena	–	Not applicable
–	F Nzobana	–	Not applicable
–	H Gwai	–	Not applicable
–	G Manganye	–	Not applicable
–	W Jojoji	–	Not applicable
–	M November	–	Not applicable

MOROKO

Name	Armament	Fired
Captain S van der Linde	.38 Pistol	No
Sergeant J Oosthuizen	Sten Gun	64 Rounds
Bantu Dep-Sgt J Mkize	Bayonet; Knobkerrie	Not applicable
– M Seleke	–	Not applicable
Bantu Constable S Padi	–	Not applicable
– D Tsoali	–	Not applicable
– J Mpaka	–	Not applicable
– R Mkwanazi	–	Not applicable
– L Ngobeni	–	Not applicable

–	W Madikane	–	Not applicable
–	J Gwabezi	–	Not applicable
–	S Khusu	–	Not applicable
–	P Kaula	–	Not applicable
–	A Gulwa	–	Not applicable
–	J Motolkoane	–	Not applicable
–	K Sithole	–	Not applicable
–	M Montshe	–	Not applicable
–	L Mokoena	–	Not applicable
–	M Nkosi	–	Not applicable
–	P Kutu	–	Not applicable
–	U Setuni	–	Not applicable
–	M Seabe	–	Not applicable
–	K Kekana	–	Not applicable

KLIPTOWN

Name	Armament	Fired
Captain A Brummer	Saracen Personnel	No
Constable F Brits	303	No

SPRINGS

Name	Armament	Fired
Captain H Theron	.38 Pistol	No
Chief Constable A Muller	Sten Gun	No
Sergeant J Kapp	.38 Pistol; .303 Rifle	No
– W Smit	.38 Pistol; .303 Rifle	No
Dep-Sgt C Breytenbach	.38 Pistol; .303 Rifle	6 Rounds x 303
Constable L Hattingh	.38 Pistol; .303 Rifle	No
– D Roets	.38 Pistol; .303 Rifle	12 Rounds x 303

– J Tinderholm	.38 Pistol; .303 Rifle	8 Rounds x 303
– F van Zyl	.38 Pistol; .303 Rifle	14 Rounds x 303
– J Muller	.38 Pistol; .303 Rifle	7 Rounds x 303
– N Nel	.38 Pistol; .303 Rifle	10 Rounds x 303
– A de Vries	.38 Pistol; .303 Rifle	15 Rounds x 303
– J de Kock	.38 Pistol; .303 Rifle	No
– F Kruger	.38 Pistol; .303 Rifle	No
– J Joubert	Sten Gun	25 Rounds
– P van Schalkwyk	.303 Rifle	15 Rounds
– C Spies	.38 Pistol; .303 Rifle	6 Rounds x 303
Bantu Constable 'Masilo'	Knobkerrie	Not applicable
– 'Nowet'	–	Not applicable
– 'Thomas'	–	Not applicable
– 'Paulus'	–	Not applicable
– 'Johannes'	–	Not applicable
– 'Archibald'	–	Not applicable
– 'Jacob'	–	Not applicable
– 'George'	–	Not applicable
– 'Alfred'	–	Not applicable

BOKSBURG

Name	Armament	Fired
Lieutenant A Fremantle	.38 Pistol	No
Sergeant P Napier	.38 Pistol	No
Constable R Olivier	.38 Pistol; .303 Rifle	7 Rounds x 303
– J Coetzee	.38 Pistol; .303 Rifle	6 Rounds x 303
– D Prinsloo	.38 Pistol; .303 Rifle	11 Rounds x 303
– J Steyn	.38 Pistol; .303 Rifle	8 Rounds x 303

APPENDIX 2A

THE VICTIMS

'NATIVES WHO DIED OF GUN WOUNDS'
(FROM THE REGISTER OF THE SHARPEVILLE NATIVES'
CEMETERY)

Name	Age
Daniel Mono	40
Jackie Lefakane	50
Ephraim Chaka	36
Solomon Mabephogodche	36
Maria Molebatse	13
Ezekiel Mareletse	33
Elizabeth Mtimkulu	36
William Sedisa	19
Philemon Mokoena	30
Maggie Bakela	40
Islabet Mgomezulu	30
Edward Tsela	16
Isaac Nkhi	40
Martha Thesani	22
Sanana Sethoane	18
Isaac Raletapi	20
Johannes Selanyane	17
John Phutheho	30
Swaart Moseia	28
Petrus Nkesaal	28
Samuel Moahloli	30

Merton Sekitla	34
Jean Mafogane	36
Kaifas Motsepe	45
Christona Motsepe	· 18
Kaseleng Matunye	45
Joseph Mochologi	30
Pauline Madiku	22
Richard Molefe	30
Ezekal Mayelo	44
Paulina Mafulatsi	25
Jemina Letse	37
Daniel Mamakgotle	31
Jeremiah Tlanyane	28
Ben Nchaupe	45
Azael Mangala	39
David Makhela	14
Elisabeth Manyane	18
James Bessie	12
Jacob Rasikusana	35
Gilbert Dimo	58
Philemon Sepanpuru	48
Jan Mogemi	24
Kepano Mtsega	50
Samuel Makhume	39
Isaac Mashiya	30
Edwin Moshebatsi	45
Alfeas Selepe	22
Thomas Hlongwane	24
Elias Molotse	29
Paulus Mabisela	18
Abraham Mazibuko	22
Ephraim Nyembezi	30
Jacob Mafabela	35
Frank Mokoena	34

APPENDIX 2B

THE VICTIMS

(NAMES ON THE TOMBSTONES AT THE SHARPEVILLE ·
NATIVES' CEMETERY)

Isaiah Mangala	Christina Motsepe
Mrs Toroki Sekete	Khaselini Samson Mathinge
Mr Toroki Sekete	D. H. Moono
Elias Masilo	Amos Mthimkulu
Irene Modiko	Jospeh Mochologi
Simon Masilo	Samuel Setatsa
Enuell Mpeka	Paulina Malikoe
Peter Mabenyane	Zaccheus Maysiels
Elliot Sekoala	Paulina Mofulatis
Anna Ramohloa	Motsabi Mosoetsa
Solomon Mapogoshe	Daniel Monnakgotla
Isaac Nkhi	Jan Mnguni
Martha Thinane	Gilbert Dimo
Moeketsi Mosia	Philimon Sepampuru
Samuel Moahlali	Edwin Mashoabathe
John Motsoahe	Norah Mobheklzizwe

APPENDIX 2C

THE VICTIMS

THE 'LYS VAN OORLEDENES' (LIST OF THE DEAD)
(THE OFFICIAL LIST OF THE SOUTH AFRICAN POLICE)

Naam (Name)	Geslag (Gender)	Ouderdom (Age)
Willem Sedisa	Manlik (Male)	28
John Mofokeng	M	44
Abraham Mazebuko	M	23
Walter Mbatha	M	35
George Sekete	M	39
Jacob Mafobela	M	35
Jemina Potse	Vroulik (Female)	37
Petrus Ntshoesane	M	25
David Makhoba	M	14
Anual Mohlasane	M	35
Shadrack Mahlong	M	19
Aron Mavizela	M	24
Elliot Kabe	M	24
Simon Maselo	M	35
Elias Maselo	M	17
David Maphika	M	50
Martha Tinane	V	22
Jeremiah Tlanyane	M	28
Samuel Mokhuma	M	39
Anna Ramothla	V	22

Gilbert Monyane	M	18
Christina Motsepe	V	18
Kopana Mtsoga	M	50
Gilbert Demo	M	53
Ben Nchaupe	M	45
Geelbooi Mofokeng	M	28
Maria Molebatsi	V	13
Wiggi Bakela	V	40
Frank Makoena	M	34
Joseph Mochologi	M	50
Ezekiel Maroletsi	M	33
Samuel Mahlele	M	30
Daniel Monkgotla	M	31
Elisa Moletsi	M	29
Jan Mnguni	M	24
Philemon Sepanpuru	M	48
Zekia Lefakane	M	50
Johannes Selanyane	M	36
Edward Tsela	M	12
Jonas Mailane	M	36
James Besche	M	12
Nora Mbele	V	23
Paulus Mavizela	M	28
Miriam Sekitla	V	36
John Phutheho	M	30
Daniel Mono	M	40
Malefane Nyembesi	M	30
Alfons Selepe	M	22
Ephraim Chaka	M	36
Ezekiel Maselo	M	44
Naphtali Maine	M	25
Izak Mashiya	M	30
Richard Molefe	M	50
Jacob Ramokoena	M	35

Azael Mangala	M	37
Thomas Hlongwane	M	24
Samuel Sefatsa	M	28
Kaselien Matinye	M	45
Piet Mabenjane	M	36
Edwin Moshabate	M	45
Elizabeth Mtimkulu	V	36
Izak Rabotapi	M	20
Solomon Mapogoshe	M	36
Philemon Makoena	M	30
Talbert Mazomba	M	30
Izak Nkhi	M	40
Kaifas Motsepe	M	45
Paulina Mafulatse	V	25
Paulina Malikhoe	V	22

SELECT BIBLIOGRAPHY

AUTHORS NOTE

There are few good secondary resources on the Sharpeville massacre. Most of what little exists is hagiographic, repetitive, polemical or designed to serve one or another political agenda on the part of the major role players on the South African stage in the past forty years. As Lodge has noted in his study of black politics in post-World War II South Africa, which appeared in 1983, the official report of the Commission was not fully and properly published almost twenty years after the event. This remains the case today.

This work has therefore had to rely mainly on primary resources – 117 interviews conducted between June 1999 and August 2000 to be precise – with participants both in the Sharpeville community and in state circles. I have not listed these interviews one-by-one since almost all only took on life once the respondents were guaranteed complete confidentiality, anonymity or the luxury of a pseudonymous identity. This was particularly the case with almost all state operatives. I saw no purpose in listing a date without a name, or a name accompanied by a (*) to denote that this was not the real name. My debt to many of these people, named or otherwise, is acknowledged in the introductory sections.

The following bibliography contains a number of key works on massacres and the recapturing of historic memory which are designed to help us recast Sharpeville in more comprehensibly universal terms. It also contains some of the more critical of the several hundred official depositions which lie in yellowed files in the South African Police Services Museum in Pretoria. For reasons of space, the bibliography contains only a portion of these previously 'reserved' documents which somehow escaped the orgy of paper-shredding that accompanied South Africa's democratic transition. Most of the large report of the Wessels Commission is also to be found on these dusty shelves, although the tidy and full micro-filmed version currently resides at the University of York.

BOOKS, THESES AND DISSERTATIONS

Arendt, Hannah. *Eichmann in Jerusalem: A Report on the Banality of Evil* (New York: Penguin Books, Penguin 20th Century Classics, revised edition, 1994).

Baumann, Zygmunt. *Modernity and the Holocaust* (Ithaca: Cornell University Press, 1989).

Barrington Moore, Jnr. *Injustice: The Social Bases of Obedience and Revolt* (London: Macmillan, 1978).

Brink, Lourens. Die Onluste van Sharpeville. Master's Dissertation, University of the Orange Free State, 1984.

Browning, Christopher. *Ordinary Men: Reserve Battalion 101 and the Final Solution in Poland* (New York: Harper Perennial, 1993).

Canetti, Elias. *Crowds and Power* (Harmondsworth; Penguin Books, 1973).

Calvocoressi, Peter. *South Africa and World Opinion* (Oxford: Oxford University Press, 1961).

Dippenaar, Marius de Witt. *The History of the South African Police, 1913-88* (Pretoria: Promedia Publications, 1988).

Dower, John. *War Without Mercy: Race and Power in the Pacific War* (New York: Pantheon Books, 1987).

Farmer, Sarah. *Martyred Village: Commemorating the 1944 Massacre at Oradour-sur-Glane* (Berkeley: University of California Press, 1999).

Goodwin, June & Schiff, Ben. *Heart of Whiteness: Afrikaners Face Black Rule in the New South Africa* (New York: Scribner, 1995).

Grest, Jeremy. The Crisis of Local Government in South Africa. In Philip Frankel, Noam Pines and Mark Swilling (eds). *State, Resistance and Change in South Africa* (London: Croom Helm, 1988).

Halbwachs, Maurice. *Les Cadres sociaux de la memoire* (Paris: Libraire Felix Alcan, 1925).

Henton, Calvin. *Sex and Racism* (London: Andre Deutsch, 1969).

Ignatieff, Michael. *Blood and Belonging: Journeys into the New Nationalism* (London: Chatto & Windus, 1994).

Jeffrey, Ian. Cultural Trends and Community Formation in a South African Township: Sharpeville, 1943-85. Master's Dissertation, Department of Anthropology, University of the Witwatersrand, Johannesburg, 1991.

Leigh, RL. *Vereeniging, South Africa, 1892-1967* (Johannesburg: Courier-Gazette Publishers, 1968).

Levene, Mark and Roberts, Penny (eds). *The Massacre in History* (New York: Berghahn Books, 1999).

Lifton, Robert Jay. *Home From the War: Vietnam Veterans – Neither Victims Nor Executioners* (New York: Beacon Books, 1985).

Ngoaketsi, Joseph Mahlomola. An Introduction to the History of Sharpeville, 1942-96. Honours Dissertation, Potchefstroom University, Vaal Triangle Campus, 1998.

Langer, Lawrence. *Holocaust Testimonies: The Ruins of Memory* (New Haven: Yale University Press, 1991).

Levi, Primo. *The Drowned and the Saved* (London: Abacus Books, 1989).

Lodge, Tom. *Black Politics in South Africa Since 1945* (Johannesburg: Ravan Press, 1983).

Nora, Pierre (ed). *Les Lieux de memoire. Vol 1* (Paris: Gallimard, 1984 – 93).

Oosterbroek, T (ed). *Vaal River Complex: Industrial Growth Point of the Eighties* (Johannesburg: Thompson Publications, 1983).

Parker, Peter and Parker-Mokhesi, Joyce. *In the Shadow of Sharpeville; Apartheid and Criminal Justice* (New York: New York University Press, 1998).

Pogrund, Benjamin. *How Can Man Die Better: The Life of Robert Sobukwe* (Johannesburg: Jonathan Ball Publishers, 1990).

Rantete, Johannes. *The Third Day of September: An Eye-Witness Account of the Sebokeng Rebellion of 1984* (Johannesburg: Ravan Press, 1984).

Reeves, Ambrose. *Shooting at Sharpeville: The Agony of South Africa* (London: Victor Gollancz, 1960).

—— *South Africa Today: A Challenge to Christians* (London: Victor Gollancz, 1962).

Rousso, Henry. *The Vichy Syndrome: History and Memory in France Since 1944* (Cambridge: Harvard University Press, 1991).

Rude, George. *The Crowd in the French Revolution* (Oxford: Oxford University Press, 1959).

Seekings, Jeremy. Political Mobilisation in the Black Townships of the Transvaal. In Philip Frankel, Noam Pines and Mark Swilling (eds). *State, Resistance and Change in South Africa* (London: Croom Helm, 1988).

Shakinovsky, T. The Local State in Crisis: The Shaping of the Black Working Class, Vereeniging, 1939-49. Honours Dissertation, Department of History, University of the Witwatersrand, 1984.

Tom, Petrus. *My Life Struggle* (Johannesburg: Ravan Press, 1985).

Tyler, Humphrey. *Life in the Time of Sharpeville* (Cape Town: Kwela Books, 1995).

Van Aswegen, FOF. Die Geskiedenis van Vereeniging, 1912-39. Master's Dissertation, Rand Afrikaans University, 1958.

Vanderbijlpark Publicity Association. *Vanderbijlpark: Twenty One Years of Progress* (Johannesburg: Felstar Publications, 1964).

Van Zyl, ME. Swartverstedeliking in Vereeniging, 1923-60. Doctoral Thesis, Vista University Vaal Campus, 1993.

Ward, Andrew. *Our Bones Are Scattered: The Cawnpore Massacres and the Indian Mutiny of 1857* (New York: Henry Holt & Co, 1996).

Young, James E. *Writing and Rewriting the Holocaust: Narrative and the Consequences of Interpretation* (Bloomington: Indiana University Press, 1988).

ARTICLES, MIMEOGRAPHS AND MEMORANDA

Bekker, S. The Local Government and Community of Sebokeng. Occasional Paper No 3, Department of Sociology, University of Stellenbosch, 1978.

Chaskalson, M. The Road to Sharpeville: A History of Vereeniging's African Townships in the Fifties. Seminar Paper, African Studies Institute, University of the Witwatersrand, 1986.

—— Jochelson, K and Seekings, J. Rent Boycotts and the Urban Political Economy. In Glenn Moss and Ingrid Obery (ed). *South African Review IV* (Johannesburg: Ravan Press, 1987).

Dixon, FCH. The Story of Sharpeville. Vereeniging Town Council: Engineers Department. Mimeo, nd.

Emendo. Sharpeville Local First Socio-Economic Survey (Midrand 1999).

Frankel, Philip. The Politics of the Passes: Control and Change in South Africa. *Journal of Modern African Studies* 17(2), June 1979.

────── South Africa: The Politics of Police Control. *Comparative Politics* 12(14), July 1980.

────── Race and Counter-Revolution: South Africa's 'Total Strategy'. *Journal of Commonwealth and Comparative Politics* XVIII (3), November 1980.

────── Business Development and Economic Revitalisation in Sharpeville: Conclusions of an Analysis into SMME's in the Sharpeville Area. Unpublished Study for the Australian Agency for International Development, 2000.

Labuschagne, MA. Sharpeville. Mimeo, nd.

Lodge, Tom. Review: Humphrey Tyler, Life in the Time of Sharpeville. *Financial Mail,* 12 January 1996.

Prinsloo, PJJ. Die Geskiedenis van Vereeniging. Research Report, Potchefstroom University, nd.

Schwartz, Pat. The Vaal Triangle Upheaval. *Reality,* January 1985.

Swilling, Mark. Stayaways, Urban Protest and the State. In *South African Review III* (Johannesburg: Ravan Press, 1986).

Transvaal Inter-Denominational African Ministers Association (Vereeniging Branch). On the Disturbances at Sharpeville Township, Vereeniging, on Monday, 21 March 1960, nd.

Vaal Technorama. A Few Facts About Bantu Town Vereeniging. Doc VTB 03/ 5168. 1961

────── Geskiedkundige Feite oor die Swartdorp Sharpeville. Doc VTB 03/5/68 nd.

Van der Bliek, Jasper. *The Sharpeville Scars.* Tilburg-Lekoa Vaal Association, 2000.

Van der Schyff, P. Historiese Perspectief, III. 1960 – Jaar van Storms. Mimeo, nd.

Van der Westhuizen, JW. Sharpeville, Evaton and Sebokeng: A Short History. Transvaal Provincial Administration Museum Services, July 1977.

OFFICIAL REPORTS

Union of South Africa. Summary of the Commission of Inquiry into the Events which Occurred in the Districts of Vereeniging and Vanderbijlpark. Mimeograph, 1960.

—— Verslag van die Kommissie wat Benoem is om Ondersoek in te skep na en verslag uit to bring oor die Gebeure in die Distrikte Vereeniging en Vanderbijlpark, Provinsie Transvaal op 21ˢᵗ Maart 1960, 1960.

SELECTIVE DEPOSITIONS

Berry, Ian (Journalist: Drum Publications)

Botes, Barend Hendrick (Constable: SAP)

Calder, David William (Journalist: Drum Publications)

Channon, Charles Percival (Journalist: *The Star*)

Cawood, Edward George (Captain: SAP)

Dhlamini, Samuel (Sharpeville Resident)

Els, CW (Constable: SAP)

Foster, Rupert Bailey (Inspector: Dept. of Non-European Affairs, Sharpeville)

Fourie, Quartus Stefanus (Lieutenant: SAP)

Friedman, Jack (Senior District Surgeon, Johannesburg)

Griffith, Benedict (Vereeniging Resident)

Grobler, Johannes Lodewickus (Sergeant: SAP)

Gush, O (Magistrate: Vereeniging Court)

Hlongwane, J (Sharpeville Resident)

Hoek, Jan (Photographer, *Rand Daily Mail*)

Jones, Elwyn (MP Cardiff and Observer, International Commission of Jurists)

Keen, Paul (Surgeon-in-Charge, Baragwanath Hospital)

Klopper, Theunis Christoffel (Native Commissioner, Evaton)

Kukard, Charles Edward (Chief Constable: SAP)

Kutoane, A (Sharpeville Resident)

Landen, CKG (Prosecutor: Vereeniging Court.)

Labuschagne, MA (Location Superintendent, Sharpeville)

Lelia, Elias (Sharpeville Resident)

Lepee, Stefaans (Executive Member PAC)

Lethege. A (Sharpeville Resident)

Maja, Robert (Reverend, Sharpeville)

Maboti, Abiel (Sharpeville Resident)

Makhalamele, Simon (Evaton shop owner)

Manyosi, Ronnie (Journalist, *Golden City Post*)

Matlala, A (Sharpeville Resident)

Mokanyane, L (Sharpeville Resident)

Monyake, Johannes (Executive Member PAC)

Modigo, Gladwin (Sharpeville Resident)

Mokwa, R (Sharpeville Resident)

Molefe, P (Sharpeville Resident)

Mooi, M (Sharpeville Resident)

More, Thomas (Executive Member PAC)

Mostert, Barend Daniel (Senior Inspector Dept. Non-European Affairs, Sharpeville)

Motaung, I (Sharpeville Resident)

Msimanga, T (Sharpeville Resident)

Napier, Patrick Joseph (Sergeant: SAP)

Nkosi, Lewis (Journalist, *Golden City Post*)

Nkosi, Moses ('Bantoe' Sergeant, SAP)

Nyapisa, Jan (Sharpeville Resident)

Ntoampe, Thaddea (Executive Member PAC)

Olivier, Willem Jacobus (Storeman, SAFIM)

Pienaar, GD (Lieutenant-Colonel, SAP)

Pitse, Ben (Sergeant, Vereeniging Municipal Police)

Prinsloo, Willem Carl Ernst (Colonel, SAP)

Ptawaya, George (Sharpeville Resident)

Ramodibe, David (Executive Member, PAC)

Robinson, Warwick (Journalist, *Rand Daily Mail*)

Sacks, Bernard (Journalist, *Rand Daily Mail*)

Sakwane, A (Sharpeville Resident)

Sebonyane, Pierce (Detective Constable, SAP)

Selanyane, Joseph (Sharpeville Resident)

Seretho, J (Sharpeville Resident)

Sithole, D (Sharpeville Resident)

Smuts, M (Chief Native Commissioner, Witwatersrand)

Spengler, AT (Colonel, SAP)

Steyn, H (District Surgeon, Vanderbijlpark)

Swanepoel, PD (Superintendent, Vereeniging Hospital)
Teketsi, Emmanuel (Executive Member PAC)
Theron, Barend Johannes (Constable, SAP)
Theron, Hendrik Gert (Captain, SAP)
Tsolo, Nyakane (Executive Member PAC)
Tyler, Humphrey (Journalist, Drum Publications)
Van den Bergh, JJP (Captain, SAP)
Van Eeden, Eric Alfred (Lieutenant, SAP)
Van Vuuren, Rudolph Petrus Gerhardus (Chief Fire Officer, Vereeniging)
Van Wyk, JC (Inspector, Non-European Affairs Department, Vereeniging)
Van Zyl, Willem Abraham (Major, SAP)
White, Thomas (Constable, SAP)

NEWSPAPERS AND JOURNALS

Bona
Drum
Lekoa City Council Newsletter
New Age
Pace
Post
Rand Daily Mail
Reality
The Star
Sowetan
Vaal Vision
Vereeniging News
Vereeniging & Vanderbijlpark News
Weekly Mail
The World
Zonk

INDEX